GIPS® Standards Handbook
for Asset Owners

Explanation of the
Provisions in Sections 21–26

November 2020

CFA Institute®
Global Investment
Performance Standards

ISBN 978-1-953337-00-9

CONTENTS

INTRODUCTION

The Global Investment Performance Standards (GIPS®) for Asset Owners are divided into six sections, which are as follows:

21. Fundamentals of Compliance
22. Input Data and Calculation Methodology
23. Total Fund and Composite Maintenance
24. Total Fund and Composite Time-Weighted Return Report
25. Additional Composite Money-Weighted Return Report
26. GIPS Advertising Guidelines

The Explanation of the Provisions in Sections 21–26 provides interpretation of each provision contained in Sections 21–26. Asset Owners that choose to comply with the GIPS standards must comply with all applicable requirements of the GIPS standards, including any Guidance Statements, interpretations, and Questions and Answers (Q&As) published by CFA Institute and the GIPS standards governing bodies.

Section 21: Fundamentals of Compliance. The Fundamentals of Compliance section includes several core principles that create the foundation for the GIPS standards, including properly defining the asset owner, providing GIPS Asset Owner Reports to those who have direct oversight responsibility for total fund assets and total asset owner assets, adhering to applicable laws and regulations, and ensuring that information presented is not false or misleading.

Section 22: Input Data and Calculation Methodology. Consistency of input data used to calculate performance is critical to effective compliance with the GIPS standards and establishes the foundation for full and fair investment performance presentations. Achieving transparency among asset owner's performance presentations requires uniformity in methods used to calculate returns. The GIPS standards mandate the use of certain calculation methodologies to facilitate a clear understanding of the information. It is important that the data being presented to the oversight body is consistent and transparent to aid in the evaluation of performance information and foster strong investment decision-making.

Section 23: Total Fund and Composite Maintenance. A total fund is a pool of assets managed by an asset owner according to a specific investment mandate, which is typically composed of multiple asset classes. The total fund is typically composed of underlying portfolios, each representing one of the strategies used to achieve the asset owner's investment mandate. The asset owner is required to create a total fund and present total fund information to the oversight body.

A composite is an aggregation of one or more portfolios managed according to a similar investment mandate, objective, or strategy. The composite return is the asset-weighted average of the performance of all portfolios in the composite. Asset owners are not required to present composites in compliance with the GIPS standards but may choose to do so. If an asset owner chooses to create an additional composite and present it in a GIPS Asset Owner Report, it must present the GIPS Asset Owner Report to the oversight body.

Section 24: Total Fund and Composite Time-Weighted Return Report. Section 24 includes the requirements and recommendations for preparing a GIPS Asset Owner Report that includes time-weighted returns. Asset owners that prepare a GIPS Asset Owner Report that includes time-weighted returns must include the required numerical information and disclosures specified in Section 24, if applicable to the specific total fund or composite.

Section 25: Additional Composite Money-Weighted Return Report. Section 25 includes the requirements and recommendations that apply to asset owners that calculate and report additional composite performance in a GIPS Asset Owner Report using money-weighted returns. An additional composite is a grouping of portfolios representing a particular strategy or asset class that the asset owner chooses to present in a GIPS Asset Owner Report.

Section 26: GIPS Advertising Guidelines. The Explanation of the Provisions in Section 26 provides interpretation of each provision that is included in Section 26—GIPS Advertising Guidelines. Asset owners may wish to prepare materials that are widely distributed, such as annual reports provided to beneficiaries and posted on the asset owner's website. The asset owner may wish to include the fact that the asset owner claims compliance with the GIPS standards but does not wish to include a lengthy GIPS Asset Owner Report for the total fund. The asset owner may instead choose to prepare these materials following the GIPS Advertising Guidelines. To claim compliance with the GIPS standards in an advertisement, asset owners must adhere to the GIPS Advertising Guidelines or include a GIPS Asset Owner Report.

Each provision is included in a grey text box. Within the provisions are words appearing in small capital letters. This indicates defined terms that can be found in the GIPS Standards Glossary. Below each provision is a discussion that provides interpretive guidance to help readers understand the provision.

vi | www.cfainstitute.org

21. FUNDAMENTALS OF COMPLIANCE

21.A. Fundamentals of Compliance–Requirements

Provision 21.A.1

The GIPS standards MUST be applied on an ASSET OWNER–wide basis. Compliance MUST be met on an ASSET OWNER–wide basis and cannot be met on a TOTAL FUND, COMPOSITE, POOLED FUND, or PORTFOLIO basis.

Discussion

The GIPS standards provide an ethical framework for calculating and presenting an asset owner's investment performance history. The definition of the asset owner is the foundation for asset owner–wide compliance and creates defined boundaries for determining total asset owner assets. Only asset owners that have discretion over total fund assets, either by managing assets directly or by having the discretion to hire and fire external managers, may claim compliance with the GIPS standards.

To claim compliance, an asset owner must comply with all the applicable requirements of the GIPS standards. Compliance cannot be met on a total fund, composite, pooled fund, or portfolio basis and can be met only on an asset owner–wide basis. For example, if an asset owner definition includes both equity and fixed-income assets, the asset owner cannot present only its equity assets as being in compliance with the GIPS standards. If an asset owner definition includes two total funds, the asset owner cannot present only one total fund as being in compliance with the GIPS standards.

Some asset owners, such as pension funds, manage the assets of other related asset owners to gain efficiencies and cost savings. For example, a state employee pension plan may also manage employee pension plans of local municipalities within that state. These asset owners would follow the guidance and requirements of the GIPS Standards for Asset Owners.

Some asset owners have the authority to compete for business by marketing to prospective clients, as traditional investment managers do. These asset owners would follow the guidance and requirements of the GIPS Standards for Firms, rather than the GIPS Standards for Asset Owners.

See Provisions 21.A.2 and 21.A.24 for guidance on when an asset owner competes for business.

 |

Provision 21.A.2

An ASSET OWNER MUST be defined as an entity that manages investments, directly and/or through the use of EXTERNAL MANAGERS, on behalf of participants, beneficiaries, or the organization itself. These entities include, but are not limited to, public and private pension funds, endowments, foundations, family offices, provident funds, insurers and reinsurers, sovereign wealth funds, and fiduciaries.

Discussion

It is the asset owner's responsibility to ensure that the definition of the asset owner is appropriate, rational, and fair, reflecting the organization or entity that has discretion over the total assets managed by the organization or entity. An asset owner's definition will reflect the specific circumstances of the asset owner and how it manages investments, either directly and/or indirectly through the use of external managers. For a public pension fund, the asset owner is generally defined by legislation. In the case of foundations, endowments, or family offices, the asset owner would be the entity established by the governing body to manage the pool of assets. Asset owners claiming compliance must apply the GIPS standards to the entire entity defined as the asset owner.

There are situations in which an organization may act as both an asset owner, where investment authority and ownership are vested with the organization itself, as well as a firm (asset manager) that competes for assets whose vesting lies with external clients. In such cases, the asset owner has two choices in how to define itself for the purpose of complying with the GIPS standards.

- The asset owner bifurcates its assets into two entities: one defined as an asset owner and one defined as a firm.
- The asset owner does not bifurcate its assets and instead defines itself as both an asset owner and a firm. When calculating and presenting performance to the oversight body, the asset owner follows the GIPS Standards for Asset Owners. When calculating and presenting performance to prospective clients or prospective investors, the asset owner follows the GIPS Standards for Firms.

See Provision 21.A.24 for additional guidance on situations in which an asset owner competes for business, including those instances in which an asset owner acts as both an asset owner and a firm that competes for business.

Provision 21.A.3

The ASSET OWNER MUST have discretion over TOTAL FUND assets, either by managing assets directly or by having the discretion to hire and fire EXTERNAL MANAGERS.

Discussion

The GIPS standards are applicable only to asset owners that have discretion over total fund assets, either by managing assets internally and/or by having control over asset allocation decisions and the ability to hire and fire external managers. An external manager is a third-party investment manager that is hired by an asset owner to manage some or all of the total asset owner assets.

If the asset owner has discretion to assign assets to an external manager, those assets must be included in total asset owner assets. Once the assets are given to an external manager to manage, the asset owner will not have control over exactly how those assets are invested. Nevertheless, the asset owner chose to invest the assets by placing them with an external manager and has the discretion to hire and fire the external manager. Although the external manager is not required to comply with the GIPS standards, it may be helpful to the asset owner if the external manager is familiar with the GIPS standards.

Asset owners must treat the assets assigned to an external manager as they would other assets that are managed in-house and must include them in total asset owner assets, assign them to the appropriate total fund, and include them in the total fund performance calculation. The asset owner can include the assets managed by the external manager and the external manager's performance record in the total fund only for the periods that the asset owner assigned the assets to the external manager.

Provision 21.A.4

To initially claim compliance with the GIPS standards, an ASSET OWNER MUST attain compliance for a minimum of one year or for the period since the ASSET OWNER inception if the ASSET OWNER has been in existence for less than one year.

Because of the unique nature of assets owners, in that they do not typically compete for clients, instead of requiring an initial five years of compliance with the GIPS standards as is required for firms, an asset owner must initially attain compliance for a minimum of one year or for the period since the asset owner inception if the asset owner has been in existence for less than one year. Importantly, this exception is allowed only for asset owners that do not compete for business. It applies only to asset owners that manage an entity's assets solely for the purpose of supporting the organization and are accountable only to their respective oversight bodies.

Being in compliance for a minimum one-year period, or for the period since inception if less than one year, means that, for this period, the asset owner has complied with all applicable requirements of the GIPS standards, including any Guidance Statements, interpretations, and Questions & Answers (Q&As) published by CFA Institute and the GIPS standards governing bodies.

Assuming an asset owner initially attains compliance for the minimum one-year period, and the asset owner is presenting time-weighted returns (TWRs) in a GIPS Asset Owner Report, the asset owner is required to present one year of GIPS-compliant performance, or performance since inception of the total fund or composite if it has been in existence less than one year. A GIPS Asset Owner Report is a presentation for a total fund or composite that contains all the information required by the GIPS standards and may also include recommended information or supplemental information. The ability to present one year of GIPS-compliant performance does not mean, however, that the asset owner is able to claim compliance with the GIPS standards. The asset owner must fulfill all of the requirements of the GIPS standards for at least the initial one-year period or since inception if the asset owner has been in existence for less than one year, not simply the requirements relating to the presentation of performance in a GIPS Asset Owner Report.

An additional composite is a grouping of portfolios representing a particular strategy or asset class that the asset owner chooses to present in a GIPS Asset Owner Report. If an asset owner has chosen to present a money-weighted return (MWR) for an additional composite in a GIPS Asset Owner Report, it is required to present only one return: the annualized since-inception MWR of the composite through the most recent annual period end. If the asset owner does not have records to support the track record since the composite's inception date, the asset owner must present the composite's annualized MWR for the longest period for which the asset owner has such records, through the most recent annual period end. Regardless of the period encompassed in this MWR, the asset owner cannot claim compliance with the GIPS standards until it has fulfilled all of the requirements of the GIPS standards, including but not limited to all of the input data and calculation requirements, for a full one-year period or since inception of the composite if the composite has been in existence for less than one year. If the composite has been in existence for longer than one year but the asset owner is initially claiming compliance with the GIPS standards for the minimum one-year period, the asset owner is still required to present the annualized MWR for the longest period for which the asset owner has records—not only for the period for which the asset owner claims compliance with the GIPS standards.

If an asset owner initially claims compliance for a period longer than one year, the asset owner must present a track record for the entire period for which it claims compliance. This condition applies whether the asset owner presents TWRs, MWRs, or both in its GIPS Asset Owner Reports.

Once an asset owner has claimed compliance for a one-year period, or since inception of the asset owner if the asset owner has existed for less than one year, the asset owner must include in GIPS Asset Owner Reports an additional year of performance each year, building up to a minimum of 10 years of GIPS-compliant performance. Although an asset owner is required to present only 10 years of performance in a GIPS Asset Owner Report, it is recommended that asset owners present more than 10 years of performance in a GIPS Asset Owner Report.

Consider the following examples of periods required to be presented when first claiming compliance with the GIPS standards and TWRs are presented.

Example 1:

An asset owner has been in existence since 1 January 2011 and wishes to claim compliance starting with GIPS Asset Owner Reports for periods ending 31 December 2020. The asset owner decides to attain compliance for the minimum one-year period and chooses to present performance on a calendar-year basis. The asset owner has one total fund with a track record starting on 1 January 2011.

The asset owner must comply with all applicable requirements of the GIPS standards on an asset owner–wide basis for an initial one-year period, in this case from 1 January 2020 through 31 December 2020. The asset owner must prepare a GIPS Asset Owner Report that includes one year of GIPS-compliant performance for its total fund for the one-year period ended 31 December 2020. The asset owner must then continue to add one year of additional performance to its GIPS Asset Owner Report each year prospectively, building to a minimum of 10 years of GIPS-compliant performance. An asset owner is not required to present a track record longer than 10 years but is recommended to do so.

Example 2:

An asset owner has been in existence since 2013 and wishes to claim compliance starting in 2020. For various reasons, the asset owner can create a GIPS-compliant track record only beginning 1 July 2019.

The asset owner may not claim compliance with the GIPS standards until it can present one year of GIPS-compliant performance. In this case, the asset owner must wait until it has GIPS-compliant returns from 1 July 2019 through 30 June 2020. Only then can the asset owner claim compliance with the GIPS standards. The asset owner must then continue to add one year of additional performance to its GIPS Asset Owner Reports each year, building to a minimum of 10 years of GIPS-compliant performance for each of its GIPS Asset Owner Reports. An asset owner is not required to present a track record longer than 10 years but is recommended to do so.

Example 3:

A asset owner has been in existence for less than one year and has no annual total fund returns to report.

The asset owner may claim compliance with the GIPS standards as soon as it meets all of the applicable requirements of the GIPS standards and has performance to report. If the asset owner is less than 12 months old, it is permitted to present since-inception performance in a GIPS Asset Owner Report for its total fund and claim compliance with the GIPS standards. The asset owner must then continue to add one year of additional performance to its GIPS Asset Owner Reports each year, building to a minimum of 10 years of GIPS-compliant performance. An asset owner is not required to present a track record longer than 10 years but is recommended to do so.

Returns for periods of less than one year must not be annualized.

 |

Provision 21.A.5

The ASSET OWNER MUST comply with all applicable REQUIREMENTS of the GIPS standards, including any Guidance Statements, interpretations, and Questions & Answers (Q&As) published by CFA Institute and the GIPS standards governing bodies.

Discussion

The GIPS standards are ethical standards for investment performance presentation to ensure fair representation and full disclosure of an asset owner's performance. Asset owners must comply with all the requirements of the GIPS standards that apply to the asset owner, including requirements found within the provisions of the GIPS standards as well as within any Guidance Statements, interpretations, and Questions & Answers (Q&As) published by CFA Institute and the GIPS standards governing bodies. Asset owners must also comply with all updates and clarifications published by these entities. Asset owners must review all of the provisions and other requirements of the GIPS standards to determine each requirement's applicability.

The GIPS standards must be applied with the objectives of full disclosure and fair representation of investment performance. Meeting the objectives of full disclosure and fair representation will likely require more than compliance with the minimum requirements of the GIPS standards. If an asset owner applies the GIPS standards in a performance situation that is not addressed specifically by the GIPS standards or is open to interpretation, disclosures other than those required by the GIPS standards may be necessary. To fully explain the performance included in a GIPS Asset Owner Report, asset owners are encouraged to present all relevant information, beyond required and recommended information, that will help the oversight body understand the information presented. Asset owners are also encouraged to adopt the recommendations included in the GIPS standards.

Provision 21.A.6

The ASSET OWNER MUST:

a. Document its policies and procedures used in establishing and maintaining compliance with the REQUIREMENTS of the GIPS standards, as well as any RECOMMENDATIONS it has chosen to adopt, and apply them consistently.

b. Create policies and procedures to monitor and identify changes and additions to all of the Guidance Statements, interpretations, and Q&As published by CFA Institute and the GIPS standards governing bodies.

Discussion

Policies and procedures are essential to implementing adequate business controls at all stages of the investment performance process—from data input to preparing materials for oversight bodies—to ensure the validity of the claim of compliance. An asset owner must document all of the policies and procedures it follows for meeting the requirements of the GIPS standards, as well as any recommendations the asset owner has chosen to adopt. There is no requirement to create and document policies and procedures to comply with requirements that do not apply to the asset owner. However, asset owners must actively make a determination about the applicability of all the requirements of the GIPS standards and document their policies and procedures accordingly.

Once an asset owner establishes its policies and procedures, it must apply them consistently. Policies and procedures should be reviewed regularly to determine if they should be changed or improved, but it is not expected that they will change frequently. An asset owner must not change a policy retroactively solely to enhance performance or to present the asset owner in a better light. Retroactive changes to policies and procedures should be avoided.

Asset owners must also create policies and procedures to monitor and identify changes and additions to all of the Guidance Statements, interpretations, Q&As, and any other guidance published by CFA Institute and the GIPS standards governing bodies. An asset owner should assign at least one person internally who is responsible for monitoring its compliance with the GIPS standards. Depending on the asset owner's size and complexity, it might have a team of people responsible for GIPS compliance, and maintaining compliance may require coordination across multiple departments, including but not limited to operations, performance, portfolio management, and compliance.

Provision 21.A.7

The ASSET OWNER MUST:

a. Comply with all applicable laws and regulations regarding the calculation and presentation of performance.

b. Create policies and procedures to monitor and identify changes and additions to laws and regulations regarding the calculation and presentation of performance.

Discussion

The GIPS standards provide an ethical framework for calculating and presenting an asset owner's investment performance history. Asset owners must also comply with all applicable laws and regulations regarding the calculation and presentation of performance. Asset owners must create policies and procedures to ensure that they adhere to all applicable laws and regulations regarding the calculation and presentation of performance. Asset owners must also have policies and procedures to identify and monitor changes and additions to laws and regulations regarding the calculation and presentation of performance.

Compliance with applicable laws and regulations does not necessarily result in compliance with the GIPS standards. Asset owners claiming compliance must comply with the GIPS standards in addition to all applicable laws and regulations. In the rare cases when laws and regulations conflict with the GIPS standards, asset owners are required to comply with the laws and regulations and disclose the manner in which the laws or regulations conflict with the GIPS standards.

Provision 21.A.8

The ASSET OWNER MUST NOT present performance or PERFORMANCE-RELATED INFORMATION that is false or misleading. This REQUIREMENT applies to all performance or PERFORMANCE-RELATED INFORMATION on an ASSET OWNER–wide basis and is not limited to those materials that reference the GIPS standards. The ASSET OWNER may provide any performance or PERFORMANCE-RELATED INFORMATION that is specifically requested by the OVERSIGHT BODY.

Discussion

The underlying principles of the GIPS standards, fair representation and full disclosure, help to ensure that oversight bodies are not given performance or performance-related information that is incomplete, inaccurate, biased, or fraudulent. Asset owners must not present any performance or performance-related information that is known to be inaccurate or that may mislead the oversight body. This concept applies to all performance or performance-related materials on an asset owner–wide basis and is not limited to those materials that reference the GIPS standards. An example of information that is misleading is model performance that is presented as actual performance.

Asset owners are not limited to providing only GIPS-compliant information to oversight bodies. Asset owners may present other performance or performance-related information as long as it is not false or misleading.

The following information has an especially high risk of being interpreted by oversight bodies in a way that is likely to be false and misleading:

• Actual performance linked to model, hypothetical, backtested, or simulated historical results; and

• Performance compared with an inappropriate benchmark.

This information must not be presented in a GIPS Asset Owner Report.

Outside of a GIPS Asset Owner Report, an asset owner may present this information if asked to do so by the oversight body. The information may be presented in a presentation that is created for and will be used only by the oversight body.

An asset owner may wish to present performance for select periods, other than the period(s) required and recommended by the GIPS standards. For example, if the market experienced a sharp decline during the first two months of the calendar year and became more stable in March, the asset owner may want to show performance of its strategy from 1 January through 28 February and from 1 March through 31 December. If the performance for these select periods is presented in addition to the performance for the required periods, it may be presented in a GIPS Asset Owner Report. This presentation is permitted because the select periods are being presented in addition to the required periods. To present only performance for the select periods without performance for the required periods, especially if the select periods were chosen because the periods had the highest performance, would be false and misleading and is not permitted for asset owners that claim compliance with the GIPS standards. Asset owners may present performance for select periods outside of GIPS Asset Owner Reports with the appropriate disclosure and labeling.

The asset owner may provide to an oversight body any information requested by the oversight body. Such information must be accompanied by comprehensive disclosures that explain the information being presented.

Provision 21.A.9

If the ASSET OWNER does not meet all the applicable REQUIREMENTS of the GIPS standards, the ASSET OWNER MUST NOT represent or state that it is "in compliance with the Global Investment Performance Standards except for..." or make any other statements that may indicate compliance or partial compliance with the GIPS standards.

Discussion

When the asset owner makes the claim of compliance with the GIPS standards, it is representing that all of the applicable requirements of the GIPS standards have been met on an asset owner–wide basis. Either an asset owner meets all of the applicable requirements of the GIPS standards and may claim compliance, or an asset owner does not meet all of the applicable requirements of the GIPS standards and must not claim compliance or partial compliance with the GIPS standards. If the asset owner does not meet all the applicable requirements of the GIPS standards, the asset owner must not represent or state that it is "in compliance with the Global Investment

 |

Performance Standards except for…" or make any other statements that may indicate compliance or partial compliance with the GIPS standards.

Provision 21.A.10

Statements referring to the calculation methodology as being "in accordance," "in compliance," or "consistent" with the Global Investment Performance Standards, or similar statements, are prohibited.

Discussion

Only asset owners that manage actual assets may claim compliance with the GIPS standards. For asset owners that do manage actual assets, either directly or by having the discretion to hire and fire external managers, compliance can be achieved only when the asset owner has met all of the applicable requirements of the GIPS standards on an asset owner–wide basis. Compliance with the GIPS standards involves more than just the use of a particular calculation methodology. To avoid any confusion, references to the GIPS standards must not be used in the context of reporting performance or performance presentations when the asset owner is not in compliance with the GIPS standards.

Software vendors, custodians, and other service providers do not manage actual assets and cannot claim compliance with the GIPS standards. They may make reference to the fact that their software or services may help an asset owner achieve or maintain compliance with the GIPS standards, if that is the case. For example, a software vendor may state that its software system calculates performance that satisfies the calculation requirements of the GIPS standards, but the vendor must not state or imply that using its system automatically makes an asset owner compliant with the GIPS standards or that its system complies with the GIPS standards.

Provision 21.A.11

The ASSET OWNER MUST:

a. Provide a GIPS ASSET OWNER REPORT for all TOTAL FUNDS and any additional COMPOSITES that have been created to the OVERSIGHT BODY.

b. Provide an updated GIPS ASSET OWNER REPORT for all TOTAL FUNDS and any additional COMPOSITES that have been created to the OVERSIGHT BODY at least once every 12 months.

Discussion

A GIPS Asset Owner Report is defined as an asset owner's presentation for a total fund or composite that contains all the information required by the GIPS standards and may also include recommended information or supplemental information. An oversight body is defined as those who have direct oversight responsibility for total fund assets and total asset owner assets. Asset owners claiming compliance with the GIPS standards must provide the respective oversight body with a GIPS Asset Owner Report for each total fund that it manages, as well as a GIPS Asset Owner Report for any additional composites the asset owner has chosen to create. (An additional composite is a grouping of portfolios representing a particular strategy or asset class that the asset owner chooses to present in a GIPS Asset Owner Report.) An updated GIPS Asset Owner Report for all total funds and any additional composites must be provided to the oversight body at least once every 12 months. Asset owners are not required to present all composites, including those used for internal reporting purposes, in a GIPS Asset Owner Report. Asset owners must provide a GIPS Asset Owner Report to the oversight body only for those additional composites that the asset owner has chosen to create and present in a GIPS Asset Owner Report.

If an asset owner manages more than one total fund according to the same investment strategy, the asset owner has a choice regarding how the total funds are presented to the oversight body. The asset owner may choose to present each total fund separately to the oversight body, creating a separate GIPS Asset Owner Report for each total fund. Alternatively, the asset owner may include all total funds managed according to the same investment strategy in one total fund composite and create one GIPS Asset Owner Report for the total fund composite to present to the oversight body.

If the asset owner has more than one oversight body, or manages assets on behalf of another organization, each GIPS Asset Owner Report must be provided to the respective oversight body.

Because an asset owner is required to demonstrate that it provided the oversight body with the required GIPS Asset Owner Reports (see Provision 21.A.14), an asset owner should establish policies and procedures for tracking which GIPS Asset Owner Reports were provided to the oversight body and any other entities and when they were provided. Doing so will allow an asset owner to determine when the oversight body must receive an updated GIPS Asset Owner Report. It will also allow an asset owner to know who must receive a corrected GIPS Asset Owner Report in cases for which the asset owner determines that a previously distributed GIPS Asset Owner Report contained a material error. (See Provision 21.A.16.)

Asset owners that wish to distribute a GIPS Asset Owner Report more broadly may include it on their websites and in their annual reports, newsletters, and other distributed materials. Asset owners may also refer to their claim of compliance with the GIPS standards on their websites and in their annual reports, newsletters, and other distributed materials in accordance with the GIPS Advertising Guidelines. (See Section 26 for the GIPS Advertising Guidelines.)

 |

Asset owners are not limited to providing only GIPS Asset Owner Reports to their oversight bodies. Asset owners may present other performance or performance-related information, in addition to the GIPS Asset Owner Report, as long as it is not false or misleading. Asset owners may also provide any performance or performance-related information their oversight bodies request. Such information must be accompanied by comprehensive disclosures that explain the information being presented.

Provision 21.A.12

The ASSET OWNER may provide a GIPS ASSET OWNER REPORT to those who have a more indirect fiduciary role but is not REQUIRED to do so.

Discussion

Asset owners are not required to provide a GIPS Asset Owner Report to those who have a more indirect fiduciary role, such as a member of the legislative body that drafts the legislation establishing a public pension plan, but may do so if they wish. For those total funds that have beneficiaries or regulators, the asset owner should provide a GIPS Asset Owner Report to the beneficiaries or regulators upon request. Asset owners are required to comply with all applicable laws and regulations regarding the calculation and presentation of performance.

Provision 21.A.13

When providing GIPS ASSET OWNER REPORTS to an OVERSIGHT BODY, the ASSET OWNER MUST update these reports to include information through the most recent annual period end within 12 months of that annual period end.

Discussion

GIPS Asset Owner Reports are designed to provide information to oversight bodies that will help them understand the investment mandate, characteristics, and performance of the total fund(s) and any additional composites that have been created by the asset owner. (An additional composite is a grouping of portfolios representing a particular strategy or asset class that the asset owner chooses to present in a GIPS Asset Owner Report.) Although a GIPS Asset Owner Report contains important information, the value and relevance of that information are affected by the timeliness with which the GIPS Asset Owner Report is updated. A GIPS Asset Owner Report that presents returns that are significantly out of date is not helpful to the oversight body. It is therefore required that any GIPS Asset Owner Report that is provided to an oversight body must be updated within 12 months of the end of the most recent annual period end. It is recommended that GIPS Asset Owner Reports be updated quarterly to provide more timely information to the asset owner's oversight body (see Provision 21.B.2).

As an example, suppose that an asset owner presents calendar-year returns in GIPS Asset Owner Reports. GIPS Asset Owner Reports with information through 31 December 2020 must be available no later than 31 December 2021. The lack of the completion of an annual verification is not a valid reason for delaying the updating of a GIPS Asset Owner Report.

Provision 21.A.14

The ASSET OWNER MUST be able to demonstrate how it provided GIPS ASSET OWNER REPORTS to the OVERSIGHT BODY.

Discussion

Asset owners are required by the GIPS standards to provide GIPS Asset Owner Reports to their oversight bodies. Asset owners are also required to have policies and procedures in place that are used to establish and maintain compliance with the requirements of the GIPS standards. Therefore, an asset owner claiming compliance with the GIPS standards must have specific policies and procedures to ensure that the required GIPS Asset Owner Report(s) have been provided to the oversight body. These should include policies and procedures for tracking which GIPS Asset Owner Reports were provided to the oversight body and when. For example, an asset owner's policies and procedures might specify that the required GIPS Asset Owner Report(s) will be included as part of the standard package of materials prepared for the oversight body, and that a checklist will be used to indicate the dates on which a GIPS Asset Owner Report was provided to the oversight body and which version of the GIPS Asset Owner Report was provided. Documenting the date on which the GIPS Asset Owner Report was last provided to the oversight body, as well as which version was provided, will help an asset owner fulfill the requirement to provide the required GIPS Asset Owner Report(s) to the oversight body at least once every 12 months. The most effective policies and procedures for an asset owner will depend on the circumstances surrounding the typical interactions between the asset owner and the oversight body.

To demonstrate that the asset owner provided the GIPS Asset Owner Report to the oversight body, it is necessary for the asset owner to document both the relevant policies and procedures for providing the required reports to the oversight body and the steps taken to implement the relevant policies and procedures.

Provision 21.A.15

A BENCHMARK used in a GIPS ASSET OWNER REPORT MUST reflect the investment mandate, objective, or strategy of the TOTAL FUND or COMPOSITE. The ASSET OWNER MUST NOT use a price-only BENCHMARK in a GIPS ASSET OWNER REPORT.

Discussion

Benchmarks are important tools that aid in the planning, implementation, and evaluation of a total fund's or additional composite's investment policy. (An additional composite is a grouping of portfolios representing a particular strategy or asset class that the asset owner chooses to present in a GIPS Asset Owner Report.) They also help facilitate discussions with an asset owner's oversight body regarding the relationship between risk and return. As a result, asset owners are required to present the total return for a benchmark that reflects the total fund's or additional composite's investment mandate, objective, or strategy in all GIPS Asset Owner Reports.

GIPS Asset Owner Reports that include time-weighted returns must include total fund or additional composite returns for each annual period. GIPS Asset Owner Reports that include money-weighted returns must include the additional composite return for the longest period for which the asset owner has records through the most recent annual period end. Asset owners must present benchmark returns for these required periods and for any additional periods for which total fund or additional composite returns are presented. For example, if a GIPS Asset Owner Report includes quarterly total fund returns, quarterly benchmark returns must also be included.

The benchmark that appears in a GIPS Asset Owner Report may be different from the benchmark(s) used for the portfolios that are included in the total fund or additional composite. For example, an asset owner may decide that it is appropriate to include portfolios with different benchmarks in the same additional composite. Additionally, an asset owner may present more than one benchmark in a GIPS Asset Owner Report. The asset owner must determine the appropriate benchmark or benchmarks for each total fund and additional composite.

There may be situations in which there is no appropriate benchmark for a total fund, total fund composite, or an additional composite—that is, no benchmark exists that reflects the total fund's, total fund composite's, or additional composite's investment mandate, objective, or strategy. In such cases, the asset owner must not present a benchmark in the GIPS Asset Owner Report and must disclose why no benchmark is presented.

Because the GIPS standards require that the total return for the benchmark be presented, a price-only index would not satisfy the requirements of the GIPS standards. This also applies to benchmarks that are components of a blended benchmark. A blended benchmark is the combination of two or more indexes, such as a benchmark that consists of 50% of the ABC Index and 50% of the DEF Index. In this example, both the ABC Index and the DEF Index must be total return benchmarks, not price-only benchmarks. However, when there is an appropriate total return benchmark, a price-only benchmark may be presented in a GIPS Asset Owner Report as supplemental information, as well as outside of a GIPS Asset Owner Report, if the price-only benchmark is accompanied by a total return benchmark. If a price-only benchmark is included in a GIPS Asset Owner Report as supplemental information or presented outside of a GIPS Asset Owner Report, it must be identified as a price-only benchmark, and there must be sufficient disclosures so that an oversight body understands the difference between the return of a price-only benchmark and the return of a total return benchmark. If no appropriate total return benchmark exists, the asset owner may not present a price-only benchmark in a GIPS Asset Owner Report but may present it outside of a GIPS Asset Owner Report. In such cases, "price only" must be included in the label or the name of the benchmark. As in all cases where a price-only benchmark is presented, there must be sufficient disclosures so that an oversight body understands the difference between the return of a price-only benchmark and the return of a total return benchmark.

Some benchmarks may appear to be price-only benchmarks because they do not include income, but they should be considered total return benchmarks. These include the following:

- public market equivalent (PME) benchmarks,
- commodity benchmarks, and similar benchmarks, that do not have income because of the nature of the benchmark constituents, and
- target returns, such as an 8% hurdle rate.

Please refer to Provision 25.C.28 for more information on PME benchmarks.

Provision 21.A.16

The ASSET OWNER MUST correct MATERIAL ERRORS in GIPS ASSET OWNER REPORTS and MUST:

a. Provide the corrected GIPS ASSET OWNER REPORT to the current verifier.

b. Provide the corrected GIPS ASSET OWNER REPORT to any former verifiers that received the GIPS ASSET OWNER REPORT that had the MATERIAL ERROR.

c. Provide the corrected GIPS ASSET OWNER REPORT to any OVERSIGHT BODY that received the GIPS ASSET OWNER REPORT that had the MATERIAL ERROR.

 |

Discussion

Asset owners claiming compliance with the GIPS standards are likely to face situations in which errors are discovered that must be specifically addressed. Even with the tightest of controls, errors will occur. An error, which can be qualitative or quantitative, is any component of a GIPS Asset Owner Report that is missing or inaccurate. Errors in GIPS Asset Owner Reports can result from, but are not limited to, incorrect, incomplete, or missing:

- total fund or composite returns or assets,
- asset owner assets,
- benchmark returns,
- number of portfolios in a composite,
- three-year annualized ex post standard deviation, and
- disclosures.

Asset owners must establish error correction policies and procedures, and materiality must be defined in the error correction policies.

If a GIPS Asset Owner Report contains a material error, the GIPS Asset Owner Report must be corrected and the corrected GIPS Asset Owner Report that includes a disclosure of the error must be provided to the current verifier and to any former verifiers that received the GIPS Asset Owner Report with the material error. Former verifiers that received the GIPS Asset Owner Report with the material error must receive the corrected GIPS Asset Owner Report with a disclosure of the error in case the error affects a previously issued verification report or performance examination report. The asset owner must also provide the corrected GIPS Asset Owner Report to any oversight body that received the GIPS Asset Owner Report that had the material error.

The asset owner generally has three options for dealing with non-material errors in GIPS Asset Owner Reports:

1. *Take no action.*

   The error is deemed immaterial and does not require a change to any data or disclosures in the GIPS Asset Owner Report.

2. *Correct the GIPS Asset Owner Report with no disclosure of the change and no distribution of the corrected GIPS Asset Owner Report.*

   The correction of the error results in a change to one or more items in the GIPS Asset Owner Report, but these changes are deemed not material and therefore do not require disclosure of the change or distribution of the corrected GIPS Asset Owner Report.

3. *Correct the GIPS Asset Owner Report with disclosure of the change and no distribution of the corrected GIPS Asset Owner Report.*

   The correction of the error results in a change to one or more items in the GIPS Asset Owner Report, but these changes are deemed not material. The asset owner does not distribute the corrected GIPS Asset Owner Report but, according to the asset owner's pre-established error correction policies and procedures, the error does require disclosure in the corrected GIPS Asset Owner Report.

An asset owner must decide what criteria it will use to determine materiality. The following is a definition of materiality that asset owners might find useful as a starting point:

   An error (or item) is material if the magnitude of the omission or misstatement of performance information, in light of surrounding circumstances, makes it probable that the judgment of a reasonable person relying on the information would have been changed by the omission or misstatement.

When determining materiality, an asset owner may consider the following factors:

- magnitude of the error, in absolute and relative terms,
- whether the error is material relative to the benchmark,
- whether returns are overstated or understated,
- significance of the missing or incorrect disclosures,
- whether the error affects returns over time or is a timing issue,
- period(s) affected by the error,
- if these policies will be applied asset owner–wide or on a total fund–specific or composite-specific basis, and
- whether the asset owner has any legal or regulatory obligations related to error correction.

The size and effect of the error may vary for different asset types (e.g., equities, fixed income, emerging market equities), reporting periods (e.g., monthly, quarterly, or annual returns), and by time period (e.g., prior to a specific date, more than five years ago).

It is important to remember that the omission of required information is considered an error, as well as a misstatement in the information presented. The GIPS Asset Owner Report must be corrected to include the required information, and the asset owner must apply its error correction policies to determine if the error is material.

Asset owners must establish and document error correction policies and procedures and must implement them consistently. An asset owner should strive to create an unambiguous process that includes specific steps to discover errors.

 |

Provision 21.A.17

The ASSET OWNER MUST maintain a complete list of TOTAL FUND DESCRIPTIONS and COM-POSITE DESCRIPTIONS for any COMPOSITE that has been presented in a GIPS ASSET OWNER REPORT. The ASSET OWNER MUST include terminated TOTAL FUNDS and COMPOSITES on this list for at least five years after the TOTAL FUND TERMINATION DATE or COMPOSITE TERMINATION DATE. If the ASSET OWNER has only one REQUIRED TOTAL FUND and has not chosen to create any additional COMPOSITES, the GIPS ASSET OWNER REPORT for the TOTAL FUND may be used.

Discussion

Asset owners must maintain a complete list of total fund descriptions and composite descriptions for any total fund, total fund composite, or additional composite that has been presented in a GIPS Asset Owner Report. (An additional composite is a grouping of portfolios representing a particular strategy or asset class that the asset owner chooses to present in a GIPS Asset Owner Report.) If the asset owner has only one total fund or only one total fund composite and has not chosen to create any additional composites, the GIPS Asset Owner Report for the total fund or the total fund composite represents the asset owner's list of total fund and composite descriptions. This is because the composite description in the GIPS Asset Report for the total fund or the total fund composite is required to be included in the GIPS Asset Owner Report, and the GIPS Asset Owner Report can be used to meet this requirement. If the asset owner chooses to create additional composites representing one or more strategies within a total fund, or the asset owner has more than one required GIPS Asset Owner Report for its total funds, a list of total fund descriptions and composite descriptions must be maintained.

If the asset owner competes for business and claims compliance with the GIPS standards when doing so, this list must also include the strategies that the asset owner uses when it competes for business.

Asset owners must include terminated total funds and terminated composites on the asset owner's list of total fund descriptions and composite descriptions for at least five years after the total fund termination date or composite termination date.

The total fund description or composite description is general information regarding the investment mandate, objective, or strategy of the total fund or composite. The description must include enough information to allow the oversight body to understand the key characteristics of the total fund's or composite's investment mandate, objective, or strategy, including the risks of the strategy; how leverage, derivatives, and short positions are used if they are a material part of the strategy; and whether or not illiquid assets are a material part of the strategy. In addition to these factors, the total fund description is expected to include the following:

- the total fund's asset allocation as of the most recent annual period end,

- the actuarial rate of return or spending policy description, and
- a description of the asset classes and/or other groupings within the total fund, such as the composition of the asset class, strategy used, types of management used (e.g., active, passive, internal, external), and relevant exposures.

A total fund description or composite description must include the material risks of the total fund's or composite's strategy. All investment products or strategies have some degree of inherent common risk, such as, but not limited to, market, currency, investment-specific, inflation, or interest rate risk. Asset owners may include these generic, systemic risks in a total fund description or composite description but are not required to do so. It is not expected that the total fund description or composite description will include reference to every one of these generic, systemic risks unless any is materially more significant to a total fund strategy or composite strategy than typically expected. The following are some of the risks that should be discussed in a total fund description or composite description if the risks could have had significant influence on the historical returns or are a key feature of the strategy and need to be considered alongside future expected returns:

- liquidity risk,
- leverage and derivatives risk,
- credit/issuer risk,
- counterparty risk,
- interest rate risk, and
- currency risk.

Some strategies can be highly volatile or may be profoundly affected by market-driven events. Asset owners are reminded that total fund descriptions and composite descriptions must reflect material changes in the risks of the strategies that would be caused by market events or changes imposed by the asset owner.

A sample list of total fund descriptions and composite descriptions is provided in Appendix D of the GIPS standards.

Provision 21.A.18

The ASSET OWNER MUST provide the complete list of TOTAL FUND DESCRIPTIONS and COMPOSITE DESCRIPTIONS to the OVERSIGHT BODY if it makes such a request. If the ASSET OWNER has only one REQUIRED TOTAL FUND and has not chosen to create any additional COMPOSITES, the GIPS ASSET OWNER REPORT for the TOTAL FUND may be used.

|

Discussion

In addition to maintaining a complete list of total fund descriptions and composite descriptions, as applicable to the asset owner, asset owners must provide this list to the oversight body upon request. If the asset owner has only one required total fund or only one required total fund composite, and has not chosen to create any additional composites, the GIPS Asset Owner Report for the total fund or the total fund composite may be used. (An additional composite is a grouping of portfolios representing a particular strategy or asset class that the asset owner chooses to present in a GIPS Asset Owner Report.)

Although asset owners are required to provide the complete list of total fund descriptions and composite descriptions to the oversight body upon request, they are encouraged to provide this information to anyone else who makes the request.

Provision 21.A.19

All data and information necessary to support all items included in GIPS ASSET OWNER REPORTS and GIPS ADVERTISEMENTS MUST be captured, maintained, and available within a reasonable time frame, for all periods presented in these reports and advertisements.

Discussion

A fundamental principle of the GIPS standards is the need for asset owners to be able to ensure the validity of their claim of compliance. It is, therefore, important for oversight bodies, verifiers, and regulators to have confidence that all items included in a GIPS Asset Owner Report or GIPS Advertisement are supported by the appropriate records.

Asset owners must maintain records to be able to recalculate their performance history as well as substantiate all other information, including supplemental information, included in a GIPS Asset Owner Report or GIPS Advertisement, for all periods shown. This requirement applies regardless of the period for which performance is presented in the GIPS Asset Owner Report or GIPS Advertisement (e.g., 1 year, 5 years, 10 years, or more than 10 years). This requirement is consistent with the regulatory requirements of many countries. In some jurisdictions, however, regulators require records to be kept for longer periods than those required by the GIPS standards. Care should be taken to ensure that the asset owner follows the strictest of the recordkeeping requirements applicable to the asset owner.

It is understood that the required data may not be immediately available. For example, data may need to be retrieved from an offsite location or from a third-party service provider.

However, the data and information required to be maintained by this provision must be available in a usable format within a reasonable time frame. In all instances, either paper (hard-copy) records or electronically stored records will suffice. If records are stored electronically, the records must be accessible and able to be printed or downloaded, if needed. Records stored in a system that is not operable and from which data cannot be retrieved will not satisfy the recordkeeping requirements.

Although most asset owners are looking for a very precise list of the minimum documents that must be maintained to support all parts of the GIPS Asset Owner Report or GIPS Advertisement, including the ability to recalculate the asset owner's performance history, there is no single list of records that will suffice in all situations. Each asset owner must determine for itself which records must be maintained. The following lists include records that asset owners should consider maintaining to meet the recordkeeping requirements of this provision. None of these lists should be considered exhaustive. The actual records required will depend on the asset owner's particular circumstances.

Records to Support Portfolio-Level Returns

1. portfolio statements, including positions and valuations, as well as information supporting the determination of fair value,
2. information to prove that performance is based on actual assets, including bank/custodial statements and reconciliations,
3. portfolio transactions reports,
4. outstanding trades reports,
5. corporate action reports,
6. income received/earned reports,
7. accrued income reports,
8. foreign or other withholding tax reclaim reports,
9. cash flow/weighted cash flow reports,
10. foreign exchange rates,
11. information on calculation methodology used,
12. information provided by a third party (e.g., an external manager or custodian) for which an asset owner may need to take additional steps to ensure the information can be relied on to meet the requirements of the GIPS standards,
13. investment management fee information, and
14. pooled fund profit and loss allocation reports.

Records to Support Total Fund and Composite-Level Returns and Other Total Fund and Composite-Level Data

1. portfolios included in the total fund or composite,
   a. when each portfolio entered (and exited, if applicable) the total fund or composite,
   b. each portfolio's return for each period, and
   c. value used to weight each portfolio (beginning value or beginning value plus weighted external cash flows) for each period,
2. number of total funds or portfolios in the composite and the total fund or composite assets as of each annual period end and any other period for which this information is presented in GIPS Asset Owner Reports,
3. support for investment management costs used to calculated net-of-fees returns, and support for the three-year annualized ex post standard deviation calculation and any additional risk measures, and
4. exchange rates used to convert investments or returns from different currencies.

Records to Support the Inclusion of a Total Fund or Portfolio in a Specific Composite

1. total fund or composite definition,
2. investment management agreements and investment guidelines for externally managed portfolios, as well as amendments thereto, and
3. documentation regarding changes to a total fund's or portfolio's investment mandate, objective, or strategy.

Records to Support Other Information Included in a GIPS Asset Owner Report

1. composite cumulative committed capital,
2. composite since-inception paid-in-capital,
3. composite since-inception distributions,
4. composite investment multiple, realization multiple, PIC multiple, and unrealized multiple,
5. audited financial statements,
6. investment management fee schedules charged by external managers,
7. pooled fund expense ratio and investment management fee schedules charged by external managers, if full gross-of-fees returns are calculated,
8. performance-fee calculations for performance fees paid to external managers,
9. benchmark returns, including custom benchmark calculations,

10. estimated transaction costs, and

11. supplemental information.

Records to Support an Asset Owner's Claim of Compliance

1. GIPS standards policies and procedures, covering all periods for which the asset owner claims compliance with the GIPS standards,

2. definition of the asset owner, historically and current,

3. supporting calculation for total asset owner assets as of each annual period end and any other period for which total asset owner assets are presented in GIPS Asset Owner Reports,

4. total fund and composite inception dates and composite creation dates,

5. list of total fund descriptions and composite descriptions, and

6. GIPS Asset Owner Reports for all total funds, total fund composites, and additional composites (an additional composite is a grouping of portfolios representing a particular strategy or asset class that the asset owner chooses to present in a GIPS Asset Owner Report).

Any Additional Records Necessary to Support a Claim of Compliance

1. system and control reports from independent accountants or other third parties (e.g., accounting reports, other internal controls/compliance reports for custodians),

2. third-party (e.g., external manager, custodial, performance data provider) agreements,

3. minutes of relevant decision-making committees (e.g., a board, an investment committee, a GIPS compliance committee),

4. systems manuals, especially for the systems that generate the portfolio, total fund, and composite returns, as well as for GIPS Asset Owner Reports (including both numerical information and disclosures),

5. documentation of providing GIPS Asset Owner Reports to the oversight body,

6. documentation that the asset owner followed its error correction policy, including providing, in the case of a material error, a corrected GIPS Asset Owner Report, including disclosure of the error, to all appropriate parties in accordance with the asset owner's error correction policy,

7. underlying benchmark data (if not publicly available), and

8. documentation of providing the following to any oversight body that requested:

   a. a list of total fund descriptions and composite descriptions,

   b. portfolio-weighted custom benchmark component weights for prior periods,

   c. policies for valuing portfolios,

d. policies for calculating performance,

e. policies for preparing GIPS Asset Owner Reports,

f. verification report(s), and

g. performance examination report(s).

It is expected that all asset owners will have disaster recovery plans to mitigate the loss of records for any reason, whether it is a catastrophic event beyond the control of the asset owner or a situation within the control of the asset owner. If an asset owner that claims compliance with the GIPS standards experiences a catastrophic event that destroys all of its records and electronic or other backup systems, the asset owner should try to reconstruct the necessary information by obtaining the information from custodians, consultants, verifiers, or any other party outside the asset owner that might have duplicate copies of those records. If the underlying data to support the GIPS Asset Owner Report was destroyed because of extreme circumstances beyond the asset owner's control and is unavailable from other sources, however, the asset owner may continue to claim compliance and show performance if the lack of records for the unavailable period(s) is disclosed.

For example, assume Asset Owner A claims compliance with the GIPS standards, and the records for Asset Owner A from its inception on 1 January 2017 through 31 December 2017 were destroyed under extreme circumstances beyond the asset owner's control. The asset owner can continue to claim compliance with the GIPS standards for that period but must disclose that the asset owner's records for the period from 1 January 2017 through 31 December 2017 were destroyed under extreme circumstances beyond the asset owner's control and the data are unavailable from other sources. The asset owner must also consider any applicable regulatory requirements and must remember that the GIPS standards are ethical standards based on the principles of fair representation and full disclosure. Any performance information that is presented must adhere to these principles.

Asset owners that have not yet claimed compliance with the GIPS standards and want to do so but do not have records to support the recordkeeping requirements because they experienced a catastrophic event in the past cannot take advantage of this exception from the recordkeeping requirement. They cannot claim compliance until they have complied with all the requirements of the GIPS standards, including the requirement to have the records to support at least a one-year performance track record.

All asset owners are reminded that, above all else, they must follow all applicable laws and regulations regarding the calculation and presentation of performance, including all recordkeeping requirements.

Provision 21.A.20

The ASSET OWNER is responsible for its claim of compliance with the GIPS standards and MUST ensure that the records and information provided by any third party on which the ASSET OWNER relies meet the REQUIREMENTS of the GIPS standards.

Discussion

An asset owner that claims compliance with the GIPS standards is responsible for its claim of compliance. Therefore, an asset owner that uses a third party to provide any service (e.g., custody, external management, performance measurement), and relies on that service, must ensure that the records and information provided by the third-party service provider meet the requirements of the GIPS standards. The asset owner is responsible for ensuring that the data received from various external sources is accurate and must be able to aggregate any information supplied by external service providers as needed. An asset owner should carefully research any third-party service provider and should engage only reputable service providers.

It is acknowledged that, in some cases, it may be challenging to obtain information from a third party that meets the requirements of the GIPS standards. An asset owner has the option of bringing performance in house rather than relying on a third party. An asset owner can also make adjustments to the information provided by a third party so that it meets the requirements of the GIPS standards. For example, if an asset owner received composite data from a third party, and the third party weighted portfolio returns by ending value instead of beginning value, the asset owner could weight the returns itself using beginning-of-period values to calculate composite returns. As another example, suppose that a custodian reflects interest income on a cash basis. The asset owner may make adjustments to the income information from the custodian to properly reflect accrued income.

When using third-party service providers, asset owners are encouraged to ensure that adequate service-level agreements are in place to provide the historical records necessary, both currently and as needed in the future. It may be helpful to partner with custodians, external managers, and other service providers that understand what is needed to comply with the GIPS standards.

Asset owners must establish policies and procedures to ensure that third-party information, such as the information provided by a custodian or an external manager, adheres to the requirements of the GIPS standards, if the asset owner relies on that information. A thorough examination of third-party service providers' policies and procedures should be conducted when they are hired. It is recommended that asset owners that claim compliance with the GIPS standards conduct periodic testing or other monitoring procedures that ensure that the policies and procedures of any third-party service provider on which the asset owner relies have not changed since the service provider was first hired and are being applied consistently and appropriately.

Finally, this provision does not require the asset owner to "look through" net asset value (NAV) valuations of externally managed pooled funds. Asset owners may rely on NAVs of pooled funds that reflect the fund's tradable value and use that as the pooled fund's fair value.

Provision 21.A.21

The ASSET OWNER MUST NOT LINK actual performance to historical THEORETICAL PERFORMANCE.

Discussion

Theoretical performance is a broad term encompassing different types of performance that is not derived from a total fund, composite, or portfolio with actual assets invested in the strategy or fund presented ("non-actual" performance). There are several names for this type of information: model, backtested, hypothetical, simulated, indicative, and forward-looking, among others. Asset owners may present theoretical performance but, within a GIPS Asset Owner Report, historical theoretical performance must not be linked to the performance of a total fund or composite that includes actual portfolios. As an example, an asset owner that has a composite with a one-year track record must not extend the history to five years using backtested performance for four years linked to the actual one-year performance. As a second example, a composite that lost all its constituent portfolios for two months cannot continue the track record without interruption by using the benchmark return for the missing months of performance to simulate performance. In this case, the asset owner also cannot link the periods prior to the break and after the break to create a continuous track record as if there was no break. Historical total fund or composite returns must represent performance of only actual discretionary assets managed by the asset owner.

Theoretical performance, such as simulated or model performance, may be included in a GIPS Asset Owner Report. If theoretical performance is included in a GIPS Asset Owner Report, it must not be linked to actual performance and must be clearly labeled as supplemental information. Theoretical performance should be provided only to those parties who are sufficiently experienced and knowledgeable to assess the relevance and limitations of theoretical performance.

Outside of a GIPS Asset Owner Report, asset owners may present actual performance linked to historical theoretical performance to the oversight body. The linked information may be presented in a presentation that is created for and will be used only by the oversight body. There must be sufficient disclosures regarding the linked performance so that the oversight body understands the relevance and limitations of the information.

Provision 21.A.22

Changes in an ASSET OWNER's organization MUST NOT lead to alteration of historical performance.

Discussion

Over time, the organization of an asset owner may change. Regardless of the reason for the change in the asset owner's organization, historical total fund or composite performance must remain part of the asset owner's history. In considering issues regarding the use of historical performance, it is important to remember that performance is the record of the asset owner, not of the individual. For example, suppose that a sole investment decision maker for a portfolio managed internally leaves the asset owner and the new portfolio manager continues to manage the portfolio according to the same investment mandate or strategy as the previous portfolio manager. The asset owner must link the historical performance of the portfolio to the ongoing performance achieved by the new portfolio manager.

Provision 21.A.23

The ASSET OWNER MUST NOT present non-GIPS-compliant performance in GIPS ASSET OWNER REPORTS.

Discussion

Only GIPS-compliant performance is allowed to be presented in a GIPS Asset Owner Report. Outside of a GIPS Asset Owner Report, asset owners may present their entire performance history, which may include both non-compliant and compliant performance.

As an example for presenting time-weighted returns, suppose that an asset owner with a six-year track record is newly coming into compliance with the GIPS standards. The asset owner has elected to bring only one year of its performance history into compliance. The asset owner may present the entire six-year track record outside of a GIPS Asset Owner Report by linking the compliant and the non-compliant track record. However, the GIPS Asset Owner Report must include only the portion of the track record that is compliant with the GIPS standards.

When presenting money-weighted returns (MWRs) for an additional composite in a GIPS Asset Owner Report, the asset owner must not present non-GIPS-compliant performance. (An additional composite is a grouping of portfolios representing a particular strategy or asset class that the asset owner chooses to present in a GIPS Asset Owner Report.) The measurement period for the MWR is from inception of the composite through the most recent annual period end. If the asset owner does not have the records to support the track record from the composite's inception through the most recent annual period end, the asset owner must present the annualized MWR for the longest period for which the asset owner has such records, through the most recent annual period end. All inputs to the MWR calculation must meet any applicable requirements of the GIPS standards. This includes using fair value for periods beginning on or after 1 January 2011 and using daily external cash flows beginning 1 January 2020. See the discussion of Provisions 22.A.22 and 22.A.23. MWRs that are calculated using inputs that do not meet all applicable requirements of the GIPS standards must not be presented in GIPS Asset Owner Reports.

Any MWRs that the asset owner chooses to include in the GIPS Asset Owner Report for a total fund or a total fund composite must be calculated using inputs that meet the applicable requirements of the GIPS standards, as described above.

Provision 21.A.24

If an ASSET OWNER competes for business, the ASSET OWNER MUST follow all sections of the GIPS Standards for Firms and all applicable REQUIREMENTS when competing for business.

Discussion

Most asset owners do not compete for business. An asset owner that does not compete for business and chooses to comply with the GIPS standards must comply with the GIPS Standards for Asset Owners and not the GIPS Standards for Firms when reporting performance to the oversight body. This means that the asset owner must calculate and present total fund and total fund composite returns that are net-of-fees. (A net-of-fees return reflects the deduction of transaction costs, all fees and expenses for externally managed pooled fund, investment management fees for externally managed segregated accounts, and investment management costs.) These net-of-fees returns must be included in a GIPS Asset Owner Report that is presented annually to the oversight body.

Some asset owners have the authority to compete for business by marketing to prospective clients and prospective investors, as traditional investment managers do. Asset owners that choose to comply with the GIPS standards when competing for business must follow the guidance and requirements of the GIPS Standards for Firms rather than the GIPS Standards for Asset Owners when competing for business.

It is also possible that an organization may act as both an asset owner, where investment authority and ownership are vested with the organization itself, as well as an asset manager, where it is competing for assets whose vesting lies with external clients. In such cases, the asset owner has two choices for how to define itself for the purpose of complying with the GIPS standards.

Option 1:

The asset owner bifurcates its assets into two entities: one defined as an asset owner and one defined as a firm. If an asset owner bifurcates its assets into two entities, it is not required to claim compliance with the GIPS standards for both entities.

As an example, suppose that Asset Owner ABC, which acts as both an asset owner and an asset manager that competes for business and has been in existence for more than five years, has decided to bifurcate its assets into two separate entities for the purposes of complying with the GIPS standards: Asset Owner A, an asset owner, and Firm A, which competes for business.

- If Asset Owner A chooses to claim compliance, it must follow the GIPS Standards for Asset Owners. The total asset owner assets of Asset Owner A must include only those assets managed on behalf of the organization itself. It must not include the assets that are managed on behalf of clients and are included in Firm A. Asset Owner A must create a GIPS Asset Owner Report for its total funds, total fund composites, and any additional composites that it chooses to create and present in a GIPS Asset Owner Report, based on the assets in Asset Owner A. (An additional composite is a grouping of portfolios representing a particular strategy or asset class that the asset owner chooses to present in a GIPS Asset Owner Report.)

  When preparing its required GIPS Asset Owner Report(s), Asset Owner A must follow the GIPS Standards for Asset Owners. For example, it must include a period of at least one year in its GIPS Asset Owner Reports when initially coming into compliance with the GIPS standards, and GIPS Asset Owner Reports for a total fund must present net-of-fees returns using time-weighted returns. Asset Owner A must follow all of the other requirements of the GIPS Standards for Asset Owners as well. If Asset Owner A is required by laws or regulations to report to the oversight body on all assets that it manages, or is requested to do so by the oversight body, it would report on the combined assets of Asset Owner A and Firm A outside of a GIPS Asset Owner Report.

- If Firm A, which competes for business, chooses to claim compliance, it must follow the GIPS Standards for Firms. The assets of Firm A must include only those assets that Firm A obtained by competing for business, and Firm A will report performance to prospective clients and prospective investors, rather than to an oversight body.

  When competing for business, Firm A must create and present GIPS Composite Reports and/or GIPS Pooled Fund Reports, following all of the requirements of the GIPS Standards for Firms regarding the presentation and reporting of performance and performance-related information to prospective clients and prospective investors. For example, Firm A must be able to claim compliance for a period of a minimum of five years, and it must include in its GIPS Composite Reports and GIPS Pooled Fund Reports at least five years of compliant performance when it initially comes into compliance with the GIPS Standards for Firms.

  Firm A may present gross-of-fees returns, net-of-fees returns, or both in its GIPS Composite Reports and GIPS Pooled Fund Reports. Because Firm A is defined to include only those assets obtained by competing for assets, it must not present the performance history of assets included in the Asset Owner A–defined entity in its GIPS Composite Reports or GIPS Pooled Fund Reports. Firm A may present the performance history of Asset Owner A assets as supplemental information as long as this performance history is clearly labeled as such. Please refer to Provision 24.A.8 for more information on presenting supplemental information.

Option 2:

The asset owner does not bifurcate its assets and instead defines itself as both an asset owner and a firm. If the asset owner chooses this option, the asset owner is defined as one entity but must follow different GIPS standards for the calculation and presentation of performance when dealing with different parties. When calculating and presenting performance to the oversight body, the asset owner must follow the GIPS Standards for Asset Owners. When calculating and presenting performance to prospective clients and prospective investors, the asset owner must follow the GIPS Standards for Firms. (This assumes that the asset owner has chosen to comply with the GIPS standards when reporting performance to the oversight body as well as when it competes for business. An asset owner that does not bifurcate its assets is not required to claim compliance with both the GIPS Standards for Firms and the GIPS Standards for Asset Owners.)

- When the asset owner is calculating and presenting performance to the oversight body, it follows the GIPS Standards for Asset Owners. It must prepare a GIPS Asset Owner Report for all total funds, total fund composites, and additional composites it has chosen to present in a GIPS Asset Owner Report managed in its role as asset owner for the oversight body. In its GIPS Asset Owner Reports, it must be able to claim compliance for at least one year and must present at least one year of compliant performance when it first claims compliance with the GIPS standards. Its GIPS Asset Owner Report for its total fund(s) and total fund composites must present net-of-fees returns, and all total funds and total fund composites must be calculated using time-weighted returns. Total asset owner assets reported in its GIPS Asset Owner Reports must include all assets managed by the asset owner, including assets managed by the asset owner and those assets that were obtained through competition, because they are all part of one defined entity.

  Because the oversight body would generally have responsibility for the entire organization, the asset owner should provide information to the oversight body about all assets managed by the asset owner. The asset owner is required to provide the oversight body with a list of composite descriptions upon request by the oversight body. This list must include all composites managed by the asset owner for external clients as well as those total funds and composites managed on behalf of the organization. The asset owner should offer to provide GIPS-compliant information for assets managed for external clients. The asset owner should also inform the oversight body about the amount of assets managed on behalf of the organization and assets managed on behalf of external clients.

- When the asset owner is marketing to external clients, it must follow the GIPS Standards for Firms. It must be able to claim compliance for a minimum period of five years, and it must include in its GIPS Composite Reports or GIPS Pooled Fund Reports at least five years of compliant performance when initially claiming compliance. It may present gross-of-fees returns, net-of-fees returns, or both in its GIPS Composite Reports and GIPS Pooled Fund Reports. It must prepare and present to prospective clients and prospective investors the appropriate GIPS Composite Report or GIPS Pooled Fund Report for the composite or pooled fund that it is marketing to that prospective client or prospective investor. Total firm assets reported in its GIPS Composite Reports or GIPS Pooled Fund Reports would include all assets managed by the asset owner, whether the assets are managed in its role as asset owner or in its role as an asset manager that competes for business.

Provision 21.A.25

The ASSET OWNER MUST present TIME-WEIGHTED RETURNS for all TOTAL FUNDS.
The ASSET OWNER may present MONEY-WEIGHTED RETURNS in addition to TIME-WEIGHTED RETURNS for TOTAL FUNDS.

Discussion

For an asset owner, the total fund is typically a multi-asset class fund, including such asset classes as equity, fixed income, real estate, and private equity, designed to fulfill the investment mandate. Although different types of assets are included in the total fund, total fund performance must be calculated using a consistently applied time-weighted return (TWR) methodology that adheres to the requirements of the GIPS standards.

Although asset owners must present TWRs for total funds and total fund composites in GIPS Asset Owner Reports, it is recommended that money-weighted returns (MWRs) also be presented if the asset owner believes that the presentation of MWRs would be helpful and important in understanding the performance of the total fund. While required TWRs represent the performance of the asset owner, MWRs represent the combination of the asset owner's performance and the effect of cash flows. In the case of a pension plan, although neither the pension plan sponsor nor the pension fund participants typically control the timing of the cash flows into or out of the total fund, MWRs may be informative in determining how the timing of plan contributions and withdrawals has impacted the total fund's performance. MWRs may also be a better indicator of profitability of the total fund. In addition, local regulations may require some asset owners to report MWRs in financial statements.

Provision 21.A.26

The ASSET OWNER MUST choose to present TIME-WEIGHTED RETURNS, MONEY-WEIGHTED RETURNS, or both for each additional COMPOSITE and MUST consistently present the selected returns for each additional COMPOSITE.

Discussion

In addition to the required GIPS Asset Owner Report for each total fund or total fund composite, the asset owner may choose to create additional composites. (An additional composite is a grouping of portfolios representing a particular strategy or asset class that the asset owner chooses to present in a GIPS Asset Owner Report.) As an example, an asset owner may wish to create an additional composite that represents all domestic equities within a total fund. If the asset owner chooses to create any additional composites, it must prepare a GIPS Asset Owner Report for each additional composite.

A time-weighted return (TWR) is required to be presented in all GIPS Asset Owner Reports representing a total fund or total fund composite. For GIPS Asset Owner Reports representing additional composites, the asset owner may choose to present either TWRs, money-weighted returns (MWRs), or both. There are no criteria that must be met for an MWR to be presented in a GIPS Asset Owner Report for an additional composite. (In contrast, the GIPS Standards for Firms require certain criteria to be met if MWRs are presented in a GIPS Composite Report or GIPS Pooled Fund Report.) Once an asset owner has chosen which return(s) it will present in a GIPS Asset Owner Report for an additional composite, the asset owner must consistently present the return(s) selected for each additional composite.

To "consistently present" the selected returns means that, once an asset owner has chosen the type of return to present in a GIPS Asset Owner Report for an additional composite (TWR, MWR, or both), it must continue to present the selected return(s) unless there is a compelling reason to change the type of return presented. Doing so is important for consistency in the presentation of an asset owner's track record and to prevent the changing of the type of return presented in order to present more-favorable returns.

The following are some of the appropriate reasons for an asset owner to change the type of return presented:

- There is a change in the GIPS standards with respect to the requirements for the use of a TWR or MWR;
- There are new legal or regulatory requirements that require a change in the type of return presented;
- The asset owner decides to present both TWRs and MWRs in GIPS Asset Owner Reports for additional composites, rather than the one type of return that had been presented, in order to provide a more comprehensive view of performance;
- A review of the asset owner's strategy leads to a changed view regarding the type of return that most accurately reflects the strategy (this should be a very infrequent occurrence); or
- There is a change in the strategy's key features that would lead to a change in the type of return that is presented (for example, there may be a change in the investments used for the strategy).

Once a change in the type of return(s) presented is made, however, the newly selected return(s) type must be presented unless there is a compelling reason to make another change.

Provision 21.A.27

The ASSET OWNER MUST notify CFA Institute of its claim of compliance by submitting the GIPS COMPLIANCE NOTIFICATION FORM. This form:

a. MUST be filed when the ASSET OWNER initially claims compliance with the GIPS standards.

b. MUST be updated annually with information as of the most recent 31 December, with the exception of ASSET OWNER contact information, which MUST be current as of the form submission date.

c. MUST be filed annually thereafter by 30 June.

Discussion

Asset owners must notify CFA Institute of their claim of compliance by submitting the GIPS Compliance Notification Form, which can be found on the GIPS standards website (gipsstandards.org).

When an asset owner is first coming into compliance, the asset owner must submit the GIPS Compliance Notification Form to CFA Institute once it has met all of the requirements of the GIPS standards and is at the point of initially claiming compliance with the GIPS standards. The asset owner must not claim compliance with the GIPS standards unless the GIPS Compliance Notification Form has been submitted to CFA Institute.

After the initial filing, the form must be filed annually by 30 June. Information provided in the GIPS Compliance Notification Form must be as of the most recent 31 December, with the exception of the asset owner's contact information. Contact information must be current as of the form's submission date. The period of any verification performed would not impact the notification submission date or the date as of which the information is provided. Asset owners must establish policies and procedures to ensure the form is submitted by the deadline.

The GIPS Compliance Notification Form must reflect the definition of the asset owner used to determine asset owner–wide compliance with the GIPS standards even when the definition of the asset owner is different from the legal entity of the asset owner. If an asset owner competes for business and complies with the GIPS Standards for Firms as well as the GIPS Standards for Asset Owners, the asset owner would submit a GIPS Compliance Notification Form for each entity.

 |

Provision 21.A.28

If an ASSET OWNER chooses to be verified, it MUST gain an understanding of the verifier's policies for maintaining independence and MUST consider the verifier's assessment of independence.

Discussion

Verification is a process by which a verification firm (verifier) conducts testing of an asset owner on an asset owner–wide basis, in accordance with the required verification procedures of the GIPS Standards for Verifiers. Verification provides assurance on whether the asset owner's policies and procedures related to total fund and composite maintenance, as well as the calculation, presentation, and distribution of performance, have been designed in compliance with the GIPS standards and have been implemented on an asset owner–wide basis. Crucial to the verification process is the assumption by all interested parties that the verifier performs its service in an unbiased manner and is not testing its own work. Therefore, verification must be performed by an independent third party. If an asset owner chooses to be verified, the asset owner must understand the verifier's policies for ensuring that the verifier is independent from the asset owner. To do so, the asset owner should obtain a summary of the verifier's policies for ensuring independence and should have sufficient discussions with the verifier to understand the policies.

Although an asset owner is not responsible for a verifier's independence assessment, the asset owner must understand the issues encountered and the conclusions reached by the verifier regarding independence from the asset owner, particularly when the verifier provides other GIPS-compliance-related services. This understanding is important because the asset owner may have knowledge that the verifier does not have. The asset owner is obligated to inform the verifier if the asset owner believes that the verifier missed some factor in its independence assessment or if the asset owner believes the assessment is incorrect.

When considering verifier independence, both the asset owner and the verifier must keep in mind the following question: If the asset owner's oversight body relies on the fact that the asset owner has been verified, could the oversight body's perception of the verification's value potentially change if the oversight body knew about other existing relationships between the asset owner and the verifier? An asset owner must gain enough of an understanding of the verifier's policies and procedures for maintaining independence to lead to a strong "no" to this question.

The asset owner's understanding of the verifier's policies and procedures for maintaining independence is not a one-time event. It is an ongoing process and must be performed in connection with each verification engagement.

It may be helpful for both the verifier and the asset owner to consider independence as a continuum. At one extreme of the continuum is a verifier that has no other relationships with the asset owner. At the other extreme is a verifier with existing relationships and independence issues with the asset owner that cannot be resolved, such that the verifier cannot conduct the engagement because independence cannot be achieved. The asset owner and the verifier must determine where their relationship lies on this continuum and whether it is appropriate to proceed with the verification engagement.

21.B. Fundamentals of Compliance—Recommendations

Provision 21.B.1

The ASSET OWNER SHOULD comply with the RECOMMENDATIONS of the GIPS standards, including RECOMMENDATIONS in any Guidance Statements, interpretations, and Q&As published by CFA Institute and the GIPS standards governing bodies.

Discussion

The recommendations contained in the GIPS standards are suggested tasks or actions that are considered best practice and should be followed or performed, although they are not required. The GIPS standards must be applied with the objectives of fair representation and full disclosure of investment performance. However, meeting the objectives of fair representation and full disclosure, which are the fundamental principles of the GIPS standards, may mean that an asset owner must follow the recommendations in addition to the requirements of the GIPS standards. If an asset owner chooses to adopt any recommendations, its policies and procedures must reflect how that recommendation is applied.

Provision 21.B.2

The ASSET OWNER SHOULD update GIPS ASSET OWNER REPORTS quarterly.

Discussion

GIPS Asset Owner Reports contain important information, but the value and relevance of that information are affected by the timeliness with which the GIPS Asset Owner Report is updated. A GIPS Asset Owner Report that includes returns that are significantly out of date is not helpful to the asset owner's oversight body. For this reason, it is required that asset owners update GIPS Asset Owner Reports within 12 months of the end of the most recent annual period, even if a

 |

GIPS standards verification for the asset owner, or a performance examination of a total fund or composite, is not yet completed. In the interest of fair representation and full disclosure, however, it is recommended that GIPS Asset Owner Reports be updated quarterly to provide more timely information to the asset owner's oversight body.

When updating a GIPS Asset Owner Report that presents time-weighted returns to include monthly, quarterly, or year-to-date returns, asset owners are required to update only the following information:

- total fund or composite returns,
- benchmark returns, and
- significant events that would help an oversight body understand the GIPS Asset Owner Report.

When performance in a GIPS Asset Owner Report that presents money-weighted returns is updated more frequently than the required annual update, asset owners are required to update only the following information:

- the total fund or composite return,
- the benchmark return,
- the information required by Provision 25.A.3, such as the paid-in capital (PIC) multiple, the investment multiple (TVPI), and the unrealized multiple (RVPI) as of the most recent quarter end or month end, and
- significant events that would help an oversight body understand the GIPS Asset Owner Report.

Asset owners may also update other information in the GIPS Asset Owner Report, such as total asset owner assets and the number of portfolios in a composite, but are not required to do so.

Provision 21.B.3

The ASSET OWNER SHOULD be verified.

Discussion

Verification is intended to provide an asset owner and its oversight body additional confidence in the asset owner's claim of compliance with the GIPS standards. It is recommended that asset owners be verified for all period(s) for which compliance with the GIPS standards is claimed. Verification may increase the knowledge of the asset owner's performance measurement team and improve the consistency and quality of the asset owner's GIPS standards–related performance information. Verification may also result in improved internal policies and procedures. Verification does not provide assurance, however, about the performance of any specific total fund or composite or the accuracy of any specific GIPS Asset Owner Report. Although verification brings additional credibility to the claim of compliance, it does not provide assurance on the asset owner's claim of compliance with the GIPS standards in its entirety.

|

22. INPUT DATA AND CALCULATION METHODOLOGY

22.A. Input Data and Calculation Methodology—Requirements

Assets

> **Provision 22.A.1**
>
> TOTAL ASSET OWNER ASSETS MUST be the aggregate FAIR VALUE of all discretionary and non-discretionary assets managed by the ASSET OWNER. This includes both fee-paying and non-fee-paying PORTFOLIOS.[1]

Discussion

Asset owners include (but are not limited to) pension funds (both public and private), endowments, foundations, family offices, provident funds, insurers and reinsurers, sovereign wealth funds, and fiduciaries that have investment responsibility for a pool of assets. They typically do not have external clients. Total asset owner assets include all discretionary and non-discretionary assets for which an asset owner has investment management responsibility. Total asset owner assets include assets assigned to an external manager provided the asset owner has discretion over the selection of the external manager. All portfolios included in total asset owner assets must be included in a total fund.

For periods beginning on or after 1 January 2011, asset owners must value all discretionary and non-discretionary assets in accordance with the definition of fair value. Fair value is defined in the GIPS standards as the amount at which an investment could be sold in an arm's-length transaction between willing parties in an orderly transaction. The valuation must be determined using the objective, observable, unadjusted quoted market price for an identical investment in an active market on the measurement date, if available. In the absence of an objective, observable, unadjusted quoted market price for an identical investment in an active market on the measurement date, the valuation must represent the asset owner's best estimate of the fair value. Fair value must include any accrued income.

---

[1] REQUIRED for periods beginning on or after 1 January 2011. For periods prior to 1 January 2011, TOTAL ASSET OWNER ASSETS MUST be the aggregate of either the FAIR VALUE or the MARKET VALUE of all discretionary and non-discretionary assets managed by the ASSET OWNER.

The requirement to value all assets at fair value applies to assets in both fee-paying and non-fee-paying portfolios. One example of a non-fee-paying portfolio is one that is internally managed and no explicit investment management fees are charged for managing those assets. Total asset owner assets must reflect the fair value of all discretionary and non-discretionary assets within the asset owner definition. For periods prior to 1 January 2011, total asset owner assets must be the aggregate of the fair value or market value of all discretionary and non-discretionary assets under management within the defined asset owner.

Some asset owners use an external manager to manage some or all of the total asset owner assets. If an asset owner has discretion over selecting (i.e., can hire and/or fire) the external manager, the asset owner must include the assets managed by the external manger in total asset owner assets. If the asset owner does not have discretion over external manager selection, it must not include the assets managed by the external manager in total asset owner assets, total fund assets, or composite assets.

An asset owner retains the responsibility for its claim of compliance for all of its assets, including its discretionary assets managed by external managers and their reported performance. Therefore, all discretionary assets managed by an external manager must be treated by the asset owner in the same manner as assets managed internally and must be subject to the same policies and procedures as internally managed assets. If the asset owner intends to place reliance on information from external managers, it must ensure that the records and information provided by the external manager meet the requirements of the GIPS standards. For reliance on third-party records and information, please refer to Provision 21.A.20.

Total asset owner assets must include:

- assets for which the asset owner has either conditional or unconditional authority to make investment decisions;
- fee-paying assets and non-fee-paying assets;
- assets managed outside the asset owner (e.g., by external managers) for which the asset owner has asset allocation (assignment) authority (i.e., the asset owner has discretion over the selection of the external manager); and
- cash and cash equivalents (substitutes). (See Provision 22.A.8 for additional guidance on the inclusion of cash and cash equivalents in total asset owner assets.)

Provision 22.A.2

TOTAL ASSET OWNER ASSETS, TOTAL FUND assets, and COMPOSITE assets MUST:

a. Include only actual assets managed by the ASSET OWNER.
b. Be calculated net of leverage and not grossed up as if the leverage did not exist.

Discussion

Total asset owner assets, total fund assets, and composite assets must include only actual assets managed by the asset owner. Assets represented by simulated, backtested, or model performance must not be included in total asset owner assets, total fund assets, or composite assets because such assets do not represent actual assets managed by the asset owner.

Total asset owner assets, total fund assets, and composite assets must include any externally managed assets for which the asset owner has discretion in selecting the external manager.

When a total fund or composite strategy employs leverage, the total fund or composite assets and total asset owner assets must be presented net of the leverage and not grossed up as if the leverage did not exist. For example, if an asset owner is managing a total fund that has $200 million in assets and the asset owner chooses to borrow $50 million, the total fund's net assets are $200 million, and its gross assets are $250 million. Because the asset owner chose to lever the total fund, the asset owner must use $200 million when calculating total asset owner assets, total fund assets, and composite assets if the total fund is in a composite.

Provision 22.A.3

The ASSET OWNER MUST NOT double count assets when calculating TOTAL ASSET OWNER ASSETS, TOTAL FUND assets, and COMPOSITE assets.

Discussion

Asset owners are prohibited from double counting assets when calculating total asset owner assets, total fund assets, or composite assets. If double counting is not eliminated, assets reported will be inflated and result in a misleading GIPS Asset Owner Report. For asset owners that create additional composites that include portfolios included in the total fund, or include portfolios in more than one composite, care must be taken to ensure assets are not counted more than once. (An additional composite is a grouping of portfolios representing a particular strategy or asset class that the asset owner chooses to present in a GIPS Asset Owner Report.)

As an example, suppose that Asset Owner XYZ has created two additional composites, the All Equity Composite and the Externally Managed Equity Composite. Asset Owner XYZ has the following three equity portfolios:

Portfolio 1 is internally managed and invested in domestic equities, with net assets of €20 million.

Portfolio 2 is an externally managed segregated account invested in international equities, with net assets of €30 million.

 |

Portfolio 3 is an externally managed pooled fund invested in global equities, with net assets of €20 million.

The All Equity Composite includes Portfolio 1, Portfolio 2, and Portfolio 3 and has net assets of €70 million.

The Externally Managed Equity Composite includes Portfolio 2 and Portfolio 3 and has net assets of €50 million.

Each of these portfolios must be included only once in the calculation of total fund assets and total asset owner assets.

Provision 22.A.4

TOTAL FUND and COMPOSITE performance MUST be calculated using only actual assets managed by the ASSET OWNER.

Discussion

Total fund and composite performance must be calculated using only actual assets managed by the asset owner. This performance must include any externally managed assets for which the asset owner has discretion in selecting the external manager.

Simulated, backtested, or model performance must not be included in any total fund or composite because such performance does not represent actual assets managed by the asset owner. Similarly, asset owners must not blend the history of two existing total funds or composites to create simulated performance for a "hybrid" or model total fund or composite and present it as a GIPS-compliant track record. For example, if the performance of actual portfolios in an equity additional composite is combined with the performance of actual portfolios in a fixed-income additional composite to show what the results might have been had the equity and fixed-income portfolios been combined, the results would be considered a simulated strategy. (An additional composite is a grouping of portfolios representing a particular strategy or asset class that the asset owner chooses to present in a GIPS Asset Owner Report.) This "hybrid" or model composite may be presented as supplemental information only if all of the component parts are presented. Even though the returns for the equity and fixed-income additional composites are based on actual assets managed by the asset owner, the arbitrary method of combining them historically is subject to manipulation and does not represent real-time, actual asset allocation decisions. The performance results of this simulated strategy would, therefore, be considered hypothetical performance.

Asset owners may present theoretical performance in GIPS Asset Owner Reports. Theoretical performance is not derived from actual assets invested in the strategy presented, and it includes model, backtested, hypothetical, simulated, indicative, ex ante, and forward-looking performance. Theoretical performance must be clearly labeled as supplemental information. Asset owners must not link historical theoretical performance with actual performance.

General/Accounting

Provision 22.A.5

TOTAL RETURNS MUST be used.

Discussion

Total return, which is measured over a specified period, has two components: (1) the appreciation or depreciation (capital change) of the assets in the total fund or portfolio over the specified period and (2) the income earned on the assets in the total fund or portfolio over the specified period. When calculating the performance of a total fund or portfolio, the GIPS standards require asset owners to use a total return.

Provision 22.A.6

TRADE DATE ACCOUNTING MUST be used.[2]

Discussion

For periods beginning on or after 1 January 2005, trade date accounting must be used. For the purpose of complying with the GIPS standards, trade date accounting is defined as recognizing the asset or liability on the date of purchase or sale and not on the settlement date. Recognizing the asset or liability within three business days of the date the transaction is entered into (the trade date T, T + 1, T + 2, or T + 3) satisfies the trade date accounting requirement for purposes of the GIPS standards. Settlement date accounting recognizes the asset or liability on the date when the exchange of cash and investments is completed.

For purchases, when using settlement date accounting, any movement in value between the trade date or booking date and the settlement date will not affect performance until the settlement date. For purchases, when using trade date accounting, the change in value will be reflected for each valuation between trade date and settlement date. Performance comparisons between total funds,

---

[2] REQUIRED for periods beginning on or after 1 January 2005.

portfolios, and/or composites that use settlement date accounting and those that use trade date accounting may not be valid. The same problem occurs when comparing settlement date total funds, portfolios, and composites with their benchmarks.

The principle behind requiring trade date accounting is to ensure there is not a significant lag between trade execution and reflecting the trade in the performance of a portfolio. For the purpose of compliance with the GIPS standards, portfolios are considered to satisfy the trade date accounting requirement provided that transactions are recorded and recognized consistently and within normal market practice—typically, a period between the trade date and up to three business days after the trade date (T + 3).

External cash flows are typically booked on the date when they are actually received or distributed. If an asset owner receives notification of incoming funds and trades on a pre-announced external cash inflow before it is received into the portfolio, the portfolio will become leveraged during the period between the trade date and the date when the external cash inflow is physically received. To "cover" this additional exposure and eliminate the leverage effect, asset owners may choose to apply the trade date and settlement date principles to pre-arranged external cash flows by booking the external cash flow with a trade date that reflects the date the asset owner may trade in advance of the external cash inflow and a settlement date that reflects the date when the cash is received. If the asset owner chooses to match the trade date of pre-announced external cash flows to the trade date of trades related to those external cash flows, it should establish this as its policy and treat all pre-announced external cash flows consistently.

Provision 22.A.7

ACCRUAL ACCOUNTING MUST be used for fixed-income securities and all other investments that earn interest income, except that interest income on cash and cash equivalents may be recognized on a cash basis. Any accrued income MUST be included in the beginning and ending TOTAL FUND and PORTFOLIO values when performance is calculated.

Discussion

Accrual accounting allows the recording of financial transactions as they come into existence rather than when they are paid or settled. When determining the valuation for a security that pays interest income, asset owners must include the income that would have been received at the end of the performance period had the security actually paid interest income earned during the performance period.

Accrued interest income must be included in both the beginning and ending total fund and portfolio values when performance is calculated. Interest should be accrued for a security in the total fund or portfolio using whatever method is customary and appropriate for that security.

Some instruments already include accrued income as part of the security's market price. If income for these instruments is being accrued as part of the income recognition process, steps should be taken to ensure that the income is not double counted.

Income on cash and cash equivalents may be recognized on either an accrual or cash basis. Accrued income for cash and cash equivalents can be difficult to calculate. Unlike bonds with a known coupon rate, some short-term securities (e.g., overnight deposits) may not have a published interest rate. Asset owners must develop a methodology for accounting for short-term interest earnings and consistently apply the method selected. Asset owners could consider using the last actual known interest rate to accrue income for the most recent period. When the actual rate becomes known, an adjustment can then be made to allocate the actual income earned to the proper period. In this way, there is no systematic underestimation or overestimation of income, and income is also properly assigned to the period when earned. Cash basis accounting (recording the income for short-term cash and cash equivalents as it is actually received) will tend to lag the suggested accrual method by recognizing income a month after it was earned. Either method is acceptable, however, and the method chosen must be used consistently.

An issue that may arise is how to calculate the performance of a bond, including the accrual of interest, when a bond goes into default. In this situation, the asset owner must recognize the loss when it occurred, and the historical performance must not be recalculated. The accrual of interest must be included in the calculation method up until the point of the bond's default. At that point, the calculation method would reflect the loss of accrued interest by adjusting the amount of accrued interest to zero. When and if the bond comes out of default and there is a reasonable expectation that the bond will commence paying interest, including back interest, the asset owner must begin accruing for such interest payments. The asset owner must not allocate such payments over periods when they were originally due but not paid.

Provision 22.A.8

Cash and cash equivalents that are considered discretionary and part of the investable assets of the TOTAL FUND MUST be included in TOTAL FUND assets and performance calculations.

Discussion

Asset owners often maintain a number of cash accounts. Some are held within the total fund and are available for investment along with other total fund assets. When cash and cash equivalents are considered discretionary and part of the investable assets of the total fund, they must be included in all total fund assets and performance calculations. The asset owner's asset allocation decisions, including allocation to cash, are a component of the investment strategy implementation and thus part of the total fund's return.

 |

If the asset owner does not control the actual investment of cash (e.g., cash is always invested in a custodial money market fund) but does control the amount of the total fund that is allocated to cash, then the cash assets must be included in the asset owner's total fund assets and the performance of cash must be included in the total fund performance. The fact that the investment of cash is technically not under the asset owner's control will not generally affect the total fund's returns as much as the allocation of assets to cash, which is under the asset owner's control.

Operating cash accounts that are not available for investment, such as a checking account used for payments to beneficiaries, vendors, and others, should not be included in total fund assets and performance calculations.

If a cash account has multiple purposes and is available for investment as well as used as an operating cash account, and an asset owner is unable to differentiate the portion of the cash account that is available for investment, it is recommended that a conservative approach be taken. The entire cash account should be considered available for investment and included in total fund assets and performance calculations.

Cash accounts that are not included in total fund assets because they are not available for investment must not be used in the calculation of total asset owner assets. Asset owners must create policies and procedures for the treatment of cash accounts and apply them consistently.

Provision 22.A.9

Returns for periods of less than one year MUST NOT be annualized.

Discussion

Total fund or composite performance reflects only the performance of actual assets managed by the asset owner. When returns for periods of less than one year are annualized, the partial-year return is "extended" in order to create an annual return. The extrapolation of the partial-year return produces a simulated return and does not reflect the performance of actual assets. Therefore, performance for periods of less than one year must not be annualized.

Care must be taken when money-weighted returns (MWRs) are calculated and the total fund or composite has less than a year of performance. Many asset owners use Excel to calculate MWRs using the XIRR function. The XIRR function calculates an annualized internal rate of return (IRR) (an IRR is a method that can be used to calculate an MWR). When calculating an XIRR for a period of less than one year, the annualized return generated must be "de-annualized."

The non-annualized since-inception IRR (SI-IRR) can be calculated as follows:

$$R_{SI-IRR} = \left[(1 + r_{SI-IRR})^{\frac{TD}{365}} \right] - 1,$$

where

R_{SI-IRR}	=	non-annualized since-inception internal rate of return
r_{SI-IRR}	=	annualized since-inception internal rate of return
TD	=	total number of calendar days in the measurement period (less than one year)

For example, a portfolio is funded with $1,000,000 cash on 1 September 2020. Another $75,000 is contributed on 10 September 2020. At the end of the month, 30 September 2020, the portfolio is valued at $1,100,000. Also assume that end-of-day cash flows are used. Using Excel's XIRR formula, the annualized SI-IRR is 34.41%.

Dates	External Cash Flows & Ending Valuation	Explanation
1 Sep 20	$(1,000,000)	Contribution
10 Sep 20	$(75,000)	Contribution
30 Sep 20	$1,100,000	Portfolio value as of 30 September 2020
	34.41%	Calculated annualized return using XIRR

To calculate the non-annualized return in Excel, using the non-annualized SI-IRR formula, the calculation is as follows:

= (1+0.3441)^(29/365)−1

= 2.38%

Provision 22.A.10

All returns MUST be calculated after the deduction of TRANSACTION COSTS incurred during the period. The ASSET OWNER may use estimated TRANSACTION COSTS only for those PORTFOLIOS for which actual TRANSACTION COSTS are not known.

|

Discussion

Transaction costs are defined as the costs of buying or selling investments. These costs typically take the form of brokerage commissions, exchange fees and/or taxes, and/or bid–offer spreads from either internal or external brokers. Custodial fees charged per transaction should be considered custody fees and not transaction costs. For real estate, private equity, and other private market investments, transaction costs include all legal, financial, advisory, and investment banking fees related to buying, selling, restructuring, and/or recapitalizing investments but do not include dead deal costs.

Gross-of-fees returns, net-of-external-costs-only returns, and net-of-fees returns must reflect the deduction of transaction costs incurred in the purchase or sale of investments. Transaction costs must be deducted when calculating performance because these are costs that must be paid in order to implement the investment strategy. An asset owner may use estimated transaction costs only for those portfolios whose actual transaction costs are not known. It is the asset owner's responsibility to determine if there are any regulatory requirements that would prohibit the use of estimated transaction costs. If such regulatory requirements exist, estimated transaction costs must not be used.

When a portfolio's transaction costs are not known, a reasonable estimate of transaction costs (i.e., an estimate that the asset owner judges to be a fair approximation of actual transaction costs) may be used. Some approaches for determining a reasonable estimate of transaction costs include basing estimated transaction costs on:

- actual transaction costs for portfolios that the asset owner manages in the same or a similar strategy, or
- actual transaction costs for similar securities that trade in a similar market.

The estimate of transaction costs may take the form of a percentage cost that can be applied to the portfolio return to determine the portfolio return after the deduction of those costs, or as a monetary value. If a monetary value is used, for costs that are based on the size of the transaction, the asset owner should scale the monetary transaction cost estimate sourced from a similarly managed portfolio to the monetary value of the portfolio.

For the treatment of estimated transaction costs in bundled fee portfolios, please refer to Provision 22.A.11.

Regardless of the approach used, the asset owner must have documentation supporting the transaction costs on which the estimate is based.

Asset owners that use estimated transaction costs must document their policies and procedures for estimating transaction costs, along with the rationale for their method of estimating transaction costs, and apply the policies consistently. The methodology and assumptions used to estimate transaction costs must be periodically reviewed to ensure that the policies are still judged to result in a reasonable estimate of transaction costs.

Provision 22.A.11

For PORTFOLIOS with BUNDLED FEES, if the ASSET OWNER cannot estimate TRANSACTION COSTS or if actual TRANSACTION COSTS cannot be segregated from a BUNDLED FEE, when calculating GROSS-OF-FEES returns or NET-OF-EXTERNAL-COSTS-ONLY returns, these returns MUST be reduced by the entire BUNDLED FEE or the portion of the BUNDLED FEE that includes the TRANSACTION COSTS.

Discussion

A bundled fee portfolio is an externally managed segregated account that has a fee structure that combines multiple fees into one total or "bundled" fee. Bundled fees can include any combination of investment management fees, transaction costs, custody fees, and/or administrative fees. An example of a bundled fee is an all-in fee, a type of bundled fee that is typically offered in certain jurisdictions where asset management, brokerage, and custody services are offered by the same company. Calculations of gross-of-fees and net-of-external-costs-only returns for all portfolios, including bundled fee portfolios, must reflect the deduction of transaction costs incurred by the portfolio during the measurement period.

A gross-of-fees return is the return on investments reduced by transaction costs and all fees and expenses for externally managed pooled funds incurred during the period. When calculating a bundled fee portfolio's gross-of-fees return, if the asset owner can identify the portion of the bundled fee that includes the transaction costs, that is the only portion of the bundled fee that must be deducted when calculating gross-of-fees returns. If the asset owner is unable to determine the portion of the bundled fee that includes the transaction costs and is unable to determine an appropriate estimate of transaction costs, then the entire bundled fee must be deducted when calculating the bundled fee portfolio's gross-of-fees return.

A net-of-external-costs-only return is the gross-of-fees return reduced by investment management fees for externally managed segregated accounts.[A] A net-of-external-costs-only return must, therefore, reflect the deduction of transaction costs and investment management fees. To meet the requirements of the GIPS standards when calculating a bundled fee portfolio's net-of-external-costs-only return, if the asset owner can identify the portion of the bundled fee that includes transaction costs and investment management fees, that is the only portion of the bundled fee that must be deducted when calculating net-of-external-costs-only returns. If the asset owner is unable to identify the portion of the bundled fee that includes transaction costs and investment

---

[A] The definition of NET-OF-EXTERNAL-COSTS-ONLY included in the Glossary in the 2020 edition of the GIPS standards is incorrect and should state:

NET-OF-EXTERNAL-COSTS-ONLY: The GROSS-OF-FEES return reduced by ~~all costs~~ INVESTMENT MANAGEMENT FEES for externally managed SEGREGATED ACCOUNTS.

 |

management fees, and it is unable to determine an appropriate estimate of transaction costs, then the entire bundled fee must be reflected (i.e., reduce performance) when calculating the bundled fee portfolio's net-of-external-costs-only return.

Provision 22.A.12

All REQUIRED returns MUST be calculated net of leverage.

Discussion

All required returns must be calculated net of leverage. Leverage refers to loans taken at the discretion of the asset owner. For example, suppose that an asset owner is managing a real estate portfolio internally with a value of $1.5 million and borrowed $500,000 to fund a portion of the investments. The net of leverage amount (i.e., the assets on which performance is calculated) is $1 million, not $1.5 million, which is the gross of leverage amount.

Externally managed segregated accounts may also be levered. Using the same example, assume instead that this real estate portfolio was managed by an external manager. The asset owner funded the portfolio with cash, and the external manager borrowed $500,000. The net of leverage amount, $1 million, must be used to calculate this portfolio's performance, not the grossed-up amount of $1.5 million.

The rationale for requiring that all returns be calculated net of leverage is that an unlevered return (i.e., a return that is gross of leverage) is hypothetical, and it is not appropriate for an asset owner to include such a return when calculating performance of a portfolio, total fund, or composite. Unlevered performance is permitted to be presented only as supplemental information.

Provision 22.A.13

The ASSET OWNER MUST calculate performance in accordance with its TOTAL FUND–specific or COMPOSITE-specific calculation policies.

Discussion

An asset owner must create total fund–specific and composite-specific policies for calculating the performance of its total fund(s) and composites. It must apply these policies consistently when calculating performance. An asset owner must ensure that its policies for calculating performance address not only assets managed internally but also those managed externally or for which performance is calculated externally. An asset owner claiming compliance with the GIPS standards that uses external managers and service providers is responsible for having policies and procedures in place to ensure that the relevant outsourced services produce information on which the asset owner relies that is consistent with the requirements of the GIPS standards and that all GIPS standards requirements have been met. (See Provision 21.A.20.)

Although it is not possible to list all of the items that must be included in an asset owner's policies and procedures for calculating the performance of its total funds, portfolios, and any composites, the following are examples of some of the items that an asset owner must address in its policies and procedures relating to performance calculation.

- How the asset owner ensures that the information from external managers and other third-party service providers meets the requirements of the GIPS standards and can be used, as necessary, to produce returns that comply with the GIPS standards;
- The policies for estimating transaction costs, if estimated transaction costs are used;
- The fees and expenses deducted when calculating
    - Full gross-of-fees returns
    - Gross-of-fees returns
    - Net-of external-costs-only returns
    - Net-of-fees returns;
- The methodology for calculating a time-weighted return (TWR) for total funds, portfolios, and composites for which the asset owner presents a TWR;
- The methodology for calculating a money-weighted return (MWR) for total funds, portfolios, and composites for which the asset owner presents an MWR;
- The calculation methodology for total funds and portfolios with external cash flows;
- The treatment of reclaimable withholding taxes when recording interest income and dividends;
- The treatment of side pockets, if any;
- How the asset owner identifies the fees that are being charged, including performance-based fees, for any externally managed pooled funds and externally managed segregated accounts when calculating returns;
- How the asset owner determines the investment management costs for internally and externally managed assets; and
- How the asset owner determines how its various cash accounts are treated when calculating assets and performance.

Although an asset owner must establish a total fund–specific or composite-specific calculation policy, that policy may differentiate calculations used for different types of portfolios in the total fund or composite. For example, suppose that an asset owner has an additional composite that includes two portfolios: an internally managed portfolio that uses a daily TWR calculation methodology and an externally managed segregated account that uses a Modified Dietz return (with revaluations for large cash flows) calculation methodology. (An additional composite is a grouping of portfolios representing a particular strategy or asset class that the asset owner chooses to present in a GIPS Asset Owner Report.) The asset owner may have a different policy for the return calculation methodologies used for internally managed portfolios versus segregated accounts that are included in the same composite. The asset owner must apply the composite-specific calculation policy consistently, however, based on the return calculation methodologies for each type of portfolio in the additional composite.

It is possible that all of an asset owner's total funds and composites use the same calculation policy; however, the appropriate policy must be determined for each total fund and composite. The asset owner must not simply establish this policy on an asset owner–wide basis without considering whether the policy is appropriate for each total fund or composite.

An asset owner's policies and procedures for calculating performance must be designed to ensure that the asset owner adheres to all applicable laws and regulations regarding the calculation and presentation of performance. Asset owners must establish policies and procedures to ensure that performance and performance-related information does not include false or misleading information.

Policies and procedures should be reviewed regularly to determine if they should be changed or improved, but it is not expected that they will change frequently. An asset owner must not change a policy retroactively solely to increase performance or to present the asset owner in a better light. Retroactive changes to policies and procedures should be avoided.

The asset owner should also conduct periodic testing or other monitoring procedures to ensure that all policies and procedures of any third party on which the asset owner relies are being applied consistently and appropriately.

Provision 22.A.14

For an ASSET OWNER invested in underlying POOLED FUNDS, all returns MUST reflect the deduction of all fees and expenses charged at the underlying POOLED FUND level.

Discussion

If an asset owner invests in underlying pooled funds, it must ensure that all returns reflect the deduction of all fees and expenses charged at the underlying pooled fund level. The values of externally managed pooled funds are typically net of embedded investment management fees and other fees and expenses. In some instances, asset owners may pay investment management fees for the management of the pooled funds or other fees and expenses that are not embedded in the value of the pooled funds. All fees and expenses that are embedded in such funds or charged externally on behalf of such funds must be deducted when calculating gross-of-fees returns, net-of-external-costs-only returns, and net-of-fees returns.

Provision 22.A.15

When calculating ADDITIONAL RISK MEASURES:

a. The PERIODICITY of the TOTAL FUND or COMPOSITE returns and the BENCHMARK returns MUST be the same.

b. The risk measure calculation methodology of the TOTAL FUND or COMPOSITE and the BENCHMARK MUST be the same.

Discussion

Evaluating past performance requires an understanding of the risks taken to achieve the results. The asset owner may choose to present additional risk measures for a total fund or composite and for the benchmark that it determines are appropriate for the total fund's or composite's investment mandate, objective, or strategy. An additional risk measure is a risk measure included in a GIPS Asset Owner Report beyond those required to be presented. An asset owner may choose to present a proprietary measure of risk as an additional risk measure, but the asset owner must describe the proprietary measure of risk that is presented and explain why it was selected.

The periodicity of the total fund or composite and the benchmark must be identical when calculating additional risk measures. Periodicity refers to the length of the period over which a variable is measured (e.g., total fund or composite performance calculated monthly has monthly periodicity). As an example, if an asset owner is calculating an additional risk measure for a total fund that has monthly returns and a benchmark that has quarterly returns, the asset owner would be required to use quarterly total fund returns, not monthly returns, when calculating an additional risk measure. The asset owner must also determine that there are enough data points for the selected measure to be statistically significant so as not to be misleading.

It is also required that the risk measure calculation methodology of the total fund or composite and the benchmark be the same. Asset owners are required to select a calculation methodology on a total fund–specific or composite-specific basis, document the methodology in their policies and procedures, and consistently apply that methodology. Asset owners are required to maintain records supporting all calculations presented in GIPS Asset Owner Reports.

|

Valuation

Provision 22.A.16

TOTAL FUNDS and PORTFOLIOS MUST be valued in accordance with the definition of FAIR VALUE.[3]

Discussion

The quality of a return depends on the quality of the valuations included in the calculation of that return. Performance reporting is of little value unless the underlying valuations are based on sound valuation principles. Beginning 1 January 2011, total fund and portfolio valuations must be based on fair value.

Fair value is defined as the amount at which an investment could be sold in an arm's-length transaction between willing parties in an orderly transition. The valuation must be determined using the objective, observable, unadjusted quoted market price for an identical investment in an active market on the measurement date, if available. In the absence of an objective, observable, unadjusted quoted market price for an identical investment in an active market on the measurement date, the valuation must represent the asset owner's best estimate of the fair value. Fair value must include any accrued income.

As noted in the definition of fair value, when determining fair value, asset owners must use the objective, observable, unadjusted quoted market prices for identical investments in active markets on the measurement date, if available. Markets are not always liquid, however, and investment prices are not always objective and/or observable. For illiquid or hard-to-value investments, or for investments for which no observable market value or market price is available, additional steps are necessary. An asset owner's valuation policies and procedures must address situations in which the market prices may be available for similar but not identical investments, inputs to valuations are subjective rather than objective, and/or markets are inactive instead of active.

A very small number of circumstances exist in which cost or book value may be deemed to be fair value, such as real estate in the first year of the purchase of the property. In such a case, if an asset owner can support a determination that cost or book value and fair value are the same, it is acceptable for book value to be used when calculating asset values and returns.

---

[3] REQUIRED for periods beginning on or after 1 January 2011. For periods prior to 1 January 2011, PORTFOLIO valuations (excluding REAL ESTATE and PRIVATE EQUITY) MUST be based on FAIR VALUES or MARKET VALUES. For periods prior to 1 January 2011, REAL ESTATE investments MUST be valued at FAIR VALUE or MARKET VALUE (as previously defined for REAL ESTATE in the 2005 edition of the GIPS standards). For periods ending prior to 1 January 2011, PRIVATE EQUITY investments MUST be valued at FAIR VALUE, according to either the GIPS Private Equity Valuation Principles in Appendix D of the 2005 version of the GIPS standards or the GIPS Valuation Principles in Chapter II of the 2010 edition of the GIPS standards.

It is important that an asset owner establish fair valuation policies that take into account the specific characteristics of asset classes or investment types. For example, to fairly value an investment in an international pooled fund might require an asset owner to roll forward the valuation of the fund to the local market, in order to determine a value that reflects the more current exchange rate.

Provision 22.B.6 includes a recommended valuation hierarchy. Asset owners are not required to follow the valuation hierarchy, but it is recommended that they do so.

Although an asset owner may use external third parties to value investments, the asset owner still retains responsibility for compliance with the GIPS standards, which includes the requirement to fairly value investments.

Over time, the type of valuation required and the minimum valuation frequency have changed. Prior editions of the GIPS standards included valuation guidance specific to private equity. The 2020 edition of the GIPS standards has no private equity–specific requirements. Instead, private equity is included in the broader category of private market investments. Please see the historical valuation requirements for various asset classes in the following exhibit.

Time Frame	Valuation Method	Minimum Valuation Frequency
Total Funds and Portfolios (except private market investments)		
1 Jan 2011 to Current	Fair Value	Monthly and on the date of all large cash flows
1 Jan 2010 to 31 Dec 2010	Fair Value or Market Value	Monthly and on the date of all large cash flows
1 Jan 2001 to 31 Dec 2009	Fair Value or Market Value	Monthly
Prior to 1 Jan 2001	Fair Value or Market Value	Quarterly
Private Market Investments (except private equity and directly owned real estate)		
1 Jan 2011 to Current	Fair Value	Quarterly
Prior to 1 Jan 2011	Fair Value or Market Value	Quarterly
Private Equity		
1 Jan 2011 to Current	Fair Value	Quarterly
1 Jan 2008 to 31 Dec 2010	Fair Value (According to the GIPS Private Equity Valuation Principles in Appendix D of the 2005 edition of the GIPS standards, or the GIPS Valuation Principles in Chapter II of the 2010 edition of the GIPS standards)	Quarterly
Prior to 1 Jan 2008	Fair Value (According to the GIPS Private Equity Valuation Principles in Appendix D of the 2005 edition of the GIPS standards, or the GIPS Valuation Principles in Chapter II of the 2010 edition of the GIPS standards)	Annually

 |

Time Frame	Valuation Method	Minimum Valuation Frequency
Real Estate Directly Owned by the Asset Owner		
1 Jan 2011 to Current	Fair Value	Quarterly
1 Jan 2008 to 31 Dec 2010	Fair Value or Market Value (as previously defined for Real Estate in the 2005 edition of the GIPS standards)	Quarterly
Prior to 1 Jan 2008	Fair Value or Market Value (as previously defined for Real Estate in the 2005 edition of the GIPS standards)	Annually
1 Jan 2012 to Current	External Valuation	1. External valuation every 12 months unless the oversight body stipulates otherwise, in which case investments must be externally valued every 36 months; or 2. Annual financial statement audit
1 Jan 2006 to 31 Dec 2011	External Valuation	Every 36 months

Provision 22.A.17

The ASSET OWNER MUST value TOTAL FUNDS and PORTFOLIOS in accordance with the TOTAL FUND–specific or COMPOSITE-specific valuation policy.

Discussion

When daily calculations are not used, an asset owner must not value a total fund or portfolio "opportunistically" and must follow its total fund–specific or composite-specific valuation policies consistently. For example, assume that an asset owner's valuation policy is to value portfolios for large cash flows, defined in the composite-specific valuation policy as a single external cash flow equal to or greater than 5% of the portfolio's beginning-of-month value. For any single external cash flow that is less than 5% of the portfolio's beginning-of-month value, the asset owner must not value the portfolio. For any single external cash flow that is equal to or greater than 5% of the portfolio's beginning-of-month value, the asset owner must value the portfolio. The asset owner must apply the total fund–specific or composite-specific valuation policy consistently and not "cherry-pick" when to value portfolios.

Although an asset owner must establish a total fund–specific or composite-specific valuation policy, that policy may differentiate valuation frequency for different types of portfolios in the total fund or composite. For example, suppose that an asset owner has a total fund that includes investments in underlying pooled funds, which are valued daily, and externally managed segregated accounts, which are valued monthly and for external cash flows above 5%. The asset owner may have a different policy for the frequency of valuing pooled funds versus segregated accounts that are included in the same total fund. The asset owner must apply the total fund–specific valuation policy consistently, however, based on the valuation frequency for each type of portfolio in the total fund.

It is possible that all of an asset owner's total funds or composites use the same valuation policy; however, the appropriate policy must be determined for each total fund or composite. The asset owner must not simply establish this policy on an asset owner–wide basis without considering whether the policy is appropriate for each total fund or composite.

An asset owner must ensure that its policies for valuing assets address not only assets managed internally but also those managed externally or for which valuations are performed externally. An asset owner that uses external managers and service providers is responsible for having policies and procedures in place to ensure that the relevant outsourced services produce information on which the asset owner relies that is consistent with the requirements of the GIPS standards and that all GIPS standards requirements have been met.

Policies and procedures should be reviewed regularly to determine if they should be changed or improved, but it is not expected that they will change frequently. An asset owner must not change a policy retroactively solely to increase performance or to present the asset owner in a better light. Retroactive changes to policies and procedures should be avoided.

The asset owner should also conduct periodic testing or other monitoring procedures to ensure that all outsourced policies and procedures are being applied consistently and appropriately.

Provision 22.A.18

If the ASSET OWNER uses the last available historical price or preliminary, estimated value as FAIR VALUE, the ASSET OWNER MUST:

a. Consider it to be the best approximation of the current FAIR VALUE.

b. Assess the difference between the approximation and final value and the effect on TOTAL FUND assets or COMPOSITE assets, TOTAL ASSET OWNER ASSETS, and performance, and also make any adjustments when the final value is received.

Discussion

It is not uncommon for private market investments to be valued using preliminary, estimated values. If an asset owner uses either the last available historical price or preliminary, estimated values as fair value, perhaps in order to produce a GIPS Asset Owner Report on a timely basis, the asset owner must consider the estimate of value to be the best approximation of the current fair value, and this must be defined in the asset owner's fair valuation policy. When using preliminary, estimated values, the asset owner should obtain an understanding of the process used to establish estimated values in order to determine whether reliance can be placed on the process.

Asset owners must define the use of the last available historical price or preliminary, estimated values, and the treatment of subsequent final values, in their total fund–specific or composite-specific fair valuation policies. The valuation policies must be followed consistently and made available upon request. If the asset owner uses the last available historical price or preliminary, estimated values, when final values are received, the asset owner must assess the difference between the estimate of value and the final value, as well as the effect on total fund or composite assets, total asset owner assets, and performance. If the final values and resulting performance differ materially, asset owners must determine whether any adjustments to the total fund or composite must be made on a prospective basis or retroactively. If total fund or composite valuations are revised retroactively, asset owners must consider the requirements related to error correction and the asset owner's error correction policies. Differences between final and estimated values are not considered to be errors but are treated similarly.

It is important to remember the underlying principles of the GIPS standards: fair representation and full disclosure. If differences between the estimated and final values are consistently material, the asset owner should reassess whether it is proper to continue to use the estimates of fair value.

Provision 22.A.19

Total funds and composites must have consistent beginning and ending annual valuation dates. Unless the total fund or composite is reported on a non-calendar fiscal year, the beginning and ending valuation dates must be at calendar year end or on the last business day of the year.[4]

Discussion

It is required that total funds and composites have consistent beginning and ending annual valuation dates. Such consistency will result in improved comparability of data. Unless the total fund or composite is reported on a non-calendar fiscal year, the beginning and ending valuation dates of the total fund or composite must be at calendar year end or on the last business day of the year. Portfolios in a total fund or composite must also have consistent beginning and ending valuation dates corresponding to the reporting period. If the total fund or composite beginning or ending annual valuation dates fall on a weekend or a holiday, the asset owner should use the valuation on the first or last business day of the period, respectively. If there is an available benchmark value

---

[4] Required for periods beginning on or after 1 January 2006.

on the same day as the ending valuation day for the total fund or composite, the asset owner should use the benchmark value from the ending valuation day for the total fund or composite. If the total fund or composite ending annual valuation date differs from that of the benchmark, this difference should be disclosed. For example, if the annual period end and the last valuation falls on 30 December because of the New Year's Eve holiday, but the end of the annual period for the benchmark falls on 31 December, any material difference in performance should be disclosed. The asset owner should use the benchmark value from 30 December if it is available.

Note that an asset owner's total fund(s) and/or composites may have different year-end valuation dates if one or more of the asset owner's total funds or composites is reported on a non-calendar fiscal year, whereas other total funds and/or composites are reported as of calendar year end or on the last business day of the year. The annual valuation dates must correspond to the reporting dates for the total fund or composite. It is important, however, that the annual periods within a GIPS Asset Owner Report are consistent. For example, a GIPS Asset Owner Report that reports a total fund's performance annually as of 30 June, its fiscal year end, must consistently report data for years ending 30 June for the total fund. The asset owner may decide in the future to create a GIPS Asset Owner Report for the total fund based on a 31 December valuation and reporting date; however, the asset owner may not mix 30 June and 31 December annual reporting periods in the same GIPS Asset Owner Report and must report all annual returns as of the calendar year end.

Time-Weighted Returns

Provision 22.A.20

When calculating TIME-WEIGHTED RETURNS, TOTAL FUNDS and PORTFOLIOS except PRIVATE MARKET INVESTMENT PORTFOLIOS (see 22.A.30) MUST be valued:

a. At least monthly.[5]

b. As of the calendar month end or the last business day of the month.[6]

c. On the date of all LARGE CASH FLOWS. The ASSET OWNER MUST define LARGE CASH FLOW for each TOTAL FUND and COMPOSITE to determine when the TOTAL FUND and PORTFOLIOS in a COMPOSITE MUST be valued.[7]

---

[5] REQUIRED for periods beginning on or after 1 January 2001. For periods prior to 1 January 2001, PORTFOLIOS MUST be valued at least quarterly.

[6] REQUIRED for periods beginning on or after 1 January 2010.

[7] REQUIRED for periods beginning on or after 1 January 2010.

Discussion

The requirements contained in Provision 22.A.20 apply to an asset owner's total funds and portfolios, with the exception of private market investment portfolios that are included in composites. For the valuation requirements for private market investment portfolios that are included in composites, asset owners should refer to Provision 22.A.30 and related guidance.

To improve the accuracy of time-weighted performance calculations, the GIPS standards have gradually increased the minimum required frequency of total fund and portfolio valuation from quarterly, to monthly, to the date of all large cash flows.

When calculating time-weighted returns for total funds and portfolios, all total funds and portfolios (with the exception of private market investment portfolios that are included in composites) must be valued at least monthly. Whenever the total fund is valued and performance is calculated, all investments regardless of asset class must be valued at fair value. Valuing total funds and portfolios at different end dates does not allow for comparability of information. Asset owners must be consistent in defining the monthly valuation period to allow for comparability of data for all GIPS Asset Owner Reports. It is also required that the calculation period must end on the same day as the reporting period. In other words, asset owners must value total funds and portfolios on the last day of the reporting period or the nearest business day. For periods beginning on or after 1 January 2010, asset owners must value total funds and portfolios as of the calendar month end or the last business day of the month.

In addition to the requirement for asset owners to value total funds and portfolios at least monthly, asset owners are required to value all total funds and portfolios in a composite on the date of all large cash flows, if the total fund or portfolios in a composite are not valued daily. A large cash flow, defined by the asset owner for each total fund or composite, is the level at which the asset owner determines that an external cash flow may distort performance if the total fund or portfolio is not valued and a sub-period return is not calculated. The asset owner must determine in advance (i.e., on an ex ante basis) what is considered to be a large cash flow on a total fund–specific or composite-specific basis. Asset owners must define the amount in terms of the value of cash/asset flow or in terms of a percentage of the portfolio assets, composite assets, or total fund assets. Asset owners must also determine if a large cash flow is a single external cash flow or an aggregate of a number of external cash flows within a stated period. The determination of the large cash flow level may be influenced by a variety of factors, such as the strategy's nature, its historical and expected volatility, and the targeted cash level of the total fund or composite.

An asset owner must not establish a high large cash flow level solely for the purpose of reducing the number of instances when total funds or portfolios must be valued because of large cash flows. The asset owner also must not base the policy on the degree to which the large cash flow affects the return. The large cash flow level chosen by the asset owner on a total fund–specific or composite-specific basis must represent the asset owner's estimate of the level of external cash flow that would potentially distort the accuracy of a total fund's or portfolio's performance calculation if the total fund or portfolio is not valued at the time of the external cash flow and a sub-period return is not calculated.

It is possible that all of an asset owner's total funds or composites have the same level of large cash flows; however, the appropriate level must be determined for each total fund or composite. The asset owner must not simply establish this level on an asset owner–wide basis without considering whether the level is appropriate for each portfolio, total fund, or composite.

Revaluing portfolios as of the close of the business day prior to a large external cash flow is acceptable if external cash flows are assumed to take place at the beginning of the day.

When applying these provisions, it should be remembered that private market investment portfolios have separate valuation requirements. Asset owners should refer to the valuation table included in Provision 22.A.16 for additional guidance on valuation requirements, including the valuation requirements for private market investments.

Provision 22.A.21

When calculating TIME-WEIGHTED RETURNS for TOTAL FUNDS and PORTFOLIOS except PRIVATE MARKET INVESTMENT PORTFOLIOS (see 22.A.31), the ASSET OWNER MUST:

a. Calculate returns at least monthly.[8]

b. Calculate monthly returns through the calendar month end or the last business day of the month.[9]

c. Calculate sub-period returns at the time of all LARGE CASH FLOWS, if daily returns are not calculated.[10]

d. For EXTERNAL CASH FLOWS that are not LARGE CASH FLOWS, calculate TOTAL FUND and PORTFOLIO returns that adjust for daily-weighted EXTERNAL CASH FLOWS, if daily returns are not calculated.[11]

e. Treat EXTERNAL CASH FLOWS according to the TOTAL FUND–specific or COMPOSITE-specific policy.

f. Geometrically LINK periodic and sub-period returns.

g. Consistently apply the calculation methodology used for an individual TOTAL FUND or PORTFOLIO.

---

[8] REQUIRED for periods beginning on or after 1 January 2001.
[9] REQUIRED for periods beginning on or after 1 January 2010.
[10] REQUIRED for periods beginning on or after 1 January 2010.
[11] REQUIRED for periods beginning on or after 1 January 2005.

Discussion

Provision 22.A.21 applies to all total funds and portfolios except private market investment portfolios that are included in composites. Please refer to Provision 22.A.31 for the requirements regarding the calculation of a time-weighted return (TWR) for private market investment portfolios included in composites.

TWRs measure the asset owner's performance and attempt to negate or neutralize the effect of external cash flows that enter or exit a total fund or portfolio. (Dividend and interest income payments are not considered external cash flows.) The GIPS standards do not require a specific method to be used to calculate TWRs but do require the return methodology to meet certain criteria.

Although it is required that TWRs be calculated at least monthly, many asset owners calculate daily returns. If daily returns are not calculated, an asset owner must calculate sub-period returns for total funds and portfolios at the time of all large cash flows in order to calculate a more accurate TWR. A large cash flow is the level at which the asset owner determines that an external cash flow may distort performance if the total fund or portfolio is not valued at the time of the external cash flow and a sub-period return is not calculated. A large cash flow is defined by the asset owner for each total fund and composite to determine when the portfolios in that total fund or composite are to be valued for performance calculations. Asset owners must define the amount, for each total fund and composite, in terms of the value of the cash/asset flow or in terms of a percentage of the portfolio assets, composite assets, or total fund assets. Asset owners must also determine if a large cash flow is a single external cash flow or an aggregate of a number of external cash flows within a stated period of time.

For periods beginning on or after 1 January 2001, asset owners must calculate total fund and portfolio TWRs at least monthly. When calculating and presenting performance in a GIPS Asset Owner Report, calculating returns for total funds and portfolios at different end dates does not allow for the comparability of information. Therefore, to facilitate comparability, for periods beginning on or after 1 January 2010, asset owners must calculate monthly returns as of the calendar month-end or the last business day of the month.

The actual valuation of the total fund's or portfolio's investments and calculation of return each time a large cash flow occurs will result in a more accurate TWR calculation than using either the Original Dietz method or the Modified Dietz method, but it is less accurate than a "true" TWR calculation methodology, which requires valuation and return calculation with every external cash flow.

The returns calculated for each sub-period are geometrically linked according to the following formula:

$$r_t^{TWR} = \left[(1 + r_1) \times (1 + r_2) \times \ldots \times (1 + r_I) \right] - 1,$$

where r_t^{TWR} is the time-weighted return for period t and period t consists of I sub-periods.

The chief advantage of valuing a total fund or portfolio at the time of large cash flows and calculating sub-period returns is that it calculates a better estimate than the midpoint or day-weighting methods. The major disadvantage is that it requires precise valuation of the total fund or portfolio each time a large cash flow occurs. In practice, this means that asset owners must have the ability to value total funds and portfolios on a daily basis. If all investments are not accurately priced for each sub-period valuation, errors generated in the return calculation may be greater than the errors caused by using the midpoint or day-weighting approximation methods. In such cases, it is important to be able to correct for errors, such as missed security splits, mispricings, and improperly booked transactions, because day-to-day compounding will not correct for them automatically if external cash flows occur.

As of 1 January 2005, the calculation of total fund returns or portfolio returns that adjust for daily-weighted external cash flows is required, if daily returns are not calculated. The denominator in the calculation of a TWR that adjusts for daily-weighted external cash flows reflects the weighting of external cash flows for the days they have been in the total fund or portfolio and available for investment during the period. An asset owner must create a total fund–specific or composite-specific policy for the treatment of external cash flows and apply the policy consistently. Examples of acceptable methods for calculating returns that adjust for daily-weighted external cash flows are the Modified Dietz method and internal rate of return (IRR). These methods are estimates of TWRs.

Modified Dietz Method

The Modified Dietz method improves upon the Original Dietz method, which assumes that all external cash flows occur during the midpoint of the period. In an attempt to determine a more accurate return, the Modified Dietz method weights each external cash flow in the denominator by the amount of time it is held in the portfolio. The formula for estimating the TWR using the Modified Dietz method is

$$ r_t^{MD} = \frac{V_t^E - V_t^B - \sum_{i=1}^{I} CF_{i,t}}{V_t^B + \sum_{i=1}^{I} \left(CF_{i,t} \times w_{i,t} \right)}, $$

where

r_t^{MD}	=	the Modified Dietz return for the portfolio for period t
V_t^E	=	the ending value of the portfolio for period t
V_t^B	=	the beginning value of the portfolio for period t
i	=	the number of external cash flows (1, 2, 3, . . . I) in period t
$CF_{i,t}$	=	the value of external cash flow i in period t
$w_{i,t}$	=	the weight of external cash flow i in period t (assuming the external cash flow occurred at the end of the day), as calculated according to the following formula:

$$w_{i,t} = \frac{D_t - D_{i,t}}{D_t},$$

where

$w_{i,t}$ = the weight of external cash flow i in period t, assuming the external cash flow occurred at the end of the day

D_t = the total number of calendar days in period t

$D_{i,t}$ = the number of calendar days from the beginning of period t to external cash flow i

The numerator of $w_{i,t}$ is based on the assumption that the external cash flows occur at the end of the day. If external cash flows were assumed to occur at the beginning of the day, the numerator would be $[(D_t - D_{i,t}) + 1]$. An asset owner may choose to use a beginning-of-day or end-of-day external cash flow assumption or some combination of the two. The key is to establish a policy and treat external cash flows consistently.

The chief advantage of the Modified Dietz method is that it does not require total fund or portfolio valuation on the date of each external cash flow. Its chief disadvantage is that it provides a less accurate return than when the total fund or portfolio is valued at the time of each external cash flow. The estimate suffers most when a combination of the following conditions exists: (1) one or more large external cash flows occur; and (2) external cash flows occur during periods of high market volatility—that is, the total fund's or portfolio's returns are significantly non-linear.

The following is an example of a return calculation using the Modified Dietz method. The example is for a portfolio with a beginning value of $100,000 on 31 May, an ending value of $135,000 on 30 June, and external cash flows of –$2,000 on 6 June and $20,000 on 11 June. Assume the external cash flows were reflected at the end of the day.

31 May	Beginning Value (BV)	$100,000
6 June	Cash Flow (CF)	–$2,000
11 June	Cash Flow (CF)	$20,000
30 June	Ending Value (EV)	$135,000

$$R_{Modified\,Dietz} = \frac{EV - BV - CF}{BV + (W \times CF)}$$

W is the weight of the external cash flow for the month. Because June has 30 days and the external cash flows were assumed to occur at the end of the day, the weights of the external cash flows are calculated as $(30 - 6)/30 = 0.80$ and $(30 - 11)/30 = 0.6333$, respectively.

$$R_{Modified\,Dietz} = \frac{135,000 - 100,000 - (-2,000 + 20,000)}{100,000 + (0.80 \times -2,000) + (0.6333 \times 20,000)}$$

$$R_{Modified\,Dietz} = \frac{17,000}{111,067} = 15.31\%$$

If the asset owner's policy was to treat external cash flows as occurring at the beginning of the day, the asset owner would have added 1 to the numerator in the weight calculation, and the weights to be multiplied by the external cash flows would be calculated as $(30 - 6 + 1)/30 = 0.8333$ and $(30 - 11 + 1)/30 = 0.6667$, respectively.

The following is an example of a return calculation using the Modified Dietz method and revaluing during the month for a large cash flow (assumed to be 10% in this example). To calculate performance for the month, we must calculate performance for the sub-periods before and after the large external cash flow and then geometrically link the sub-period returns. In this example, we use the same data as the prior example but instead value the portfolio at the time of the large cash flow on 11 June.

31 May	Beginning Value (BV)	$100,000
6 June	Cash Flow (CF)	-$2,000
11 June	Cash Flow (CF)	$20,000
11 June	Ending Value (EV)	$125,000
30 June	Ending Value (EV)	$135,000

Sub-period 1 calculation, from 31 May through 11 June:

Because sub-period 1 has 11 days and the external cash flows are assumed to occur at the end of the day, the weight of the external cash flow on the sixth day is $(11 - 6)/11 = 0.4545$. The weight of the cash flow on the 11th would be zero because it is assumed to happen at the end of the day on 11 June, which is when the portfolio was revalued.

$$R_{Modified\,Dietz\,(sub\text{-}period\,1)} = \frac{125,000 - 100,000 + (-2,000 + 20,000)}{100,000 + (0.4545 \times -2,000) + (0 \times 20,000)}$$

$$R_{Modified\,Dietz\,(sub\text{-}period\,1)} = \frac{7,000}{99,091} = 7.06\%$$

Sub-period 2 calculation, from 11 June through 30 June:

$$R_{Modified\,Dietz\,(sub\text{-}period\,2)} = \frac{135,000 - 125,000}{125,000}$$

$$R_{Modified\,Dietz\,(sub\text{-}period\,2)} = \frac{10,000}{125,000} = 8.00\%$$

To calculate the monthly return, geometrically link sub-period returns 1 and 2: $(1 + 0.0706) \times (1 + 0.08) - 1 = 0.1563$, or 15.63%.

Other formulas in addition to the Modified Dietz method for calculating approximate TWRs are also permitted.

Internal Rate of Return (IRR) Method

The IRR, which is a money-weighted return, is the implied discount rate or effective compounded rate of return that equates the present value of cash outflows with the present value of cash inflows. The IRR method is an acceptable method to use to calculate a TWR when no large cash flows occur during the sub-period. To create a TWR, the IRRs before and after the large cash flow are calculated and then linked together geometrically.

The IRR is the value of R that satisfies the following equation:

$$V_E = \sum_{i=0}^{n} CF_i (1 + R)^{W_i},$$

where V_E and W_i are the same as for the Modified Dietz method.

The external cash flows, CF_i, are also the same as with the Modified Dietz method with one important exception: The value at the beginning of the period is also treated as an external cash flow—that is, $V_B = CF_0$.

The IRR is obtained by selecting values for R and solving the equation until the result equals V_E. For example, if three external cash flows (including the value at the beginning of the period) have occurred, the formula will have three terms:

$$V_E = CF_0 (1 + R)^{W_0} + CF_1 (1 + R)^{W_1} + CF_2 (1 + R)^{W_2}.$$

The first term deals with the first external cash flow, CF_0, which is the value of the portfolio at the beginning of the period; W_i is the proportion of the period when the external cash flow CF_i was held in the portfolio. Because CF_0 is in for the whole period, $W_0 = 1$. The larger the value of CF_i in the term, the more it will contribute to the total; but the smaller the exponent (i.e., the value of W_i), the less the term will contribute to the sum. The usual effect is that the first term, with a large CF_0 and W_0 equal to 1, will contribute far more than the other terms.

The advantages and disadvantages of the IRR method are the same as those of the Modified Dietz method. The IRR method has the additional disadvantage of requiring an iterative process solution. It is also possible to have multiple answers if both positive and negative external cash flows occur.

When calculating the TWR for portfolios, periodic and sub-period returns must be linked geometrically.

An asset owner must create a total fund–specific and composite-specific policy for the treatment of external cash flows for each of its total funds and composites and must apply that policy consistently. For example, the same definition of a large cash flow must be used when evaluating a cash flow for all portfolios within a specific total fund or composite. Policies and procedures for the calculation methodology used for an individual portfolio must also be created and applied consistently.

Money-Weighted Returns

Provision 22.A.22

When calculating MONEY-WEIGHTED RETURNS, the ASSET OWNER MUST value PORTFOLIOS at least annually and as of the period end for any period for which performance is calculated.

Discussion

When calculating a money-weighted return (MWR), an asset owner must value portfolios at least annually and as of the period end for any period for which performance is calculated. Valuations must be in accordance with the definition of fair value. A more frequent valuation is considered good business practice and is recommended.

When calculating time-weighted returns (TWRs), valuations at the time of large cash flows and at period end are needed because those valuations are inputs to the TWR calculation. In a true TWR calculation, sub-period returns are calculated either daily or at the time of each external cash flow and then geometrically linked together to derive a return for the period.

For MWRs, valuations are needed only at the end of the period being measured. In addition, many portfolios for which MWRs are calculated involve private market investments with valuations that are generally performed on a less frequent basis because they are illiquid securities. For these reasons, when calculating an MWR, asset owners must value portfolios at least annually and as of the period end for any period for which performance is calculated, rather than monthly and at the time of large cash flows.

More-frequent valuations are generally required for oversight body reporting purposes and are considered good business practice.

Provision 22.A.23

When calculating MONEY-WEIGHTED RETURNS, the ASSET OWNER MUST:

a. Calculate annualized SINCE-INCEPTION MONEY-WEIGHTED RETURNS or the annualized MONEY-WEIGHTED RETURN for the longest period for which the ASSET OWNER has sufficient records.

b. Calculate MONEY-WEIGHTED RETURNS using daily EXTERNAL CASH FLOWS.[12]

c. Include stock DISTRIBUTIONS as EXTERNAL CASH FLOWS and value stock DISTRIBUTIONS at the time of DISTRIBUTION.

Discussion

A money-weighted return (MWR) is a return that reflects the change in value and the timing and size of external cash flows. One commonly used method for calculating an MWR is to calculate an internal rate of return (IRR). In general, the IRR is the implied discount rate or effective compounded rate of return that equates the present value of cash outflows with the present value of cash inflows. The since-inception IRR (SI-IRR) is a specific version of the IRR in which the measurement period of the MWR covers the entire investment period since inception.

Unlike when using IRR to calculate a time-weighted return (TWR), using IRR to calculate an MWR does not involve the calculation or linking of sub-period returns. A single IRR is calculated for the entire period.

The IRR is the return for which the net present value of a cash flow series is equated to zero and is calculated by solving for the return that satisfies the following equation:

$$0 = \sum_{i=0}^{I} CF_i (1 + r_{IRR})^{-\left(\frac{t_i}{365}\right)},$$

where

CF_i = external cash flow i (negative values for outflows [capital calls] and positive values for inflows [distributions])

i = number of external cash flows (1, 2, 3, ..., I) during the measurement period

r_{IRR} = annualized internal rate of return

t_i = number of calendar days between the beginning of the measurement period and the date of external cash flow i

---

[12] Daily EXTERNAL CASH FLOWS are REQUIRED beginning 1 January 2020. Prior to 1 January 2020, quarterly or more frequent EXTERNAL CASH FLOWS MUST be used.

The SI-IRR is a special version of the IRR in which the period-end value of the investment is treated as a synthetic terminal cash inflow, calculated as follows:

$$0 = \left[\sum_{i=0}^{I} CF_i (1 + r_{SI-IRR})^{-\left(\frac{t_i}{365}\right)} \right] + \left[V_E (1 + r_{SI-IRR})^{-\left(\frac{TD}{365}\right)} \right],$$

where

CF_i	=	external cash flow i [negative values for outflows (capital calls) and positive values for inflows (distributions)]
i	=	number of external cash flows (1, 2, 3, ..., I) during the measurement period
r_{SI-IRR}	=	annualized since-inception internal rate of return
t_i	=	number of calendar days between the beginning of the measurement period and the date of external cash flow i
V_E	=	value of the investment at the end of the measurement period
TD	=	total number of calendar days in the measurement period

Note that the above annualized formula assumes a 365-day year convention and thus may have slight inaccuracies when the measurement period contains one or more leap years.

Asset owners must calculate and present the annualized SI-IRR or the annualized MWR for the longest period for which the asset owner has sufficient records. If the period is less than a full year, asset owners must present the non-annualized SI-IRR. The non-annualized SI-IRR is calculated as follows:

$$R_{SI-IRR} = \left[(1 + r_{SI-IRR})^{\frac{TD}{365}} \right] - 1,$$

where

R_{SI-IRR}	=	non-annualized since-inception internal rate of return
r_{SI-IRR}	=	annualized since-inception internal rate of return
TD	=	total number of calendar days in the measurement period

As of 1 January 2020, external cash flows must be reflected on a daily basis when calculating an MWR, which results in a more accurate return. Using daily external cash flows means that the external cash flows are dated on the date the external cash flows occur—for example, the date of a capital call or the date of a distribution. For periods prior to 1 January 2020, asset owners must calculate an MWR by using quarterly or more frequent external cash flows. However, asset owners should use daily external cash flows in calculating an MWR prior to 1 January 2020 if daily external cash flows are available.

In dealing with legacy cash flow streams that might be dated monthly for periods prior to 1 January 2020, the asset owner should assume that all external cash flows occurred on a particular date in the month regardless of the actual date of the external cash flow. The same is true if external cash flows are reflected on a quarterly basis. The asset owner could assume that all external cash flows within the month happened on the last business day of the respective month.

For example, the following table shows the date the cash flow could be reflected for performance purposes.

Date	Cash Flow	Quarterly Cash Flows		Monthly Cash Flows	
		Cash Flow	Date	Cash Flow	Date
4 Jan 2017	(100)			(100)	31 Jan 2017
7 Feb 2017	(100)			(100)	28 Feb 2017
9 Mar 2017	(100)	(300)	31 Mar 2017	(100)	31 Mar 2017
18 Apr 2017	(100)			(100)	30 Apr 2017
1 May 2017	(100)			(100)	31 May 2017
2 Jun 2017	(100)	(300)	30 Jun 2017	(100)	30 Jun 2017
14 Jul 2017	(100)			(100)	31 Jul 2017
8 Aug 2017	(100)			(100)	31 Aug 2017
9 Sep 2017	(100)	(300)	30 Sep 2017	(100)	30 Sep 2017
4 Oct 2017	(100)			(100)	31 Oct 2017
8 Nov 2017	(100)			(100)	30 Nov 2017
1 Dec 2017	(100)	(300)	31 Dec 2017	(100)	31 Dec 2017

Stock distributions must be included as external cash flows and must reflect the value at the time of distribution. The cash flow is reflected on the date the asset owner receives the distribution.

In addition to SI-IRR, asset owners may calculate an MWR using the Modified Dietz method over the entire period. Unlike when being used to calculate a TWR, using the Modified Dietz method to calculate an MWR does not involve the calculation or linking of sub-period returns. A single MWR is calculated for the entire period.

An example for a total fund MWR calculation for a four-year period follows.

				Modified Dietz			
Dates	Terminal Value	Cash Flow (CF)	Day of CF/ Valuation	Weighted CF	Numerator	Denominator	Return
31 Dec 2016		2,000,000	0	2,000,000			
8 Jan 2017		200,000	8	198,905			
24 Dec 2017		(50,000)	358	(37,748)			
20 Feb 2018		(200,000)	416	(143,053)			

			Modified Dietz				
Dates	Terminal Value	Cash Flow (CF)	Day of CF/ Valuation	Weighted CF	Numerator	Denominator	Return
6 Mar 2018		150,000	430	105,852			
11 Dec 2018		(20,000)	710	(10,281)			
25 Jun 2019		100,000	906	37,988			
3 Jul 2019		30,000	914	11,232			
14 Aug 2019		(50,000)	956	(17,283)			
21 Mar 2020		(200,000)	1,176	(39,014)			
4 Jun 2020		80,000	1,251	11,499			
22 Nov 2020		(50,000)	1,422	(1,335)			
3 Dec 2020		150,000	1,433	2,875			
31 Dec 2020	2,300,000		1,461		160,000	2,119,637	7.55% Cumulative
Total		2,140,000		2,119,637			1.84% Annualized

The numerator is the terminal value less the sum of the cash flows: (2,300,000 − 2,140,000), or 160,000.

The denominator is the sum of the weighted cash flows: (2,119,637).

The cumulative return is calculated as 160,000/2,119,637, or 7.55%.

To calculate the annualized return, the formula is $(1 + r)^{(1/n)} - 1$. In this example, it would be:

$$= (1 + 0.0755)^{(1/4)} - 1$$
$$= 1.84\%.$$

Gross and Net Returns

Provision 22.A.24

When the ASSET OWNER calculates TOTAL FUND and COMPOSITE NET-OF-FEES returns, these returns MUST reflect the deduction of:[13]

a. TRANSACTION COSTS.

b. All fees and expenses for externally managed POOLED FUNDS.

c. INVESTMENT MANAGEMENT FEES for externally managed SEGREGATED ACCOUNTS.

d. INVESTMENT MANAGEMENT COSTS.

---

[13] REQUIRED for periods beginning on or after 1 January 2015.

Discussion

For asset owners, a net-of-fees return is defined as the return that reflects the deduction of transaction costs, all fees and expenses for externally managed pooled funds, investment management fees for externally managed segregated accounts, and investment management costs.

For purposes of the GIPS standards, asset owners must reduce all returns, including total fund or composite net-of-fees returns, by transaction costs. Transaction costs are defined as the costs of buying or selling investments. These costs typically take the form of brokerage commissions, exchange fees and/or taxes, and/or bid–offer spreads from either internal or external brokers. Custodial fees charged per transaction should be considered custody fees and not transaction costs. For real estate, private equity, and other private market investments, transaction costs include all legal, financial, advisory, and investment banking fees related to buying, selling, restructuring, and/or recapitalizing investments but do not include dead deal costs. An asset owner may use estimated transaction costs only for those portfolios whose actual transaction costs are not known. (For additional information on the deduction of transaction costs, please refer to Provision 22.A.10.)

Investment management fees are the fees payable to external managers for externally managed assets. Investment management fees are typically asset based (percentage of assets), performance based (based on the portfolio's performance on an absolute basis or relative to a benchmark or other reference point), or a combination of the two but may take different forms as well. Investment management fees also include carried interest. Fees and expenses for externally managed pooled funds include embedded investment management fees, as well as any other investment management fees paid for the management of the pooled fund, even if the payment is made from other assets and payments do not flow through the pooled fund. Total fund and composite net-of-fees returns must reflect the deduction of investment management fees for externally managed segregated accounts, as well as all fees and expenses, including investment management fees, for externally managed pooled funds.

Investment management costs include all internal costs for both internally and externally managed assets.[B] Determining investment management costs is not a straightforward process for an asset owner. In addition to costs for portfolio management, they may also involve overhead and other related costs and fees, including data valuation fees, investment research services, custody fees, pro rata share of overhead (such as building and utilities), allocation of non-investment-department expenses (such as human resources, communications, and

---

[B] The definition of INVESTMENT MANAGEMENT COSTS included in the Glossary in the 2020 edition of the GIPS standards is incorrect and should state:

All internal costs for both internally and externally managed assets. In addition to costs for PORTFOLIO management, they may also involve overhead and other related costs and fees, including data valuation fees, investment research services, CUSTODY FEES, pro rata share of overhead (such as building and utilities), allocation of non-investment-department expenses (such as human resources, communications, and technology), and performance measurement and compliance services.

technology), and performance measurement and compliance services. Total fund and total fund composite net-of-fees returns must reflect the deduction of investment management costs.

The following table illustrates the calculations for total fund full gross-of-fees, gross-of-fees, net-of-external-costs-only, and net-of-fees returns. It starts with the return on investments before the deduction of any transaction costs, fees, or expenses.

Return Type	Return	Information Type	Glossary Definition
Total Fund return on investments	11.10%	Supplemental information only	
Transaction costs	–0.10%		
Total Fund full gross-of-fees return	11.00%	Supplemental information only	The return on investments that reflects the deduction of only transaction costs
Fees and expenses for externally managed pooled funds	–0.40%		
Total Fund gross-of-fees return	10.60%	Optional	The return on investments reduced by transaction costs and all fees and expenses for externally managed pooled funds
Investment management fees for externally managed segregated accounts	–0.65%		
Total Fund net-of-external costs-only return	9.95%	Optional	The gross-of-fees return reduced by investment management fees for externally managed segregated accounts[c]
Investment management costs	–0.16%		
Total Fund net-of-fees return	9.79%	Required	The return that reflects the deduction of transaction costs, all fees and expenses for externally managed pooled funds, investment management fees for externally managed segregated accounts, and investment management costs

---

[c] The definition of NET-OF-EXTERNAL-COSTS-ONLY included in the Glossary in the 2020 edition of the GIPS standards is incorrect and should state:

The GROSS-OF-FEES return reduced by ~~all costs~~ INVESTMENT MANAGEMENT FEES for externally managed SEGREGATED ACCOUNTS.

|

Provision 22.A.25

When the ASSET OWNER calculates TOTAL FUND and COMPOSITE NET-OF-EXTERNAL-COSTS-ONLY returns, these returns MUST reflect the deduction of:[14]

a. TRANSACTION COSTS.

b. All fees and expenses for externally managed POOLED FUNDS.

c. INVESTMENT MANAGEMENT FEES for externally managed SEGREGATED ACCOUNTS.

Discussion

For asset owners, a net-of-external-costs-only return[D] is the gross-of-fees return reduced by investment management fees for externally managed segregated accounts. It therefore reflects the deduction of transaction costs and all fees and expenses for externally managed pooled funds, which are already reflected in the calculation of the gross-of-fees return, as well as investment management fees for externally managed segregated accounts. Investment management costs for internally and externally managed assets are not deducted from this return.

For purposes of the GIPS standards, asset owners must reduce all returns, including total fund or composite net-of-external-costs-only returns, by transaction costs. Transaction costs are defined as the costs of buying or selling investments. These costs typically take the form of brokerage commissions, exchange fees and/or taxes, and/or bid–offer spreads from either internal or external brokers. Custodial fees charged per transaction should be considered custody fees and not transaction costs. For real estate, private equity, and other private market investments, transaction costs include all legal, financial, advisory, and investment banking fees related to buying, selling, restructuring, and/or recapitalizing investments but do not include dead deal costs. An asset owner may use estimated transaction costs only for those portfolios whose actual transaction costs are not known. (For additional information on the deduction of transaction costs, please refer to Provision 22.A.10.)

Investment management fees are the fees payable to external managers for externally managed assets. Investment management fees are typically asset based (percentage of assets), performance based (based on the portfolio's performance on an absolute basis or relative to a benchmark or other reference point), or a combination of the two but may take different forms as well. Investment management fees also include carried interest. Fees and expenses for externally managed pooled funds include embedded investment management fees, as well as any other

---

[14] REQUIRED for periods beginning on or after 1 January 2015.

[D] The definition of NET-OF-EXTERNAL-COSTS-ONLY included in the Glossary in the 2020 edition of the GIPS standards is incorrect and should state:

The GROSS-OF-FEES return reduced by ~~all costs~~ INVESTMENT MANAGEMENT FEES for externally managed SEGREGATED ACCOUNTS.

investment management fees paid for the management of the pooled fund, even if the payment is made from other assets and payments do not flow through the pooled fund. Total fund and composite net-of-external-costs-only returns must reflect the deduction of investment management fees for externally managed segregated accounts, as well as all fees and expenses, including investment management fees, for externally managed pooled funds.

Please see the table in Provision 22.A.24 for a demonstration of the calculations for total fund full gross-of-fees, gross-of-fees, net-of-external-costs-only, and net-of-fees returns.

Provision 22.A.26

When the ASSET OWNER calculates TOTAL FUND and COMPOSITE GROSS-OF-FEES returns, these returns MUST reflect the deduction of:[15]

a. TRANSACTION COSTS.

b. All fees and expenses for externally managed POOLED FUNDS.

Discussion

For asset owners, a gross-of-fees return is the return on investments reduced by transaction costs and all fees and expenses for externally managed pooled funds.

For purposes of the GIPS standards, asset owners must reduce all returns, including total fund and composite gross-of-fees returns, by transaction costs. Transaction costs are defined as the costs of buying or selling investments. These costs typically take the form of brokerage commissions, exchange fees and/or taxes, and/or bid–offer spreads from either internal or external brokers. Custodial fees charged per transaction should be considered custody fees and not transaction costs. For real estate, private equity, and other private market investments, transaction costs include all legal, financial, advisory, and investment banking fees related to buying, selling, restructuring, and/or recapitalizing investments but do not include dead deal costs. An asset owner may use estimated transaction costs only for those portfolios whose actual transaction costs are not known. (For additional information on the deduction of transaction costs, please refer to Provision 22.A.10.)

A gross-of-fees return must also reflect the deduction of all fees and expenses for externally managed pooled funds. This includes embedded investment management fees for externally managed pooled funds, as well as any other investment management fees paid for the management of the pooled fund, even if the payment is made from other assets and payments do not flow through the pooled fund.

---

[15] REQUIRED for periods beginning on or after 1 January 2015.

Investment management fees for externally managed segregated accounts are not deducted from the gross-of-fees return.

Please see the table in Provision 22.A.24 for a demonstration of the calculations for total fund full gross-of-fees, gross-of-fees, net-of-external-costs-only, and net-of-fees returns.

Composite Returns

Provision 22.A.27

COMPOSITE TIME-WEIGHTED RETURNS except PRIVATE MARKET INVESTMENT COMPOSITES (see 22.A.32) MUST be calculated at least monthly.[16]

Discussion

The more frequently composite returns are calculated, the more accurate the results will be. Quarterly composite calculations are permitted for periods prior to 1 January 2010; subsequently, composite returns must be calculated at least monthly. The portfolios included in the composite must be consistent for the entire performance measurement period. See Provision 22.A.28 for a discussion of composite return calculations.

Private market investment composites are excluded from this provision because private market investment portfolios that are included in private market investment composites are not required to be valued monthly.

Provision 22.A.28

COMPOSITE TIME-WEIGHTED RETURNS MUST be calculated by using one of the following approaches:

a. Asset-weighting the individual PORTFOLIO returns using beginning-of-period values;
b. Asset-weighting the individual PORTFOLIO returns using a method that reflects both beginning-of-period values and EXTERNAL CASH FLOWS; or
c. Using the aggregate method.

---

[16] REQUIRED for periods beginning on or after 1 January 2010. For periods beginning on or after 1 January 2006 and ending prior to 1 January 2010, COMPOSITE returns MUST be calculated at least quarterly.

Discussion

A composite is defined as an aggregation of one or more portfolios or total funds that are managed according to a similar investment mandate, objective, or strategy. The objective in calculating the composite's return is to use a method that will conceptually produce the same value as if the assets of all the individual portfolios in the composite were aggregated and a return is calculated as if the composite were one portfolio.

The GIPS standards are based on the principle of asset-weighted composite returns. For example, if a composite contains two portfolios, one of which is 10 times the size of the other, the rate of return for the larger portfolio should have more of an effect on the composite return than the rate of return for the smaller portfolio. The asset-weighted return methods satisfy this principle by weighting each portfolio's contribution to the composite rate of return by its beginning value (as a percentage of the composite's beginning value) or by its beginning value plus weighted external cash flows (as a percentage of the composite's beginning value plus weighted external cash flows). The GIPS standards require asset weighting of the portfolio returns within a composite by using beginning-of-period values, by using beginning-of-period values plus weighted external cash flows, or by aggregating portfolio assets and external cash flows to calculate performance as a single master portfolio.

New portfolios must be included in composites on a timely and consistent basis as soon as they are funded (see Provision 23.A.6). Terminated portfolios must be included in the historical performance of the composite through the final day the assets are managed (see Provision 23.A.7). When an asset owner needs to include in composite returns portfolios that do not have a full month of performance, the asset owner must calculate composite returns more frequently than monthly (e.g., daily) and therefore must be able to value portfolios in the composite on the day that the new portfolio joins the composite. Assuming an asset owner calculates composite returns daily, the asset owner would include in the daily composite return calculation only those portfolios that were managed for the full day. Asset owners must create and document policies and procedures for calculating composite returns and follow those policies and procedures consistently.

If the asset owner uses a transition manager upon termination of an external manager, the performance of the transition manager must be reflected in total fund performance. If the portfolio was included in any additional composites, the asset owner would need to determine if the transition strategy reflects the composite strategy to determine whether the track record of the transition manager would be included in the composite. (An additional composite is a grouping of portfolios representing a particular strategy or asset class that the asset owner chooses to present in a GIPS Asset Owner Report.)

The following are examples of methods that an asset owner may use when asset-weighting individual portfolio returns when calculating composite time-weighted returns.

|

The *Beginning Assets Weighting* method for calculating composite returns, R_t, uses the formula:

$$R_t = \frac{\sum_{k=1}^{K}\left(V_{k,t}^B \times r_{k,t}\right)}{\sum_{k=1}^{K} V_{k,t}^B},$$

where

R_t = the beginning assets weighted return for the composite for period t

k = the number of portfolios (1, 2, 3, . . . , K) in the composite at the beginning of period t

$V_{k,t}^B$ = the beginning value of portfolio k for period t

$r_{k,t}$ = the return of portfolio k for period t

The Beginning Assets Weighting method can also be expressed as

$$R_t = \sum_{k=1}^{K}\left(\frac{V_{k,t}^B}{\sum_{k=1}^{K} V_{k,t}^B} \times r_{k,t}\right) = \sum_{k=1}^{K} w_{k,t}^B r_{k,t},$$

where $w_{k,t}^B$ is the weight of the value of portfolio k as a fraction of total composite asset value based on beginning asset values for period t and can be calculated according to the following formula:

$$w_{k,t}^B = \frac{V_{k,t}^B}{\sum_{k=1}^{K} V_{k,t}^B}.$$

The *Beginning Assets Plus Weighted External Cash Flow* method represents a refinement to the Beginning Assets Weighting method. Consider the case in which one of two portfolios in a composite doubles in value as the result of a contribution on the third day of a performance period. Under the Beginning Assets Weighting method, this portfolio would be weighted in the composite based solely on its beginning value (i.e., not including the contribution). The Beginning Assets Plus Weighted External Cash Flow method resolves this problem by including the effect of external cash flows in the calculation. Assuming that external cash flows occur at the end of the day, the weighting factor for each external cash flow is calculated using the same methodology as in the Modified Dietz method as follows:

$$w_{i,k,t} = \frac{D_t - D_{i,k,t}}{D_t},$$

where

$w_{i,k,t}$ = the weight of external cash flow i in portfolio k in period t, assuming the external cash flow occurred at the end of the day

D_t = the total number of calendar days in period t

$D_{i,k,t}$ = the number of calendar days from the beginning of period t to external cash flow i in portfolio k

The numerator of $w_{i,k,t}$ is based on the assumption that the external cash flows occur at the end of the day. If external cash flows were assumed to occur at the beginning of the day, the numerator would be $[(D_t - D_{i,k,t}) + 1]$. An asset owner may choose to use a beginning-of-day or end-of-day external cash flow assumption or some combination of the two. The key is to establish a policy and treat external cash flows consistently.

The Beginning Assets Plus Weighted External Cash Flow composite return can be calculated as follows:

$$R_t = \frac{\sum_{k=1}^{K}\left\{\left[V_{k,t}^{B} + \sum_{i=1}^{I_k}\left(CF_{i,k,t} \times w_{i,k,t}\right)\right] \times r_{k,t}\right\}}{\sum_{k=1}^{K}\left[V_{k,t}^{B} + \sum_{i=1}^{I_k}\left(CF_{i,k,t} \times w_{i,k,t}\right)\right]},$$

where

R_t = the beginning assets plus weighted external cash flow composite return for period t

$V_{k,t}^{B}$ = the beginning value of portfolio k for period t

i_k = the number of external cash flows $(1, 2, 3, \ldots, I_k)$ in portfolio k

$CF_{i,k,t}$ = the ith external cash flow in portfolio k for period t

$w_{i,k,t}$ = the weight of external cash flow i in portfolio k for period t

$r_{k,t}$ = the return for portfolio k for period t

The Beginning Assets Plus Weighted External Cash Flow composite return method can also be expressed by the following formula:

$$R_t = \sum_{k=1}^{K}\left(\frac{V_{k,t}}{\sum_{k=1}^{K}V_{k,t}} \times r_{k,t}\right),$$

where

R_t = the beginning assets plus weighted external cash flow composite return for period t

$r_{k,t}$ = the return for portfolio k for period t

$V_{k,t}$ = the beginning value plus weighted external cash flows of portfolio k for period t, as calculated by the following formula:

$$V_{k,t} = V_{k,t}^{B} + \sum_{i=1}^{I_k} \left(CF_{i,k,t} \times w_{i,k,t} \right),$$

where

$V_{k,t}$ = the value of portfolio k's beginning assets plus weighted external cash flows for period t

$V_{k,t}^{B}$ = the beginning value of portfolio k for period t

i_k = the number of external cash flows $(1, 2, 3, \ldots, I_k)$ in portfolio k

$CF_{i,k,t}$ = the ith external cash flow in portfolio k for period t

$w_{i,k,t}$ = the weight of external cash flow i in portfolio k for period t

The *Aggregate Return* method combines all the composite assets and external cash flows before any calculations occur to calculate returns as if the composite were one portfolio. Therefore, unlike the Beginning Assets Weighting method or the Beginning Assets Plus Weighted External Cash Flow method, the Aggregate Return method does not use portfolio returns.

The following examples show how to calculate a composite return using the Beginning Assets Weighting method, the Beginning Assets Plus Weighted External Cash Flow method, and the Aggregate Return method, assuming that external cash flows occur at the end of the day.

Composite Return

Beginning Assets Weighting method:

Portfolio	BMV	Portfolio Weight	Portfolio Return	Weighted Return
A	450,000	17.08%	12%	2.05%
B	785,000	29.79%	14%	4.17%
C	1,400,000	53.13%	11%	5.84%
Total	2,635,000	100.00%		12.06%

$$R_{BMV} = \frac{(450,000 \times 0.12) + (785,000 \times 0.14) + (1,400,000 \times 0.11)}{(450,000 + 785,000 + 1,400,000)} = 12.06\%$$

Beginning Assets Plus Weighted External Cash Flow method:

Portfolio	BMV	Weighted Cash Flows	BMV plus Wtd CFs	BMV plus Wtd CFs	Portfolio Return	Weighted Return
A	450,000	75,000	525,000	18.95%	12%	2.27%
B	785,000	120,000	905,000	32.67%	14%	4.57%
C	1,400,000	(60,000)	1,340,000	48.38%	11%	5.32%
Total	2,635,000	135,000	2,770,000	100.00%		12.17%

$$R_{BMV+CF} = \frac{\begin{array}{c}\left[(450,000+75,000)\times 0.12\right]+\left[(785,000+120,000)\times 0.14\right]\\+\left[(1,400,000-60,000)\times 0.11\right]\end{array}}{(450,000+75,000+785,000+120,000+1,400,000-60,000)} = 12.17\%$$

Aggregate Return method (using Modified Dietz method):

(Assuming the large cash flow level is established at the composite level and none of the cash flows qualifies as a large cash flow)

Portfolio	BMV	EMV	Cash Flows	Weighted CFs	Portfolio Return
A	450,000	665,000	150,000	75,000	12%
B	785,000	1,140,000	240,000	120,000	14%
C	1,400,000	1,440,000	(120,000)	(60,000)	11%
Total	2,635,000	3,245,000	270,000	135,000	

$$\text{Composite Return } (R_{Aggregate}) = \frac{(\text{Total EMV} - \text{Total BMV} - \text{Total CF})}{(\text{Total BMV} + \text{Total Wtd CF})}$$

$$R_{Aggregate} = \frac{(3,245,000 - 2,635,000 - 270,000)}{(2,635,000 + 135,000)} = 12.27\%.$$

When using the aggregate method, an asset owner may encounter a situation in which the composite return falls outside the range of portfolio-level returns for a given period. This scenario can occur if the policies used to calculate portfolio-level returns do not flow through to the aggregate composite-level return calculation policies. "Flowing through" to the composite means that if any portfolio is valued during the month because of a large cash flow, the entire composite would also be valued and the sub-period return calculated for both the portfolio and the composite. An asset owner may establish large cash flow policies, however, such that only those portfolios in the composite that experience a large cash flow during the month are valued at the time of the large cash flow and any portfolios that did not experience a large cash flow are not valued during the month. In such a situation, the composite return may be outside the range of portfolio-level returns for a given period. To prevent this situation from occurring, the asset owner should consider establishing a policy wherein all portfolios in the composite are valued if any portfolio in the composite is valued during the month because of large cash flows. Once an asset owner has established large cash flow policies for a composite, the asset owner must apply the large cash flow policies consistently.

Provision 22.A.29

When calculating COMPOSITE MONEY-WEIGHTED RETURNS, the ASSET OWNER MUST calculate COMPOSITE returns by aggregating the PORTFOLIO-level information for those PORTFOLIOS included in the COMPOSITE.

When calculating composite money-weighted returns, an asset owner is required to aggregate the portfolio-level information for all portfolios included in the composite. This method combines the assets and external cash flows from all portfolios in the composite, so the return is calculated as if the composite were one portfolio. The following example shows how since-inception internal rates of return (SI-IRRs) can be calculated for a composite that includes multiple portfolios.

In 2019, the composite includes only Portfolio 1. The composite SI-IRR will be based solely on the cash flows and terminal value of Portfolio 1. In 2020, Portfolio 2 joins the composite, and at the end of 2020, the two-year annualized SI-IRR will be based on the combined cash flows and terminal values of Portfolios 1 and 2. In 2021, Portfolio 3 joins the composite, and at the end of 2021, the three-year annualized SI-IRR will be based on the combined cash flows and terminal values of Portfolios 1, 2, and 3.

	A	B	C	D	E	F	G
1							
2					Combined		Combined
3	Date	CF or TV	Portfolio 1	Portfolio 2	Portfolio 1 & 2	Portfolio 3	Portfolio 1, 2 & 3
4	31-Dec-2018	Cash Flow	(1,000,000)		(1,000,000)		(1,000,000)
5	15-Jan-2019	Cash Flow	(10,000)		(10,000)		(10,000)
6	31-Dec-2019	Terminal Value	1,090,000				
7	15-Feb-2020	Cash Flow		(5,000,000)	(5,000,000)		(5,000,000)
8	30-Jun-2020	Cash Flow		(1,000,000)	(1,000,000)		(1,000,000)
9	31-Dec-2020	Terminal Value	1,100,000	6,500,000	7,600,000		
10	12-Feb-2021	Cash Flow				(4,000,000)	(4,000,000)
11	15-Mar-2021	Cash Flow	500,000				500,000
12	31-Dec-2021	Terminal Value	900,000	6,700,000		4,200,000	11,800,000
13							
14							
15							
16	Year	SI-IRR Calc	Formula				
17	2019	7.92%	=XIRR(C4:C6,A4:A6,0.1)				
18	2020	8.47%	=XIRR(E4:E9,A4:A9,0.1)				
19	2021	7.33%	=XIRR(G4:G12,A4:A12,0.1)				

Private Market Investments

Provision 22.A.30

When calculating TIME-WEIGHTED RETURNS for PRIVATE MARKET INVESTMENT PORTFOLIOS that are included in COMPOSITES, PRIVATE MARKET INVESTMENT PORTFOLIOS MUST be valued:

a. At least quarterly.[17]

b. As of each quarter end or the last business day of the quarter.[18]

Discussion

A portfolio is considered a private market investment portfolio when it has an investment objective to invest primarily in private market investments. Private market investments include real assets (e.g., real estate and infrastructure), private equity, and similar investments that are illiquid, not publicly traded, and not traded on an exchange.

Investments that are not private market investments must be valued at least monthly and at the time of large cash flows. Because of the illiquidity of private market investments, private market investments that are included in composites must be valued at least quarterly if time-weighted returns are being calculated, and they are not required to be valued at the time of large cash flows. Asset owners may use the Modified Dietz method to calculate the quarterly return. Asset owners are not required to value private market investment portfolios at the time of large cash flows but may do so. The asset owner must establish a composite-specific valuation policy, but that policy may specify a different valuation frequency for different types of portfolios in the composite. There may also be cases in which an asset owner may establish different valuation frequency policies for the same types of portfolios within a composite. For example, the asset owner may have a private market investment portfolio in a composite that allows for monthly subscriptions and redemptions, and the asset owner's policy is to value this portfolio monthly. Another portfolio in this same composite may have the same structure but allows for quarterly subscriptions and redemptions, and so the asset owner values this portfolio quarterly. The asset owner must apply the composite-specific valuation policy consistently based on the specified valuation frequency for the portfolios in the composite, but that policy may differentiate valuation frequency for different types of portfolios in the composite. For example, segregated accounts are valued monthly and at the time of large cash flows, whereas investments in underlying pooled funds are valued daily. The asset owner must apply the composite-specific valuation policy consistently based on the valuation frequency for the type of portfolio.

---

[17] REQUIRED for periods beginning on or after 1 January 2008.
[18] REQUIRED for periods beginning on or after 1 January 2010.

 |

In all cases, however, each private market investment portfolio in the composite must be valued at quarter end or on the last business day of the quarter.

Quarterly valuations are important for the oversight body to be able to compare performance with private market investment benchmarks, which are typically not updated monthly. Quarterly valuations are also needed for comparability with other asset classes and for comparability of data in GIPS Asset Owner Reports. This quarterly valuation requirement can be met by either internal or external valuations.

Private market investments include real estate. For periods prior to 1 January 2008, real estate investments must be valued at least once every 12 months. The annual valuation requirement for periods prior to 1 January 2008 can be met either by internal or external valuations. An internal valuation is an asset owner's best estimate of value based on the most current and accurate information available to the asset owner. Internal valuation methodologies can include applying a discounted cash flow model, using a sales comparison or replacement cost approach, or conducting a review of all significant events (both general market events and asset-specific events) that could have a material effect on the investment. External valuations for real estate are discussed in Provisions 22.A.33, 22.A.34, and 22.A.35.

Provision 22.A.31

When calculating TIME-WEIGHTED RETURNS for PRIVATE MARKET INVESTMENT PORTFOLIOS that are included in COMPOSITES, the ASSET OWNER MUST:

a. Calculate returns at least quarterly.[19]

b. Calculate quarterly returns through the calendar quarter end or the last business day of the quarter.[20]

c. Calculate PORTFOLIO returns that adjust for daily-weighted EXTERNAL CASH FLOWS.[21]

d. Treat EXTERNAL CASH FLOWS according to the ASSET OWNER's COMPOSITE-specific policy.

e. Geometrically LINK periodic and sub-period returns.

f. Consistently apply the calculation methodology used for an individual PORTFOLIO.

---

[19] REQUIRED for periods beginning on or after 1 January 2008.
[20] REQUIRED for periods beginning on or after 1 January 2010.
[21] REQUIRED for periods beginning on or after 1 January 2010.

Discussion

A portfolio is considered a private market investment portfolio when it has an investment objective to invest primarily in private market investments. Private market investments include real assets (e.g., real estate and infrastructure), private equity, and similar investments that are illiquid, not publicly traded, and not traded on an exchange.

Because private market investments do not trade publicly like stocks and bonds do, the return calculation requirements differ for private market investment composites. The portfolio calculation frequency is aligned with the minimum valuation frequency, which is quarterly; therefore, asset owners must calculate portfolio returns at least quarterly.

As of 1 January 2010, asset owners must calculate quarterly returns through the calendar quarter end or the last business day of the quarter when calculating time-weighted returns (TWRs) for private market investments included in composites. Consistency in return calculation dates will result in improved comparability of data for all GIPS Asset Owner Reports.

Because most portfolios within a composite experience external cash flows, it is important that the calculation of portfolio TWRs adjust for daily-weighted external cash flows that occur during the calculation period. This is required for periods beginning on or after 1 January 2010. When calculating TWRs that adjust for daily-weighted external cash flows, periodic and sub-periodic returns must be geometrically linked.

Private market investments do not trade publicly like marketable securities do, and thus they do not have valuations readily available on a monthly basis or at the time of external cash flows. Therefore, asset owners are not required to value private market investment portfolios and to calculate sub-period returns at the time of large cash flows, and to geometrically link these sub-period returns to calculate monthly TWRs, as is required for portfolios that are not private market portfolios. Instead, asset owners must calculate returns for private market investment portfolios at least quarterly and may use methods that adjust for daily-weighted external cash flows, such as the Modified Dietz or the internal rate of return (IRR) methods.

As explained in the discussion for Provision 22.A.21, the Modified Dietz and IRR methods are money-weighted rate of return methods. By means of geometric linking of the periodic Modified Dietz or IRR returns, however, TWRs can be approximated. Asset owners must create composite-specific policies with respect to the methodology used in calculating returns for private market investment portfolios and must apply these policies consistently to the individual portfolios included in the composite.

Provision 22.A.32

COMPOSITE TIME-WEIGHTED RETURNS for PRIVATE MARKET INVESTMENT COMPOSITES MUST be calculated at least quarterly.

Discussion

Composite time-weighted returns for private market investment composites must be calculated at least quarterly. Quarterly returns are important for an oversight body to be able to compare performance with private market investment benchmarks, which are typically reported on a quarterly basis. Quarterly returns are also needed for comparability with other asset classes and for comparability of data in GIPS Asset Owner Reports.

Real Estate

Provision 22.A.33

REAL ESTATE investments that are directly owned by the ASSET OWNER MUST:[22]

a. Have an EXTERNAL VALUATION at least once every 12 months unless the OVERSIGHT BODY stipulates otherwise, in which case REAL ESTATE investments MUST have an EXTERNAL VALUATION at least once every 36 months or per OVERSIGHT BODY instructions if the OVERSIGHT BODY REQUIRES EXTERNAL VALUATIONS more frequently than every 36 months; or

b. Be subject to an annual financial statement audit performed by an independent public accounting firm. The REAL ESTATE investments MUST be accounted for at FAIR VALUE and the most recent audited financial statements available MUST contain an unmodified opinion issued by an independent public accounting firm.

Discussion

This provision applies to all real estate investments that are directly owned by the asset owner. This provision does not apply to real estate that may be held by pooled funds in which the asset owner invests or held by externally managed segregated accounts.

Real estate investments include wholly owned or partially owned:

- investments in land, including products grown from the land (e.g., timber, crops),
- buildings under development, completed buildings, and other structures or improvements,
- equity-oriented debt (e.g., participating mortgage loans), and
- private interest in a property for which some portion of the return to the investor at the time of investment is related to the performance of the underlying real estate.

---

[22] REQUIRED for periods beginning on or after 1 January 2012.

The following investments are not considered to be real estate investments and must follow the provisions of the GIPS standards that are not related to real estate:

- publicly traded real estate securities,
- mortgage-backed securities (MBS) and commercial mortgage-backed securities (CMBS), and
- private debt investments, including commercial and residential loans in which the expected return is solely related to contractual interest rates without any participation in the economic performance of the underlying real estate.

In addition to the requirement to fair value quarterly, real estate investments that are directly owned by the asset owner must have either:

- an external valuation: an assessment of value performed by an independent third party who is a professionally designated or certified commercial property valuer or appraiser. In markets where these professionals are not available, steps must be taken to ensure that only qualified independent property valuers or appraisers are used; or
- a financial statement audit: an audit of a property's or a portfolio's financial statements that includes the real estate investments.

If an asset owner chooses an external valuation to satisfy this requirement, the real estate investments must have an external valuation at least every 12 months unless the oversight body stipulates a different frequency for external valuations. For example, if the oversight body stipulates that external valuations will take place every 24 months, then real estate investments that are directly owned must have an external valuation completed at least once every 24 months. Regardless of the frequency stipulated by the oversight body, each real estate investment that is directly owned by the asset owner must have an external valuation at least once every 36 months. Asset owners are encouraged to discuss the importance of external valuation with their oversight body, because valuation is the major element used in the performance return calculation and the external appraisal typically provides a point of reference for subsequent internal valuations performed by the asset owner. An asset owner may not always be successful in convincing the oversight body to move to more frequent external valuations because of the cost of the appraisal. In many markets, however, the cost of obtaining external appraisals, including subsequent updates, are not significant because of technological advances as well as increased availability of market data. For additional information regarding an external valuation, please refer to Provision 22.A.34.

Asset owners that opt to have an external valuation are not required to obtain an external valuation for a property when the property is under a sales contract and the asset owner believes that the sale will be finalized.

Instead of an external valuation, an asset owner may choose to have a financial statement audit. The audit must be performed by an independent, qualified (i.e., professionally designated, certified, or licensed) accounting firm. The accounting firm chosen must be knowledgeable of the accounting rules and principles that apply to the asset owner's financial statements, including

 |

all relevant laws and regulatory requirements. The financial statement audit may be at either the property level or portfolio level.

Although the most recent financial statement audit does not need to be through the most recent period for which the asset owner is claiming compliance with the GIPS standards, a financial statement audit must be performed annually. The real estate investments must be accounted for at fair value, and the most recent audited financial statements available must contain an unmodified opinion issued by the independent public accounting firm.

Provision 22.A.34

EXTERNAL VALUATIONS for REAL ESTATE investments MUST be performed by an independent third party who is a professionally designated or certified commercial property valuer or appraiser. In markets where these professionals are not available, the ASSET OWNER MUST take necessary steps to ensure that only qualified independent property valuers or appraisers are used.

Discussion

An external valuation must be performed by an independent third party who is a professionally designated or certified commercial property valuer/appraiser. In Europe, Canada, and parts of Southeast Asia, the predominant professional designation is that of the Royal Institution of Chartered Surveyors (RICS). In the United States, the professional designation is Member of the Appraisal Institute (MAI). In Australia, the designation is Certified Practising Valuer from the Australian Property Institute. In markets where these professionals are unavailable, steps must be taken to ensure that only qualified independent valuers or appraisers are used. Even if no credentialed professionals are available, it would be unusual to not find a well-qualified independent valuer or appraiser who can value a property in a particular market.

The external valuation process must adhere to practices of the relevant valuation governing and standard setting body. Although appraisal standards may allow for a range of estimated values, it is recommended that a single value (final value conclusion) be obtained from external valuers or appraisers because only one value can be used for performance reporting.

Provision 22.A.35

The ASSET OWNER MUST NOT use EXTERNAL VALUATIONS for REAL ESTATE investments when the valuer's or appraiser's fee is contingent upon the investment's appraised value.

Discussion

The asset owner must not use external valuations when the valuer's or appraiser's fee is contingent upon the investment's appraised value. To do so could damage the objectivity of the valuer or appraiser and lead to a higher valuation than would otherwise be the case. The linking of a valuer's or appraiser's fee to the investment's appraised value will also lead to the perception that the investment's appraised value may have an upward bias, reducing the confidence of those evaluating the investment and the resulting valuation.

Side Pockets

Provision 22.A.36

All TOTAL FUND, COMPOSITE, and POOLED FUND returns MUST include the effect of any SIDE POCKETS held by TOTAL FUNDS, PORTFOLIOS, or POOLED FUNDS.

Discussion

A side pocket is a segregated investment that is used mainly in alternative investment pooled funds, such as hedge funds, funds of funds, and other alternative investment funds, to separate illiquid or distressed assets from other, more liquid investments or to segregate investments held for a special purpose from other investments. All total fund, composite, and pooled fund returns must include the effect of any side pockets held by the total fund, composite, or pooled fund.

Asset owners may choose to also present returns without side pockets as supplemental information. The oversight body may be interested in the performance history without the effect of side pockets.

22.B. Input Data and Calculation Methodology—Recommendations

Provision 22.B.1

The ASSET OWNER SHOULD value TOTAL FUNDS and PORTFOLIOS on the date of all EXTERNAL CASH FLOWS.

 |

Discussion

To improve the accuracy of time-weighted performance calculations, the GIPS standards have gradually increased the minimum required frequency of total fund valuation and portfolio valuation for many portfolio types from quarterly, to monthly, to the date of all large cash flows for periods beginning on or after 1 January 2010. Best practice, however, is to value total funds and portfolios on the date of all external cash flows. Asset owners are encouraged to create a policy to value total funds and portfolios on the date of all external cash flows as part of the total fund–specific or composite-specific valuation policy where possible.

Provision 22.B.2

Valuations SHOULD be obtained from a qualified independent third party.

Discussion

The quality of valuations used as inputs to calculate performance has a significant effect on the accuracy of total fund, portfolio, and composite returns; therefore, it is important that the valuations used are accurate. It is recommended that asset owners obtain valuations from an independent source because a third party can provide the most objective investment valuations. In most instances, obtaining valuations from an independent third party is considered to be a best practice. An asset owner claiming compliance with the GIPS standards is responsible for its claim of compliance and must ensure that the valuations obtained from a third party can be used to satisfy the requirements of the GIPS standards.

Provision 22.B.3

ACCRUAL ACCOUNTING SHOULD be used for dividends (as of the ex-dividend date).

Discussion

Accrual accounting determines the correct economic value of the total fund or portfolio assets and allows the recording of financial transactions as they come into existence rather than when they are paid or settled. It is recommended that dividends be recognized when earned on the ex-date (accrual basis) versus when paid (cash basis).

Provision 22.B.4

The ASSET OWNER SHOULD accrue INVESTMENT MANAGEMENT FEES and INVESTMENT MANAGEMENT COSTS.

Discussion

Investment management fees are defined as the fees payable to external managers for externally managed assets. They are typically asset based (based on a percentage of assets), performance based (based on the portfolio's performance either on an absolute basis or relative to a benchmark), or a combination of the two, but they may take other forms as well. Investment management fees also include carried interest. Investment management fees for externally managed pooled funds and externally managed segregated accounts are among the fees and expenses that must be deducted when calculating total fund and composite net-of-fees returns and total fund and composite net-of-external-costs only returns. Investment management fees for externally managed pooled funds are also among the fees and expenses that must be deducted when calculating total fund and composite gross-of-fees returns.

Investment management costs are defined as all internal costs for both internally and externally managed assets. In addition to costs for portfolio management, they may also involve overhead and other related costs and fees, including data valuation fees, investment research services, custody fees, pro rata share of overhead (such as building and utilities), allocation of non-investment-department expenses (such as human resources, communications, and technology), and performance measurement and compliance services.[E] Investment management costs are among the fees and expenses that must be deducted when calculating total fund and composite net-of-fees returns.

To reflect the most accurate returns, investment management fees and investment management costs should be accrued when possible. Accrual accounting allows the recording of financial transactions as they come into existence rather when they are paid or settled. Returns can be skewed if investment management fees and investment management costs are reflected in the calculation of returns as they are paid, particularly when portfolio values change significantly.

[E] The definition of INVESTMENT MANAGEMENT COSTS included in the Glossary in the 2020 edition of the GIPS standards is incorrect and should state:

All internal costs for both internally and externally managed assets. In addition to costs for PORTFOLIO management, they may also involve overhead and other related costs and fees, including data valuation fees, investment research services, CUSTODY FEES, pro rata share of overhead (such as building and utilities), allocation of non-investment-department expenses (such as human resources, communications, and technology), and performance measurement and compliance services.

Provision 22.B.5

Returns SHOULD be calculated net of non-reclaimable withholding taxes on dividends, interest, and capital gains. Reclaimable withholding taxes SHOULD be accrued.

Discussion

Global investing requires recognition of the tax consequences of investing in different countries. The GIPS standards recommend that performance be reported net of non-reclaimable withholding taxes on dividends, interest, and capital gains. Some countries allow certain types of foreign investors to reclaim a portion of the foreign withholding taxes that are paid. These reclaimable foreign withholding taxes may be credited back to the investor at a later date. It is recommended that reclaimable foreign withholding taxes be accrued, meaning that the refund for reclaimable withholding taxes should be recorded when the reclaimable withholding taxes become a receivable owed to the asset owner, rather than when the refund is actually received.

Provision 22.B.6

The ASSET OWNER SHOULD incorporate the following hierarchy into its policies and procedures for determining FAIR VALUE for PORTFOLIO investments on a TOTAL FUND–specific or COMPOSITE-specific basis.

a. Investments MUST be valued using objective, observable, unadjusted quoted market prices for identical investments in active markets on the measurement date, if available. If such prices are not available, then investments SHOULD be valued using;

b. Objective, observable quoted market prices for similar investments in active markets. If such prices are not available or appropriate, then investments SHOULD be valued using;

c. Quoted prices for identical or similar investments in markets that are not active (markets in which there are few transactions for the investment, the prices are not current, or price quotations vary substantially over time and/or between market makers). If such prices are not available or appropriate, then investments SHOULD be valued based on;

d. Market-based inputs, other than quoted prices, that are observable for the investment. If such prices are not available or appropriate, then investments SHOULD be valued based on;

e. Subjective, unobservable inputs for the investment where markets are not active at the measurement date. Unobservable inputs SHOULD be used to measure FAIR VALUE only when observable inputs and prices are not available or appropriate. Unobservable inputs reflect the ASSET OWNER'S own assumptions about the assumptions that market participants would use in pricing the investment and SHOULD be developed based on the best information available under the circumstances.

Discussion

The GIPS standards include a recommended valuation hierarchy as presented in Provision 22.B.6. It is recommended that asset owners incorporate this hierarchy into their policies for determining fair value for portfolio investments on a total fund–specific or composite-specific basis. For further information regarding fair valuation and the frequency of internal and external valuation requirements, please refer to Provision 22.A.16.

Provision 22.B.7

The ASSET OWNER SHOULD use GROSS-OF-FEES returns when calculating risk measures.

Discussion

Acknowledging that there are many acceptable calculation variations for various risk measures, the GIPS standards do not prescribe a specific methodology for calculating risk measures. It is recommended, however, that gross-of-fees returns be used when calculating risk measures. It is recommended that asset owners use gross-of-fees returns because these returns do not reflect the deduction of investment management fees for externally managed segregated accounts, which introduce additional variability of returns.

Asset owners are required to select a calculation methodology, on a total fund–specific or composite-specific basis, for each risk measure presented in a GIPS Asset Owner Report. They must document the chosen calculation methodology in their policies and procedures and then consistently apply the methodology selected.

 |

Provision 22.B.8

PRIVATE MARKET INVESTMENTS SHOULD have an EXTERNAL VALUATION at least once every 12 months.

Discussion

For periods beginning or after 1 January 2020, it is recommended that private market investments have an external valuation at least once every 12 months. (Real estate investments that are directly owned by the asset owner must have an external valuation at least once every 12 months, unless the oversight body stipulates a less frequent external valuation, or be subject to an annual financial statement audit. See Provision 22.A.33.)

Those evaluating an asset owner's private market investments, including the oversight body, typically prefer an external valuation because it is independent, unbiased, and an "expert" estimate of value that is perceived by the marketplace to be more reliable than an internal valuation.

An external valuation is an assessment of value performed by an independent third party who is a professionally designated or certified commercial property valuer or appraiser. In markets where these professionals are unavailable, steps must be taken to ensure that only qualified independent property valuers or appraisers are used. For additional information regarding an external valuation, please refer to Provision 22.A.34.

Provision 22.B.9

Operating cash accounts that are not available for investment SHOULD NOT be included in TOTAL ASSET OWNER ASSETS, TOTAL FUND assets, or COMPOSITE assets.[F]

Discussion

Asset owners often maintain a number of cash accounts. A cash account that is considered discretionary and is part of the investable assets of the total fund must be included in total asset owner assets, total fund assets, or composite assets. There may be other operating cash accounts, such as a checking account that is used for payments to beneficiaries, vendors and others, that may be associated with the total fund but are not part of the total fund from an investment standpoint.

[F] In the 2020 edition of the GIPS standards, Provision 22.B.9 incorrectly included the word "fully", and should state:

Operating cash accounts that are not ~~fully~~ available for investment SHOULD NOT be included in TOTAL ASSET OWNER ASSETS, TOTAL FUND assets, or COMPOSITE assets.

If the operating cash account (e.g., checking account) is not available for investment, it should not be included in total asset owner assets, total fund assets, or composite assets.

Note that if a cash account has multiple purposes and is available for investment as well as used as an operating cash account, and the asset owner is unable to differentiate the portion of the cash account that is available for investment, it is recommended that a conservative approach be taken. The entire cash account should be considered available for investment and included in total asset owner assets, total fund assets, and composite assets.

Provision 22.B.10

Operating cash accounts that are not available for investment SHOULD NOT be included in TOTAL FUND returns or COMPOSITE returns.[G]

Discussion

Asset owners often maintain a number of cash accounts. A cash account that is considered discretionary and is part of the investable assets of the total fund must be included in total fund returns or composite returns. There may be other operating cash accounts, such as a checking account that is used for payments to beneficiaries, vendors and others, that may be associated with the total fund but are not part of the total fund from an investment standpoint. If the operating cash account (e.g., checking account) is not available for investment, it should not be included in total fund returns or composite returns.

Note that if a cash account has multiple purposes and is available for investment as well as used as an operating cash account, and the asset owner is unable to differentiate the portion of the cash account that is available for investment, it is recommended that a conservative approach be taken. The entire cash account should be considered available for investment and included in total fund returns and composite returns.

[G] In the 2020 edition of the GIPS standards, Provision 22.B.10 incorrectly included the word "fully", and should state:

Operating cash accounts that are not ~~fully~~ available for investment SHOULD NOT be included in TOTAL FUND returns or COMPOSITE returns.

 |

23. TOTAL FUND AND COMPOSITE MAINTENANCE

23.A. Total Fund and Composite Maintenance–Requirements

Provision 23. A.1

TOTAL FUNDS MUST include all assets managed by the ASSET OWNER as part of the TOTAL FUND's investment mandate, objective, or strategy.

Discussion

A total fund is defined as a pool of assets managed by an asset owner according to a specific investment mandate, which is typically composed of multiple asset classes. The total fund usually consists of underlying portfolios, each representing one of the strategies used to achieve the asset owner's investment mandate. Each total fund must include all assets managed by the asset owner as part of the total fund's investment mandate, objective, or strategy.

Provision 23.A.2

If the ASSET OWNER manages more than one TOTAL FUND according to the same strategy, all TOTAL FUNDS managed according to the same investment strategy MUST be presented either:[23]

a. Separately to the OVERSIGHT BODY, or
b. As a COMPOSITE to the OVERSIGHT BODY.

Discussion

If an asset owner manages more than one total fund according to the same investment strategy, the asset owner has a choice regarding how the total funds are presented to the oversight body. The asset owner may choose to present each total fund separately to the oversight body, creating a separate GIPS Asset Owner Report for each total fund. Alternatively, the asset owner may include all total funds managed according to the same investment strategy in one total fund

---

[23] REQUIRED for periods beginning on or after 1 January 2015.

composite and create one GIPS Asset Owner Report for the total fund composite to present to the oversight body.

Although asset owners often use the term "composite" to refer to any grouping of accounts or assets, it has a specific meaning in the GIPS standards. In the GIPS standards, a composite is defined as an aggregation of one or more portfolios or total funds that are managed according to a similar investment mandate, objective, or strategy. By definition, therefore, a total fund composite may include only total funds managed according to a similar investment mandate, objective, or strategy.

If an asset owner manages more than two total funds according to the same strategy, the asset owner may include some of the total funds together in a total fund composite and present the remaining total fund(s) separately to the oversight body. There must be a GIPS Asset Owner Report for the total fund composite and for each total fund presented separately to the oversight body. Asset owners may create total fund composites giving consideration to the respective oversight body. As an example, suppose that an asset owner manages three total funds according to the same investment strategy. Two total funds, one managed for the police officers' retirement system and one managed for the firefighters' retirement system, have the same oversight body. The third total fund is managed for the teachers' retirement system and has a separate oversight body. The asset owner may choose to combine the total funds for the police officers' and firefighters' retirement systems into one total fund composite for presentation to the one oversight body, and the asset owner may present the total fund managed for the teachers' retirement system separately to the second oversight body. This approach would be chosen to facilitate the reporting of the total funds to the respective oversight bodies. The asset owner can also choose not to include the total funds for the police officers' and firefighters' retirement systems in a composite and would instead present each total fund separately to the oversight body.

Provision 23.A.3

If the ASSET OWNER manages TOTAL FUNDS according to different strategies, then each TOTAL FUND MUST be presented separately to the OVERSIGHT BODY.

Discussion

Only total funds that are managed according to the same investment strategy may be included together in a total fund composite. If an asset owner manages total funds according to different strategies, each total fund must be presented separately to the respective oversight body, and there must be a separate GIPS Asset Owner Report for each total fund.

Provision 23.A.4

Composites must be defined according to investment mandate, objective, or strategy. Composites must include all portfolios that meet the composite definition. If the asset owner chooses to create an additional composite, then all portfolios that meet the composite definition must be included in the additional composite.

Discussion

Although asset owners often use the term "composite" to refer to any grouping of accounts or assets, it has a specific meaning in the GIPS standards. In the GIPS standards, a composite is defined as an aggregation of one or more portfolios or total funds that are managed according to a similar investment mandate, objective, or strategy.

If an asset owner manages more than one total fund according to the same investment strategy, the asset owner has a choice regarding the use of composites. The asset owner may include all total funds managed according to the same investment strategy in a total fund composite, create a GIPS Asset Owner Report for the total fund composite, and present composite performance to its oversight body. Alternatively, the asset owner may choose to not create a composite and instead present each total fund separately to its oversight body. If an asset owner decides to create one or more total fund composites, these would be considered required composites.

In addition to any required total fund composites, an asset owner may choose to create one or more additional composites. An additional composite is a grouping of portfolios representing a particular strategy or asset class that the asset owner chooses to present in a GIPS Asset Owner Report.

As an example, asset owners often create asset class composites to represent each of the asset classes in the total fund (e.g., equity, fixed income, hedge funds, private equity, real estate). As another example, an asset owner may wish to create an additional composite for its private equity venture capital investments that consists of the venture capital investments held in all private equity portfolios. Although additional composites are not required, asset owners are encouraged to create additional composites when it is meaningful and appropriate and to present them in a GIPS Asset Owner Report. If an asset owner chooses to prepare a GIPS Asset Owner Report for an additional composite, the asset owner must present that composite's GIPS Asset Owner Report to the asset owner's oversight body. Asset owners are not required to create additional composites and present them in a GIPS Asset Owner Report but are recommended to do so.

If an asset owner chooses to create additional composites, all portfolios that meet the composite definition for an additional composite must be included in the composite. If a portfolio meets the composite definition for more than one composite, the portfolio must be included in each of the relevant composites.

 |

Additional composite returns are not required to include cash and cash equivalent returns. Asset owners may, therefore, create additional composites that do not include cash and cash equivalents. For example, an asset owner might decide to create an additional composite that includes all equity investments of the total fund. The asset owner may present this Equity Composite in a GIPS Asset Owner Report even though the Equity Composite returns do not include cash and cash equivalents. Only asset owners that are reporting performance to their oversight body and are not competing for business have the ability to present additional composite returns that do not include cash and cash equivalents as GIPS-compliant information. If the asset owner competes for business, additional composite returns must include cash and cash equivalents. (See Provision 21.A.24 for further information on what to do when the asset owner competes for business.)

Creating meaningful composites is critical to fair presentation, consistency, and comparability of results over time. Asset owners make the ultimate decision as to which portfolios belong in each composite.

To create appropriate composites, it is important to understand what is meant by a composite description and a composite definition.

A composite description is defined as general information regarding the investment mandate, objective, or strategy of the composite. The composite description may be more abbreviated than the composite definition but must include all key features of the composite and must include enough information to allow the oversight body to understand the key characteristics of the composite's investment mandate, objective, or strategy, including:

- the material risks of the composite's strategy,
- how leverage, derivatives, and short positions may be used, if they are a material part of the strategy, and
- if illiquid investments are a material part of the strategy.

A composite definition is defined as detailed criteria that determine the assignment of portfolios to composites. Criteria may include, but are not limited to, investment mandate, style or strategy, asset class, the use of derivatives, leverage and/or hedging, targeted risk metrics, investment constraints or restrictions, and/or portfolio type (e.g., segregated account or pooled fund).

Composite descriptions are disclosed in GIPS Asset Owner Reports and on the list of total fund descriptions and composite descriptions. (See Provision 21.A.17 for further information on creating the list of total fund descriptions and composite descriptions.) Composite definitions must be documented in the asset owner's policies and procedures.

To differentiate between a composite definition and a composite description, it might be helpful to think of a composite description as focused on a description of the strategy represented by the composite. In contrast, a composite definition includes not only the composite strategy, as represented by the composite description, but also the detailed criteria that determine whether a portfolio is included in a composite (e.g., if a composite includes segregated accounts versus pooled funds). Asset owners must use their judgment when determining what information is appropriate to include in a composite description and composite definition for a specific strategy. Asset owners are encouraged to include more than the required minimum information in a composite description if doing so will help the oversight body understand both the nature of the portfolios included in the composite and the strategy used. In some instances, the composite description and composite definition may be the same or have small differences. This is acceptable as long as the composite description and composite definition are complete and reflect the criteria listed in their glossary definitions.

Additional Considerations

The following are examples of composite descriptions that might be found in a GIPS Asset Owner Report created for an additional composite and the related composite definitions that are documented in policies and procedures.

US Equity Composite

Composite Description

The Domestic Equity Composite (Composite) includes all portfolios from the Total Fund for which the majority of the portfolio is invested in US equities, American depositary receipts (ADRs), REIT shares, and domestic equity derivatives. Composite returns do not include the effect of cash or cash equivalents for internally managed assets.

Composite Definition

The Domestic Equity Composite (Composite) includes all portfolios from the Total Fund for which the majority of the portfolio is invested in US equities, American depositary receipts (ADRs), REIT shares, and domestic equity derivatives. Composite returns do not include the effect of cash or cash equivalents for internally managed assets. The Composite includes internally managed assets, segregated accounts, and pooled funds.

Private Equity Composite

Composite Description

The Private Equity Composite includes all domestic and international investments in leveraged buyout and venture capital funds. These funds tend to have long lock-up periods (seven years or longer) because many of the portfolio investments are not liquid and the leveraged buyout funds use leverage extensively. We make commitments to the funds in various amounts, and capital is called as investment opportunities become available.

 |

Composite Definition

The Private Equity Composite includes all domestic and international investments in leveraged buyout and venture capital funds. These funds tend to have long lock-up periods (seven years or longer) because many of the portfolio investments are not liquid and the leveraged buyout funds use leverage extensively. We make commitments to the funds in various amounts, and capital is called as investment opportunities become available. All portfolios in the composite are pooled funds. All pooled funds with private market investments that have more liquidity are included in the hedge fund composite.

Provision 23.A.5

Any change to a COMPOSITE DEFINITION MUST NOT be applied retroactively.

Discussion

Although investment strategies can change over time, in most cases asset owners should not change the definition of a total fund composite or additional composite. (An additional composite is a grouping of portfolios representing a particular strategy or asset class that the asset owner chooses to present in a GIPS Asset Owner Report.) Generally, changes in strategy result in the creation of a new composite. In some cases, however, it may be appropriate to redefine a composite. If an asset owner determines that it is appropriate to redefine a composite, it must disclose the date and description of the redefinition. Changes to composites must not be applied retroactively.

Note that if an asset owner chooses to create a new composite to reflect a new investment strategy, the asset owner may move portfolios that meet the new composite definition into the new composite. The history of existing portfolios must remain with the original composite.

Provision 23.A.6

TOTAL FUNDS and COMPOSITES MUST include new PORTFOLIOS on a timely and consistent basis as soon as they are funded.

Discussion

A portfolio is defined as an account representing one of the strategies in or components of the asset owner's total fund, including assets managed by external managers for which the asset owner has discretion over the selection of the external manager. For a total fund, any new portfolios within the total fund must be included in the total fund as soon as they are funded. If there is a total fund composite, and if any of the total funds in the composite are being newly established, this requirement also applies.

The same is true for additional composites. (An additional composite is a grouping of portfolios representing a particular strategy or asset class that the asset owner chooses to present in a GIPS Asset Owner Report.) For any additional composite the asset owner chooses to create, any new portfolios (i.e., a portfolio is considered to be an investment) must be included in the relevant composite as soon as they are funded.

Provision 23.A.7

Terminated PORTFOLIOS MUST be included in the historical performance of the TOTAL FUND or COMPOSITE through the final day the assets are managed.

Discussion

A portfolio is defined as an account representing one of the strategies in or components of the asset owner's total fund, including assets managed by external managers for which the asset owner has discretion over the selection of the external manager. The requirement to include terminated portfolios (i.e., a portfolio is considered to be an investment) in the total fund's or composite's historical performance through the final day the assets are managed or held prevents survivorship bias by retaining the performance history of the portfolio for the entire time period for which it was managed to the total fund's or composite's strategy.

The same is true for additional composites. (An additional composite is a grouping of portfolios representing a particular strategy or asset class that the asset owner chooses to present in a GIPS Asset Owner Report.) If all portfolios are removed from an additional composite, for any reason, the performance record of the additional composite comes to an end. If, after a period of time, portfolios are again included in the additional composite, the prior performance history of the additional composite must be presented but must not be linked to the ongoing additional composite performance results. Please see Provision 24.A.6 for more information on presenting performance when there is a break in the total fund or composite track record.

|

Provision 23.A.8

If the ASSET OWNER chooses to create a COMPOSITE that includes more than one TOTAL FUND, or if the ASSET OWNER creates additional COMPOSITES, TOTAL FUNDS and PORTFOLIOS MUST NOT be moved from one COMPOSITE to another unless either (1) documented ASSET OWNER–directed changes to a TOTAL FUND's or PORTFOLIO's investment mandate, objective, or strategy or (2) the redefinition of the COMPOSITE make it appropriate. The historical performance of the TOTAL FUND or PORTFOLIO MUST remain with the original COMPOSITE. TOTAL FUNDS and PORTFOLIOS MUST NOT be moved into or out of COMPOSITES as a result of tactical changes.

Discussion

This provision is applicable if the asset owner chooses to create a composite that includes more than one total fund or if the asset owner creates additional composites. (An additional composite is a grouping of portfolios representing a particular strategy or asset class that the asset owner chooses to present in a GIPS Asset Owner Report.)

Asset owners are permitted to move total funds or portfolios into and out of composites only as a result of documented asset owner–directed changes to a total fund's or portfolio's investment mandate, objective, or strategy or if the redefinition of a composite makes such a move appropriate. Documentation of a change in a total fund's or portfolio's investment mandate, objective, or strategy can include, but is not limited to, letters, e-mails, and internal memorandums documenting the change.

This requirement seeks to preclude or at least minimize the movement of total funds and portfolios into, out of, and between composites. Theoretically, once an asset owner creates composites based on its various investment strategies, total funds and portfolios will be managed to those strategies on a long-term basis. As a result, defining composites is a critical issue when complying with the GIPS standards.

Over time, however, a total fund's investment mandate may be modified, and asset owners may adopt new investment strategies. In those instances, moving a total fund or portfolio from one composite to another may be necessary. Total funds or portfolios must not be moved from one composite to another because of changes in tactical asset allocation. As noted earlier, total funds and portfolios can be moved into different composites only in the case of documented changes to a total fund's or portfolio's investment mandate, objective, or strategy or when the redefinition of a composite makes such a move appropriate.

If the investment strategy for the total fund or portfolio has changed, the transfer of a total fund or portfolio from one composite to another is treated as a termination when it is removed from the former composite and treated as a new total fund or portfolio when moved to the new composite.

The total fund's prior history must remain in the former composite through the last full measurement period the total fund was managed in the former style. A portfolio's prior history must remain in the former additional composite through the day the assets were managed in the former style.

If the asset owner redefines the composite, it must determine if it is appropriate to include the history of the total funds and portfolios in that composite. Asset owners must create a policy, apply it consistently, and not cherry-pick total funds, portfolios, or time periods in order to make performance look better.

Example 1

An asset owner has two total funds managed according to the same investment strategy: Total Fund 1 is managed for the police officers' retirement system, and Total Fund 2 is managed for the firefighters' retirement system. The asset owner has chosen to present the two total funds as one composite to the oversight body. After several years, the investment strategy for Total Fund 1 changes, and the two total funds are no longer managed according to the same investment strategy.

Going forward, the asset owner must remove Total Fund 1 from the Total Fund Composite and present it separately to the oversight body. The asset owner may choose to present no performance history in the GIPS Asset Owner Report for Total Fund 1, because it represents a new strategy. Alternatively, the asset owner may choose to present the performance history for Total Fund 1 only in its GIPS Asset Owner Report. If the asset owner chooses to show performance history for Total Fund 1 related to its former strategy, the change in the investment strategy of Total Fund 1 is considered a significant event and must be disclosed in the GIPS Asset Owner Report. (See Provision 24.C.16.)

The GIPS Asset Owner Report for the Total Fund Composite would include the combined performance of Total Fund 1 and Total Fund 2 until Total Fund 1 was removed from the Total Fund Composite. From that point forward, the GIPS Asset Owner Report would include only the performance of Total Fund 2. Alternatively, the asset owner may choose to terminate the Total Fund Composite and present only the performance of Total Fund 2 in a GIPS Asset Owner Report.

Example 2

An asset owner has two total funds managed according to the same investment strategy. Over the years, the asset owner has presented the total funds separately to its oversight body. The asset owner has now decided to include the total funds in the same composite. It therefore creates a Total Fund Composite that includes both total funds and presents a GIPS Asset Owner Report for the new Total Fund Composite to its oversight body.

Presenting the total funds separately to the oversight body for a period of time, and subsequently choosing to combine the total funds in a composite for presentation to its oversight body, is permitted for asset owners. It is also permissible for an asset owner to have combined the total funds

 |

for a period of time and then decide that it is preferable to present the total funds separately to the oversight body. The decision to present the total funds to the oversight body in a new manner must be documented.

Once an asset owner changes the manner in which it presents the total funds to the oversight body, the new manner of presentation should be continued. It is also important to remember that fair representation is one of the fundamental principles on which the GIPS standards are based. Asset owners must not change the manner in which total funds are presented to the oversight body in order to hide poor performance or inappropriately highlight more positive returns.

Example 3

An asset owner has created two additional composites: one representing large-cap domestic equities (Large-Cap Domestic Equity Composite) and one representing small-cap and mid-cap domestic equities (Small-Cap/Mid-Cap Domestic Equity Composite). Together, these two composites include all of the domestic equities in the total fund. The asset owner subsequently decides to create a broader composite to represent all domestic equities, regardless of their market cap.

The asset owner would create a Domestic Equity Composite that includes all of the domestic equity portfolios in the total fund. All portfolios in the Large-Cap Domestic Equity Composite and the Small-Cap/Mid-Cap Domestic Equity Composite would be included in the new Domestic Equity Composite. The asset owner could either: 1) discontinue the Large-Cap Domestic Equity Composite and the Small-Cap/Mid-Cap Domestic Equity Composite; or 2) continue to maintain the Large-Cap Domestic Equity Composite and the Small-Cap/Mid-Cap Domestic Equity Composite, in addition to the broader Domestic Equity Composite.

24. TOTAL FUND AND COMPOSITE TIME-WEIGHTED RETURN REPORT

The following provisions apply to ASSET OWNERS that include TIME-WEIGHTED RETURNS in a GIPS ASSET OWNER REPORT.

24.A. Presentation and Reporting—Requirements

Provision 24.A.1

The ASSET OWNER MUST present in each GIPS ASSET OWNER REPORT:

a. At least one year of performance (or for the period since the TOTAL FUND or COMPOSITE INCEPTION DATE if the TOTAL FUND or COMPOSITE has been in existence less than one year) that meets the REQUIREMENTS of the GIPS standards. After the ASSET OWNER presents a minimum of one year of GIPS-compliant performance (or for the period since the TOTAL FUND or COMPOSITE INCEPTION DATE if the TOTAL FUND or COMPOSITE has been in existence less than one year), the ASSET OWNER MUST present an additional year of performance each year, building up to a minimum of 10 years of GIPS-compliant performance.

Discussion

To claim compliance, an asset owner is required to meet all applicable requirements of the GIPS standards on an asset owner–wide basis for at least a one-year period, or since inception of the asset owner if the asset owner has been in existence for less than one year. When initially claiming compliance with the GIPS standards, an asset owner must present a minimum of one year of total fund or composite performance, or performance since the inception of the total fund or composite if the total fund or composite has been in existence for less than one year.

Once the asset owner has its initial minimum one year of GIPS-compliant history, the asset owner must continue to add annual returns to each GIPS Asset Owner Report, so that 9 years after initially claiming compliance with the GIPS standards, the asset owner will have a 10-year performance record for its total fund(s) or composites. It is recommended that asset owners present a total fund's or composite's history for more than the minimum required periods. (See Provision 24.B.8.)

Because of the unique nature of asset owners, in that they do not compete for clients, asset owners must initially present at least one year of GIPS-compliant performance that meets the requirements of the GIPS standards, instead of requiring an initial five-year compliant track record as is required for firms. Importantly, this exception is allowed only for asset owners that do not compete for business. It applies only for asset owners that manage an entity's assets solely for the purpose of supporting the organization and are accountable only to their respective oversight boards. If an asset owner competes for business, please see Provision 21.A.24 for more information.

If an asset owner initially claims compliance for a period longer than one year, the asset owner must present a track record for the entire period for which it claims compliance. See Provision 21.A.4 for a discussion of the periods for which asset owners must initially comply with the GIPS standards.

An asset owner newly coming into compliance with the GIPS standards may have elected to bring only one year of its track record into compliance. If this asset owner has a historical track record longer than one year that it is not bringing into compliance, it may present the longer track record outside of the GIPS Asset Owner Report. It may link the compliant and the non-compliant track record outside of the GIPS Asset Owner Report. The GIPS Asset Owner Report must include only GIPS-compliant information.

Provision 24.A.1

The ASSET OWNER MUST present in each GIPS ASSET OWNER REPORT:

b. For TOTAL FUNDS, TOTAL FUND returns that are NET-OF-FEES.[24]

Discussion

Because the total fund net-of-fees return reflects performance after the deduction of transaction costs and all other fees and costs associated with management of the assets, this return is required to be presented for total funds and composites of total funds. For asset owners, a net-of-fees return is defined as the return that reflects the deduction of:

- transaction costs,
- all fees and expenses for externally managed pooled funds,
- investment management fees for externally managed segregated accounts, and
- investment management costs.

---

[24] REQUIRED for periods beginning on or after 1 January 2015.

The presentation of net-of-fees returns is required for periods beginning on or after 1 January 2015. Please see the discussion of the calculation of net-of-fees returns in Provision 22.A.24.

Asset owners may choose to present gross-of-fees returns and net-of-external-cost-only returns in addition to presenting the required net-of-fees returns in GIPS Asset Owner Reports. (Please see the related discussion in Provision 24.B.1.)

Provision 24.A.1

The ASSET OWNER MUST present in each GIPS ASSET OWNER REPORT:

c. TOTAL FUND or COMPOSITE returns for each annual period.

Discussion

The GIPS standards require the presentation of annual total fund or composite returns. Asset owners must clearly label the annual presentation periods. Asset owners must define the annual reporting period on a total fund–by–total fund or composite-by-composite basis and apply it consistently. For purposes of comparability, best practice would be for an asset owner to report total fund or composite performance on a calendar-year-end basis.

Within each GIPS Asset Owner Report, the annual periods must be consistent. For example, an asset owner that reports a total fund's or composite's performance annually as of 30 June must consistently report annual returns for years ending 30 June for that total fund or composite. The asset owner may decide in the future to change to a 31 December valuation and performance reporting date; however, the asset owner may not mix 30 June and 31 December valuation and reporting dates in the same GIPS Asset Owner Report.

More-frequent returns help the oversight body evaluate a total fund's or composite's track record. Asset owners are therefore recommended to present more-frequent returns, such as quarterly or monthly returns, in addition to the required annual returns. (See Provision 24.B.3.c.)

Provision 24.A.1

The ASSET OWNER MUST present in each GIPS ASSET OWNER REPORT:

d. When the initial period is less than a full year, the return from the TOTAL FUND or COMPOSITE INCEPTION DATE through the initial annual period end.[25]

---

[25] REQUIRED for COMPOSITES with a COMPOSITE INCEPTION DATE and TOTAL FUNDS with a TOTAL FUND INCEPTION DATE of 1 January 2011 or later. (Note that this footnote in the 2020 edition of the GIPS standards should be revised to include the underlined words.)

Discussion

When a total fund or composite has an initial period that is less than a full year, the GIPS standards require that the return be presented for the partial year from the total fund or composite inception date through the initial annual period end. This is required for total funds or composites that begin on or after 1 January 2011. Although not required to do so for total funds or composites that begin prior to this date, asset owners should consider presenting the initial partial year of performance for all total funds or composites.

For example, assume that an asset owner presents total fund or composite returns for annual periods ended 31 December, and a new composite is created with a track record beginning 1 April 2018. The initial GIPS Asset Owner Report for this composite must include the composite return for the period from 1 April 2018 through 31 December 2018. Subsequently, the asset owner must add annual returns, building up to a minimum 10-year track record.

Partial-year returns must not be annualized. As an example, a total fund or composite that began on 1 December 2020 and has a one-month initial return through 31 December 2020 of 3% (which equates to an annualized return of 42.6%) would be required to present that 3% as the partial year's performance. The annualized return of 42.6% must not be presented. Some spreadsheet and software applications automatically annualize all returns, and asset owners are reminded that for periods of less than a year, the asset owner must "de-annualize" any annualized returns that are calculated.

The method chosen to de-annualize a return is at the discretion of the asset owner, but it must be a geometric calculation. In the situation just presented, the 42.6% annualized return could be de-annualized using one of the following formulas:

$$\left\{\left[\left(1+0.426\right)^{\left(\frac{1}{12}\right)}\right]-1\right\}\times 100 = 3\%, \quad \text{or} \quad \left\{\left[\left(1+0.426\right)^{\left(\frac{31}{365}\right)}\right]-1\right\}\times 100 = 3\%,$$

both resulting in a non-annualized one-month return of 3%.

Provision 24.A.1

The ASSET OWNER MUST present in each GIPS ASSET OWNER REPORT:

e. When the TOTAL FUND or COMPOSITE terminates, the return from the last annual period end through the TOTAL FUND TERMINATION DATE or COMPOSITE TERMINATION DATE.[26]

---

[26] REQUIRED for COMPOSITES with a COMPOSITE TERMINATION DATE <u>and TOTAL FUNDS with a TOTAL FUND TERMINATION DATE</u> of 1 January 2011 or later. (Note that this footnote in the 2020 edition of the GIPS standards should be revised to include the underlined words.)

Discussion

The GIPS standards require that returns from the last annual period end through the total fund or composite termination date be presented for total funds and composites with a termination date of 1 January 2011 or later. Assume that an asset owner presents total fund and composite returns for annual periods ended 31 December, and a composite terminates so that the track record ends 31 August 2020. The GIPS Asset Owner Report for this composite must include the composite return for the period from 1 January 2020 through 31 August 2020.

Partial-year returns must not be annualized. As an example, a composite that terminates on 31 January 2020 and has a one-month return for January 2020 of 3% (which equates to an annualized return of 42.6%) would be required to present that 3% as the partial year's performance. The annualized return of 42.6% must not be presented. Some spreadsheet and software applications automatically annualize all returns, and asset owners are reminded that for periods of less than a year, the asset owner must "de-annualize" any annualized returns that are calculated.

The method chosen to de-annualize a return is at the discretion of the asset owner, but it must be a geometric calculation. In the situation just presented, the 42.6% annualized return could be de-annualized using one of the following formulas:

$$\left\{\left[\left(1+0.426\right)^{\left(\frac{1}{12}\right)}\right]-1\right\}\times100=3\%, \quad \text{or} \quad \left\{\left[\left(1+0.426\right)^{\left(\frac{31}{365}\right)}\right]-1\right\}\times100=3\%,$$

both resulting in a non-annualized one-month return of 3%.

Provision 24.A.1

The ASSET OWNER MUST present in each GIPS ASSET OWNER REPORT:

f.   The TOTAL RETURN for the BENCHMARK for each annual period and for all other periods for which TOTAL FUND or COMPOSITE returns are presented, unless the ASSET OWNER determines there is no appropriate BENCHMARK.

Discussion

Benchmarks are important tools that aid in the planning, implementation, and evaluation of a total fund's or composite's investment policy. They also help facilitate discussions with the oversight body regarding the relationship between risk and return. As a result, asset owners are required to present a total return for the benchmark that reflects the total fund's or composite's investment mandate, objective, or strategy for each annual period. An asset owner may choose

|

to present more than one benchmark in a GIPS Asset Owner Report and, if it does so, it must include all required information for all benchmarks included in a GIPS Asset Owner Report.

In addition to the required annual benchmark returns, asset owners must also present benchmark returns for the same periods for which total fund or composite returns are presented. For example, if the GIPS Asset Owner Report includes quarterly total fund or composite returns, quarterly benchmark returns must also be included.

It is important that the benchmark provide a fair comparison with the performance of the total fund or composite being presented in a GIPS Asset Owner Report. For example, comparing the performance of an international equities composite that has a preferred tax status with a benchmark that uses the highest tax rate could give the oversight body an incorrect impression of the composite's relative performance. If such a benchmark is the only possible benchmark to use and cannot be adjusted, the difference in tax rates used in calculating the performance of the composite and the benchmark should be disclosed. Please refer to the discussion of Provision 24.D.3 for sample disclosures for when there is a material difference between the benchmark and the total fund or composite.

Because the GIPS standards require that the total return for the benchmark be presented, a price-only index would not satisfy the requirements of the GIPS standards. This scenario also applies to benchmarks that are components of a blended benchmark. A price-only benchmark may be presented in a GIPS Asset Owner Report as supplemental information only if it is presented in addition to a total return benchmark. It must be labeled as a price-only benchmark, and there must be sufficient disclosures so that the oversight body understands the difference between the return of a price-only benchmark and the return of a total return benchmark. Asset owners must not present only a price-only benchmark, even if no appropriate total return benchmark is available for the total fund or composite. If an asset owner determines that no appropriate benchmark for the total fund or composite exists, it must not present a benchmark and must disclose why no benchmark is presented. (See Provision 24.C.25.)

Some benchmarks, such as commodity benchmarks, may not have income because the asset class does not create income, but they are still considered to be total return benchmarks. Target returns, such as an 8% hurdle rate, may also not have income, but this is not considered a price-only return.

Provision 24.A.1

The ASSET OWNER MUST present in each GIPS ASSET OWNER REPORT:

g. The number of TOTAL FUNDS or PORTFOLIOS in the COMPOSITE as of each annual period end.[27]

---

[27] REQUIRED for periods ending on or after 31 December 2020. For periods ending prior to 31 December 2020, if the COMPOSITE contains five or fewer PORTFOLIOS at period end, the number of PORTFOLIOS is not REQUIRED.

Discussion

For periods ending on or after 31 December 2020, each GIPS Asset Owner Report for a composite must include the number of total funds or portfolios included in the composite. These figures must be presented as of the end of each annual period that is included in a composite's GIPS Asset Owner Report. This requirement provides information to the oversight body on the size of the composite, measured by the number of total funds or portfolios in the composite. As an example, if there were two portfolios in the composite for the full year but four portfolios in the composite at year end, the asset owner would present four, the actual number of portfolios in the composite at year end.

For periods ending prior to 31 December 2020, if the composite contains five or fewer total funds or portfolios at period end, the number of total funds or portfolios in the composite is not required to be disclosed, although the asset owner may choose to present this information.

Provision 24.A.1

The ASSET OWNER MUST present in each GIPS ASSET OWNER REPORT:

h. TOTAL FUND assets or COMPOSITE assets as of each annual period end.

Discussion

Each GIPS Asset Owner Report must include the amount of total fund or composite assets as of the end of each annual period that is included in the GIPS Asset Owner Report. This requirement provides information to the oversight body on the size of the total fund or composite, measured by the amount of assets it contains. When the total fund or composite strategy uses leverage, total fund or composite assets must be presented net of the leverage and not grossed up as if the leverage did not exist. For example, if a total fund or composite has $200 million in net assets, and $50 million of those assets have been borrowed by an external manager, the total fund's or composite's gross assets are $250 million. When calculating total fund or composite assets, the asset owner must use $200 million. If any total funds or composites use leverage, the asset owner should also present to the oversight body assets that are grossed up as if the leverage did not exist.

 |

See the discussion of Provision 22.A.2 for additional guidance on the calculation of total fund or composite assets.

Provision 24.A.1

The ASSET OWNER MUST present in each GIPS ASSET OWNER REPORT:

i. TOTAL ASSET OWNER ASSETS as of each annual period end.[28]

Discussion

For annual periods ending on or after 31 December 2020, the asset owner must present total asset owner assets as of each annual period end. For annual periods ending prior to this date, the asset owner must present either total asset owner assets or total fund assets or composite assets as a percentage of total asset owner assets. Leverage must be deducted when calculating total asset owner assets. For example, if a composite has $200 million in net assets, and $50 million of those assets have been borrowed by an external manager, the composite's gross assets are $250 million. The asset owner must use $200 million when calculating total asset owner assets, not $250 million. The inclusion of both total fund assets or composite assets and total asset owner assets in a GIPS Asset Owner Report will help the oversight body understand the total fund or composite size in relation to total asset owner assets. If any total funds or composites use leverage, the asset owner should also present to the oversight body assets that are grossed up as if the leverage did not exist.

Both discretionary and non-discretionary portfolios are included in total asset owner assets. Total asset owner assets include assets assigned to an external manager provided the asset owner has discretion over the selection of the external manager. Operating cash accounts that are not available for investment should not be included in total asset owner assets.

Asset owners must be sure that assets are not double-counted because counting assets more than once would not fairly represent total asset owner assets.

See the discussion of Provision 22.A.1 for additional guidance on the calculation of total asset owner assets, Provision 22.A.3 for a discussion of double-counting assets, and Provision 22.A.8 for additional guidance on the treatment of cash and cash equivalents.

---

[28] REQUIRED for periods ending on or after 31 December 2020. For periods ending prior to 31 December 2020, the ASSET OWNER may present either TOTAL ASSET OWNER ASSETS or TOTAL FUND assets or COMPOSITE assets as a percentage of TOTAL ASSET OWNER ASSETS.

Provision 24.A.1

The ASSET OWNER MUST present in each GIPS ASSET OWNER REPORT:

j. For TOTAL FUNDS or COMPOSITES for which monthly COMPOSITE returns are available, the three-year annualized EX POST STANDARD DEVIATION (using monthly returns) of the TOTAL FUND or COMPOSITE and the BENCHMARK as of each annual period end.[29,H]

Discussion

Evaluating past performance requires an understanding of the risks taken to achieve the results. Standard deviation is universally defined as a measure of the variability of returns. For total funds or composites for which monthly returns are available, the GIPS standards require the presentation of ex post standard deviation. Ex post standard deviation is a measure of the volatility of a strategy and benchmark over time, and it is intended to measure the risk of investing in the strategy. For periods ending on or after 1 January 2011, asset owners must present, as of each annual period end, the three-year annualized ex post standard deviation using monthly returns for both the total fund or composite and the benchmark.

Standard deviation for both the total fund or composite and the benchmark must be calculated using 36 monthly returns. The same formula must be used to calculate standard deviation for the total fund or composite and the benchmark.

Some private market investment composites may not have monthly returns. For these composites, if the composite has at least three annual periods of performance in the GIPS Asset Owner Report, asset owners must disclose if the three-year annualized ex post standard deviation of the composite and/or benchmark is not presented because 36 monthly returns are not available. (See Provision 24.C.30.)

Ex Post Standard Deviation

Ex post standard deviation is calculated as follows:

$$\text{Total fund, composite, or benchmark ex post standard deviation} = \sqrt{\frac{\sum \left[R_i - MEAN(R) \right]^2}{n}},$$

---

[29] REQUIRED for periods ending on or after 1 January 2011.

[H] The provision in the 2020 edition of the GIPS standards needs to be edited to remove the words "TOTAL FUND OR" and should state:

For TOTAL FUNDS or COMPOSITES for which monthly ~~TOTAL FUND OR~~ COMPOSITE returns are available, the three-year annualized ex post standard deviation (using monthly returns) of the TOTAL FUND or COMPOSITE and the BENCHMARK as of each annual period end.

 |

where R_i is the return of the ith monthly total fund, composite or benchmark return, n is the number of monthly returns used for the external standard deviation calculation (the use of n is best practice and preferable, but either n or $n - 1$ in the denominator of the standard deviation calculation is acceptable), and $MEAN(R)$ is the mean monthly return of the total fund, composite, or benchmark over the period for which standard deviation is being calculated, where

$$MEAN(R) = \frac{R_1 + R_2 + \ldots + R_i}{n},$$

where R_1 is the time-weighted return for the first monthly total fund, composite, or benchmark return, R_i is the ith monthly total fund, composite, or benchmark return, and n is the number of returns used in the calculation (required to be 36 monthly returns to satisfy this requirement).

Asset owners are required to select a methodology (i.e., the use of n or $n—1$) on a total fund-specific or composite-specific basis, document it in their policies and procedures, and consistently apply that methodology.

To annualize the three-year ex post standard deviation calculated using monthly returns, the result of the foregoing standard deviation formula must be multiplied by the square root of 12.

The asset owner should use gross-of-fees returns to calculate the ex post standard deviation. (See Provision 22.B.7.) The asset owner must disclose which returns (gross-of-fees, net-of-external-costs-only, or net-of-fees) were used to calculate and present the ex post standard deviation. (See Provision 24.C.35.)

Provision 24.A.2

The ASSET OWNER MUST present the percentage of the total FAIR VALUE of TOTAL FUND assets or COMPOSITE assets that were valued using subjective unobservable inputs (as described in Provision 22.B.6) as of the most recent annual period end, if such investments represent a material amount of TOTAL FUND assets or COMPOSITE assets.

Discussion

Markets are not always liquid, and investment prices are not always objective and/or observable. As the last level of the recommended valuation hierarchy indicates (see Provision 22.B.6), it may be necessary for an asset owner to use subjective unobservable inputs to value an investment for which markets are not active at the measurement date. Examples of subjective unobservable inputs include an assumed discount rate, an assumed occupancy rate for a commercial building, and the default rate used for the valuation of a security in default. Examples related to insurance-linked securities include assumptions regarding hurricane damage and mortality rates. Unobservable inputs should be used to measure fair value only when observable inputs and prices are not available or appropriate. Unobservable inputs reflect the asset owner's own assumptions about the assumptions that market participants would use in pricing the investment and should be developed based on the best information available under the circumstances.

Asset owners must present the percentage of the total fair value of total fund assets or composite assets that were valued using subjective unobservable inputs as of the most recent annual period end, if such investments represent a material amount of total fund assets or composite assets. The amount of total fund assets or composite assets valued using subjective unobservable inputs would be considered material if it would likely influence a reader's judgment regarding the reliability of the valuation. The asset owner must decide on the criteria it will use to determine when subjective unobservable inputs represent a material amount of total fund assets or composite assets, include these criteria in its policy and procedures, and apply these criteria consistently.

Sample Disclosure:

"As of 31 December 2020, 29% of total fund assets were valued using subjective, unobservable inputs. These inputs are not supported by market activity and instead are based on internal proprietary pricing models."

Provision 24.A.3

The ASSET OWNER MUST clearly label or identify:

a. The periods that are presented.
b. If returns presented are GROSS-OF-FEES, NET-OF-EXTERNAL-COSTS-ONLY, or NET-OF-FEES.

Discussion

All periods presented in a GIPS Asset Owner Report must be clearly labeled or identified. This includes annual periods, partial-year periods, and any additional periods presented.

For total funds and total fund composites, asset owners must present net-of-fees returns in a GIPS Asset Owner Report and may also choose to present gross-of-fees and/or net-of-external-costs-only returns in addition to net-of-fees returns. For additional composites, asset owners may present either gross-of-fees returns, net-of-external-costs-only returns, or net-of-fees returns in a GIPS Asset Owner Report and may also choose to present more than one type of return. (An additional composite is a grouping of portfolios representing a particular strategy or asset class that the asset owner chooses to present in a GIPS Asset Owner Report.) For the oversight body to understand the nature of the returns being presented, all returns presented must be clearly labeled or identified as gross-of-fees, net-of-external costs-only, or net-of-fees.

Provision 24.A.4

If the ASSET OWNER presents FULL GROSS-OF-FEES RETURNS, the ASSET OWNER MUST identify them as SUPPLEMENTAL INFORMATION.

Discussion

A full gross-of-fees return is the return on investments that reflects the deduction of only transaction costs. It does not reflect the deduction of investment management fees paid for any externally managed segregated accounts or the fees and expenses for any externally managed pooled funds. Because it would not be possible to invest in these externally managed assets without paying these fees and costs, full gross-of-fees returns must be identified as supplemental information if they are included in a GIPS Asset Owner Report.

Supplemental information is any performance-related information included as part of a GIPS Asset Owner Report that supplements or enhances the requirements and/or recommendations of the GIPS standards. Supplemental information must relate directly to the total fund or composite presented in the GIPS Asset Owner Report. See Provision 24.A.8 for additional guidance on supplemental information.

Provision 24.A.5

If the ASSET OWNER includes more than one BENCHMARK in the GIPS ASSET OWNER REPORT, the ASSET OWNER MUST present and disclose all REQUIRED information for all BENCHMARKS presented.

Discussion

It is permissible to include more than one benchmark in a GIPS Asset Owner Report. All benchmarks included in a GIPS Asset Owner Report must adhere to the requirements of the GIPS standards that are applicable to benchmarks. Asset owners may label benchmarks as primary and secondary benchmarks, but the same requirements and recommendations apply to all benchmarks included in a GIPS Asset Owner Report. For example, a GIPS Asset Owner Report must include:

- a description for all benchmarks,
- a disclosure of changes to (or deletion of) any benchmark, and
- the three-year annualized ex post standard deviation of all benchmarks.

If the asset owner designates benchmarks as primary and secondary benchmarks, it must disclose when these designations change (e.g., if a primary benchmark becomes a secondary benchmark), because such a change in designation is considered a benchmark change. In all instances, if multiple benchmarks are presented in a GIPS Asset Owner Report and one or more of the benchmarks is removed from the GIPS Asset Owner Report, the asset owner must disclose this fact. (See Provision 24.C.26.)

An appropriate benchmark for a total fund or composite reflects the investment mandate, objective, or strategy of the total fund or composite. Additional benchmarks beyond appropriate benchmarks may be presented in a GIPS Asset Owner Report as supplemental information. There must be sufficient disclosure so that the oversight body understands the nature of the benchmark and why it is being presented. Disclosure, however, does not necessarily prevent information from being false or misleading. An additional benchmark must never be presented for the sole purpose of providing a favorable comparison with the performance of the total fund or composite. To do so would be misleading, regardless of the disclosures accompanying the benchmark.

Provision 24.A.6

If the COMPOSITE loses all of its member PORTFOLIOS, the COMPOSITE track record MUST end. If PORTFOLIOS are later added to the COMPOSITE, the COMPOSITE track record MUST restart. The periods both before and after the break in track record MUST be presented, with the break in performance clearly shown. The ASSET OWNER MUST NOT LINK performance prior to the break in track record to the performance after the break in track record.

Discussion

If all of the portfolios in a composite are either terminated or removed from the composite for some other reason, the composite's performance record would come to an end. After a period of time, portfolios may be added to the composite, and the composite's performance record would begin again. In such a case, there will be a break in the composite's performance record. The composite's prior performance history must not be linked to the ongoing composite performance results. An asset owner must not use the performance of a benchmark to link the performance track record from before and after the break in the composite's track record. Any performance table in a GIPS Asset Owner Report must clearly indicate the break.

For asset owners that claim compliance for a period longer than 10 years, if the break in performance occurred more than 10 years ago, the performance prior to the break does not need to be presented. In all other cases, the asset owner must present the performance both prior to and after the performance break.

Consider the following example for an asset owner that calculates performance on a monthly basis:

The asset owner has a composite that temporarily lost all of its portfolio members, resulting in a break in performance. The inception date for the composite is 1 January 2014, and there were four portfolios in the composite on 31 July 2015. During August 2015, two portfolios were liquidated and two portfolios were transferred out of the composite because of a change in their investment strategy, leaving the composite with no portfolios. During April 2016, two new portfolios managed according to the composite's investment strategy were funded and were added to the composite as of 1 May 2016, effectively reinstating the composite's performance. During 2017, three new portfolios were added to the composite.

Because all of the portfolios in the composite were either terminated or removed from the composite because of a change in their investment strategy, the performance record of the composite comes to an end as of 31 July 2015. The performance record begins again on 1 May 2016, when two new portfolios managed according to the composite's investment strategy were added to the composite. When presenting the performance of this composite, the prior performance history of the composite through 31 July 2015 must be shown but must not be linked to the ongoing composite performance results beginning 1 May 2016.

For the purpose of performance presentation, as of 31 December 2017, the composite had an uninterrupted performance track record from 1 January 2014 to 31 July 2015, a performance break from 1 August 2015 to 30 April 2016, and an uninterrupted performance track record from 1 May 2016 to 31 December 2017.

Under the principles of fair representation and full disclosure, the GIPS standards require asset owners to handle such cases with the highest transparency. In this instance, the asset owner must present both periods of performance. The periods before and after the break must be presented separately. The GIPS Asset Owner Report could present the information in this scenario as follows:

| Period | Period Returns (%) | | Number of Portfolios as of Period End | Assets as of Period End (USD millions) | |
	Composite (gross of fees)	Benchmark		Composite	Total Asset Owner
1 Jan–31 Dec 2017	X%	X%	5	X	X
1 May–31 Dec 2016*	X%	X%	2	X	X
1 Jan–31 Jul 2015*	X%	X%	—	—	—
1 Jan–31 Dec 2014	X%	X%	4	X	X

*There were no portfolios in the composite from 1 August 2015 through 30 April 2016.

It is important that the composite data is presented in a way that makes it clear that there were no portfolios in the composite from 1 August 2015 through 30 April 2016 and that the performance presented in the GIPS Asset Owner Report is not linked across the break. The periods presented must be clearly labeled.

Although the asset owner may present a cumulative return for the period from 1 January 2014 through 31 July 2015, it must not link periods across performance breaks and present a cumulative and/or annualized return over such periods (e.g., from 1 January 2014 to 31 December 2017). The same approach would apply to the presentation of any required or recommended risk measures based on cumulative periods (e.g., three-year annualized ex post standard deviation).

The asset owner may not choose to omit performance for the incomplete years (e.g., for 2015 and 2016 in the previous example) because they are not annual returns. Such an interpretation would not meet the goals of fair representation and full disclosure.

Provision 24.A.7

All REQUIRED and RECOMMENDED information in the GIPS ASSET OWNER REPORT MUST be presented in the same currency.

Discussion

Asset owners must present all required and recommended information in a GIPS Asset Owner Report in the same currency (e.g., total fund or composite and benchmark returns, total fund or composite assets, and risk measures). Supplemental information should also be presented in the same currency. If it is not, that fact must be disclosed. Not disclosing this fact could be misleading.

If an asset owner chooses to present a total fund or composite in a different currency, the asset owner must convert all of the required information into the new currency. If the asset owner chooses to present performance in multiple currencies in the same GIPS Asset Owner Report, the asset owner must convert all of the required information into each of the currencies and ensure it is clear in which currencies performance is reported. The asset owner must also convert any recommended information it chooses to present in the GIPS Asset Owner Report containing the converted information.

In cases where a total fund or composite contains portfolios with different currencies, the asset owner must convert the individual portfolio returns to a single currency in order to calculate a total fund or composite return. It is not permissible to do so by applying the exchange rate as of the current period end to historical data.

The GIPS standards do not require or recommend a particular method for converting portfolio performance from one currency to another. Two possible options for converting returns into a different currency are as follows:

- When using the aggregate method, convert the underlying data (values and external cash flows) into the selected currency using the exchange rate on the date of each cash flow and

 |

valuation and then calculate the total fund or composite returns based on the converted values; or

- When using the weighted average method, first calculate the individual portfolio or total fund returns, then convert the portfolio or total fund returns into the selected currency, and calculate the weighted average composite return using the converted returns.

An asset owner may instead convert total fund or composite returns. Starting with total fund or composite returns calculated in its base currency, a total fund or composite return is converted using the movement in the exchange rate between the base currency and the reporting currency over the period of the return. The following example illustrates this method:

Suppose that the return of a total fund or composite in euros for the year 2018 is +5.00%. The exchange rate for 1 euro per US dollar at the start of the year was 1.2008, and at the end of the year it was 1.14315. First calculate the movement in the exchange rate over the year:

$$FX\ return = \frac{FX_{end}}{FX_{start}} - 1$$

$$FX\ return = \frac{1.14315}{1.2008} - 1 = -0.0480 \quad or \quad -4.80\%$$

The exchange rate movement and the euro total fund or composite return are then multiplied to determine the USD total fund or composite return:

$$USD\ Total\ Fund\ or\ Composite\ Return = (1 + 0.05) \times (1 - 0.0480) - 1 = (1.05 \times 0.952) - 1$$
$$= -0.00041, \quad or \quad -0.041\%$$

It is not acceptable to convert returns by applying the exchange rate as of the current period end to the historical data, including cash flows and valuations, used to calculate returns.

It is up to the asset owner to determine the total fund–specific or composite-specific conversion method. Policies and procedures for converting returns must be established, documented, and applied consistently.

Provision 24.A.8

Any SUPPLEMENTAL INFORMATION included in the GIPS ASSET OWNER REPORT:

a. MUST relate directly to the TOTAL FUND or COMPOSITE.

b. MUST NOT contradict or conflict with the REQUIRED or RECOMMENDED information in the GIPS ASSET OWNER REPORT.

c. MUST be clearly labeled as SUPPLEMENTAL INFORMATION.

Discussion

Supplemental information is any performance-related information included as part of a GIPS Asset Owner Report that supplements or enhances the requirements and/or recommendations of the GIPS standards. Performance-related information includes:

- information expressed in terms of investment return and risk, and
- other information and input data that directly relate to the calculation of investment return and risk (e.g., portfolio holdings), as well as information derived from investment return and risk input data (e.g., performance contribution or attribution).

Supplemental information should provide users of the GIPS Asset Owner Report with the proper context in which to understand the performance results. Common examples of supplemental information include the following:

- segment returns (e.g., country or sector),
- full gross-of-fees returns, and
- a price-only benchmark presented in addition to a total return benchmark.

Supplemental information must relate directly to the total fund or composite and must not contradict or conflict with the required or recommended information in the GIPS Asset Owner Report. Examples of information that relates directly to the total fund or composite and would be considered supplemental information include segment returns (e.g., country or sector), performance attribution, and composite or portfolio-level holdings. An example of information that would conflict with the GIPS standards is a price-only benchmark presented as supplemental information in the absence of a total return benchmark.

The following is a more complete list of the principles that apply when supplemental information is presented. Supplemental information must:

- satisfy the spirit and principles of the GIPS standards—fair representation and full disclosure,
- comply with all applicable laws and regulations regarding the calculation and presentation of performance,
- not include performance or performance-related information that is false or misleading,
- relate directly to the total fund or composite and supplement or enhance the required or recommended information included in the total fund's or composite's GIPS Asset Owner Report,
- not contradict or conflict with the required or recommended information in the GIPS Asset Owner Report,
- be clearly labeled as supplemental information, and
- not be shown with greater prominence than the required total fund or composite information.

 |

24.B. Presentation and Reporting—Recommendations

Provision 24.B.1

The ASSET OWNER SHOULD present GROSS-OF-FEES and NET-OF-EXTERNAL-COSTS-ONLY TOTAL FUND returns.

Discussion

For total funds and total fund composites, an asset owner must present net-of-fees returns in a GIPS Asset Owner Report. In addition to the required net-of-fees returns, the asset owner may choose to present gross-of-fees and/or net-of-external-costs-only returns in a GIPS Asset Owner Report. Each type of return provides important information to the oversight body.

A net-of-fees return is the return that reflects the deduction of transaction costs, all fees and expenses for externally managed pooled funds, investment management fees for externally managed segregated accounts, and investment management costs. Net-of-fees returns therefore provide the best indication to the oversight body of the returns received over time, after taking into account the effect of internal and external investment management fees and costs.

A gross-of-fees return is the return on investments reduced by transaction costs and all fees and expenses for externally managed pooled funds. This return gives the clearest indication of the "investment return" for the assets included in the total fund.

A net-of-external-costs-only return is the gross-of-fees return reduced by investment management fees for externally managed segregated accounts. It therefore is the best indication of the returns received over time, after taking into account the effect of external management fees. Please see the discussion of the calculation of net-of-fees, net-of-external-costs-only, and gross-of-fees returns in Provision 22.A.24.

Because net-of-fees, net-of-external-costs-only, and gross-of-fees returns all provide important information to the oversight body, it is recommended that asset owners present all three types of returns in a GIPS Asset Owner Report. Presenting more than one type of return in a GIPS Asset Owner Report can provide the oversight body with insight on the relative sizes of the fees and costs associated with externally managed pooled funds and segregated accounts, as well as internally managed assets.

Provision 24.B.2

The ASSET OWNER SHOULD present GROSS-OF-FEES, NET-OF-EXTERNAL-COSTS-ONLY, and NET-OF-FEES COMPOSITE returns.

Discussion

Asset owners are required to present net-of-fees returns in GIPS Asset Owner Reports for total funds and composites of total funds. For additional composites, an asset owner may choose to present either gross-of-fees, net-of-external-costs-only, or net-of-fees composite returns in a GIPS Asset Owner Report. (An additional composite is a grouping of portfolios representing a particular strategy or asset class that the asset owner chooses to present in a GIPS Asset Owner Report.) In all GIPS Asset Owner Reports, the asset owner may also choose to present more than one type of return. Each type of return provides important information to the oversight body.

A composite gross-of-fees return is the return on investments reduced by transaction costs and all fees and expenses for externally managed pooled funds. This return gives the clearest indication of the "investment return" for the assets included in the composite.

A composite net-of-external-costs-only return is the gross-of-fees return reduced by investment management fees for externally managed segregated accounts. It therefore is the best indication of the returns received over time, after taking into account the effect of external investment management fees and expenses.

A composite net-of-fees return is the return that reflects the deduction of transaction costs, all fees and expenses for externally managed pooled funds, investment management fees for externally managed segregated accounts, and investment management costs. Net-of-fees returns therefore provide the best indication to the oversight body of the returns received over time, after taking into account the effect of internal and external investment management fees and costs. Please see the discussion of the calculation of net-of-fees, net-of-external-costs-only, and gross-of-fees returns in Provision 22.A.24.

Because gross-of-fees, net-of-external-costs-only, and net-of-fees composite returns all provide important information to the oversight body, it is recommended that asset owners present all three types of returns in a GIPS Asset Owner Report. Presenting more than one type of return in a GIPS Asset Owner Report can provide the oversight body with insight on the relative sizes of the fees and costs associated with externally managed pooled funds and segregated accounts, as well as internally managed assets.

Provision 24.B.3

The ASSET OWNER SHOULD present the following items:

a. Cumulative returns of the TOTAL FUND or COMPOSITE and the BENCHMARK for all periods.

 |

Discussion

Cumulative returns of the total fund or composite and the benchmark provide additional useful information to the oversight body by indicating the total rate of return for a defined period of performance. It is therefore recommended that cumulative returns for all periods presented in the GIPS Asset Owner Report be provided in addition to the required annual returns.

To calculate cumulative returns of a total fund or composite for any period, the historical daily, monthly, quarterly, or annual sub-period returns are geometrically linked according to the following formula:

$$R_{CUM} = \left[(1+R_1) \times (1+R_2) \times \ldots \times (1+R_n)\right] - 1,$$

where R_1 is the total fund or composite return for Period 1 and R_n is the total fund or composite return for the most recent period.

Example for a Composite:

Asset Owner ABC has the following annual returns that were calculated from monthly composite returns and are presented in the GIPS Asset Owner Report:

	Composite	$1 + R_n$
2015	2.3%	1.023
2016	-4.7%	0.953
2017	6.9%	1.069
2018	3.2%	1.032
2019	0.9%	1.009
Jan 2020–Jun 2020	-3.1%	0.969

To calculate the composite cumulative return for the period from January 2015 through June 2020, the returns are linked:

$$\begin{aligned} \text{Composite cumulative return} &= \left[(1.023) \times (0.953) \times (1.069) \times (1.032) \times (1.009) \times (0.969)\right] - 1 \\ &= 0.052, \quad \text{or} \quad 5.2\%. \end{aligned}$$

If the composite experiences a break in the track record, the periods before and after the break must not be linked. Therefore, in such a case, a cumulative return may be calculated up to the break and a separate cumulative return may be calculated for the performance period that begins after the break. However, the asset owner must not calculate a cumulative return across the periods that include the break. Additional guidance on how to calculate and present performance if there is a break in the track record is included in the discussion of Provision 24.A.6.

Provision 24.B.3

The ASSET OWNER SHOULD present the following items:

b. Equal-weighted COMPOSITE returns.

Discussion

The GIPS standards require that composite time-weighted returns be calculated by asset-weighting the individual total fund or portfolio returns or by using the aggregate method. (See Provision 22.A.28.) This approach allows for a larger total fund or portfolio to have more weight on a composite's return than a smaller total fund or portfolio. Equal-weighted composite returns, however, provide another useful perspective on composite performance. The simple average provides a measure of the asset owner's ability to obtain consistent returns for all total funds or portfolios regardless of size. It is therefore recommended that asset owners also include equal-weighted composite returns in a GIPS Asset Owner Report.

The formula for the equal-weighted composite return, R_{EQUAL}, is

$$R_{EQUAL} = \frac{R_{PORT1} + R_{PORT2} + \ldots + R_{PORTi}}{n},$$

where R_{PORT1} is the time-weighted return for the first total fund or portfolio in the composite, R_{PORTi} is the ith total fund or portfolio return in the composite, and n is the number of total funds or portfolios in the composite.

Provision 24.B.3

The ASSET OWNER SHOULD present the following items:

c. Quarterly and/or monthly returns.

Discussion

Although the GIPS standards require the presentation of annual returns for the total fund or composite and the benchmark (Provisions 24.A.1.c and 24.A.1.f), it is recommended that asset owners present more-frequent returns, such as quarterly or monthly returns. More-frequent returns help the oversight body evaluate a total fund's or composite's track record. Asset owners must present benchmark returns for the same periods for which total fund or composite returns are presented. If the GIPS Asset Owner Report includes annual and quarterly total fund or composite returns, annual and quarterly benchmark returns must also be presented.

Provision 24.B.3

The ASSET OWNER SHOULD present the following items:

d. Annualized TOTAL FUND or COMPOSITE and BENCHMARK returns for periods longer than 12 months.

Discussion

It is recommended that asset owners show the results of both the total fund or composite and the benchmark for periods longer than 12 months in annualized terms to help the oversight body in the evaluation of the total fund's or composite's track record. Annualized returns are created by calculating the geometric mean, not the arithmetic mean, and represent the geometric average annual compound return achieved over the defined period of more than one year. Sub-period returns during the investment period are geometrically linked to calculate the cumulative return. Then the nth root of the cumulative return is calculated, where n is the number of years in the period. Annualized performance is permitted only for periods of one year or more.

The formula for calculating annualized performance is as follows:

Annualized return (%) = $[(1 + R)^{1/n}] - 1$,

where R is the cumulative return for the period and n is the number of years in the period.

For example, assume a total fund's or composite's cumulative return for a five-year period is 150.0%. It has a five-year average annual compound return, or annualized return, of 20.11%, which is calculated as:

$$\left[(1+1.5)^{\frac{1}{5}} \right] - 1 = 0.2011 = 20.11\%.$$

If instead the 150% is achieved over 12.5 years, the 12.5-year average annual compound return, or annualized return, is 7.61%, which is calculated as:

$$\left[(1+1.5)^{\frac{1}{5}} \right] - 1 = 0.0761 = 7.61\%.$$

If a composite experiences a break in the track record, the periods before and after the break must not be linked, and annualized returns must not be calculated across the break in performance.

Provision 24.B.4

The ASSET OWNER SHOULD present MONEY-WEIGHTED RETURNS for TOTAL FUNDS when the ASSET OWNER believes MONEY-WEIGHTED RETURNS are helpful and important in understanding the performance of the TOTAL FUND.

Discussion

While asset owners must present time-weighted returns (TWRs) for total funds and composites of total funds, it is recommended that money-weighted returns (MWRs) be presented as well if the asset owner believes that MWRs are helpful and important in understanding the performance of the total fund or a composite of total funds. In addition, local regulations may require some asset owners to report MWRs in financial statements. Because asset owners are required to present net-of-fees returns for total funds or composites of total funds, it is recommended that any MWRs included in a GIPS Asset Owner Report should be net-of-fees.

While the required TWRs represent the performance of the asset owner, MWRs represent the combination of the asset owner's performance and the effect of cash flows. In the case of a pension plan, although neither the pension plan sponsor nor the pension fund participants typically control the timing of the cash flows into or out of the total fund, MWRs may be informative in determining how the timing of plan contributions and withdrawals has affected the total fund's performance. MWRs may also be a better indicator of the total fund's profitability.

Provision 24.B.5

For all periods for which an annualized EX POST STANDARD DEVIATION of the TOTAL FUND or COMPOSITE and the BENCHMARK are presented, the ASSET OWNER SHOULD present the corresponding annualized return of the TOTAL FUND or COMPOSITE and the BENCHMARK.

Discussion

To provide context so that the oversight body can better understand the ex post standard deviation, it is recommended that asset owners present annualized returns for the total fund or composite and the benchmark for the same periods for which an annualized standard deviation is presented. For example, if an asset owner chooses to present 5-year, 7-year, and 10-year annualized standard deviations in addition to the required 3-year annualized standard deviation, asset owners are encouraged to also present the corresponding 3-year, 5-year, 7-year, and 10-year annualized returns for the total fund or composite and the benchmark. This information will help the oversight body to better interpret risk and return in the context of the return distribution for all periods for which an annualized standard deviation is presented.

Provision 24.B.6

For all periods greater than three years for which an annualized return of the TOTAL FUND or COMPOSITE and the BENCHMARK are presented, the ASSET OWNER SHOULD present the corresponding annualized EX POST STANDARD DEVIATION (using monthly returns) of the TOTAL FUND or COMPOSITE and the BENCHMARK.

Discussion

To provide context so that the oversight body can interpret the annualized total fund or composite and benchmark returns, it is recommended that asset owners present the annualized ex post standard deviation (using monthly returns) for both the total fund or composite and the benchmark for the same periods that annualized total fund or composite and benchmark returns are presented. For example, if an asset owner chooses to present the 5-year, 7-year, and 10-year annualized total fund or composite and benchmark returns, asset owners are encouraged to also present the corresponding 5-year, 7-year, and 10-year annualized ex post standard deviation of the total fund or composite and benchmark. This information will help the oversight body to assess and compare risk and return for all periods for which annualized returns are presented.

Provision 24.B.7

The ASSET OWNER SHOULD present relevant EX POST ADDITIONAL RISK MEASURES for the TOTAL FUND or COMPOSITE and the BENCHMARK.

Discussion

For total funds, and for composites for which monthly composite returns are available, asset owners must present the three-year annualized ex post standard deviation (using monthly returns) of the total fund or composite and the benchmark as of each annual period end. This information is required for periods ending on or after 1 January 2011. (See Provision 24.A.1.j.) Additional risk measures are any risk measures included in a GIPS Asset Owner Report beyond those required to be presented. It is recommended that asset owners present relevant ex post additional risk measures for the total fund or composite and the benchmark in a GIPS Asset Owner Report. There may be additional risk measures that would be especially helpful to the oversight body when interpreting a total fund's or composite's returns. There are many risk and quantitative measures that are routinely calculated to help a reader evaluate and understand the return and risk characteristics of a particular investment strategy. Determining which risk measures are relevant to a strategy requires an understanding of the characteristics and limitations of each measure and insight into both the portfolio construction process and investment strategy. Several risk measures are commonly used, but there is no clear consensus on what constitutes relevant risk measures for evaluating portfolios that contain derivatives, alternatives, and/or illiquid assets.

A number of factors should be considered when selecting relevant risk measures, including the following:

- Comparability: The risk measure selected should allow objective comparisons across similar strategies to be made.
- Computational transparency: All inputs to the calculation should be readily available and understood.
- Interpretational transparency: In isolation as a single figure or presented as a time series, the risk measure should aid interpretation and provide context to the performance figures presented.
- Investment process or strategy consistency: The risk measure should provide insight into the underlying investment process.
- Risk measure stability: The selected risk measure should be sensitive to market and portfolio movements but should not exhibit excessive range swings such that interpretation of the absolute and relative values is compromised.

Provision 24.B.8

The ASSET OWNER SHOULD present more than 10 years of annual performance in the GIPS ASSET OWNER REPORT.

Discussion

Once the total fund or composite has its initial minimum 1-year (or since-inception) compliant history, the asset owner must continue to add annual returns to each GIPS Asset Owner Report for the next 9 years, at a minimum, so that the asset owner will build up to a 10-year compliant performance record for its total funds and composites.

At some point, an asset owner will have a minimum 10-year compliant track record for a specific total fund or composite. When the asset owner eventually adds an additional annual return to a 10-year track record in a GIPS Asset Owner Report, the asset owner may delete the information for the oldest year included or may instead present a longer track record. It is recommended that asset owners include more than the minimum 10 years of annual performance in a GIPS Asset Owner Report to provide more information to its oversight body.

Provision 24.B.9

If the ASSET OWNER uses preliminary, estimated values as FAIR VALUE, the ASSET OWNER SHOULD present the percentage of assets in the TOTAL FUND or COMPOSITE that were valued using preliminary, estimated values as of each annual period end.

Discussion

The use of preliminary, estimated values as fair value is common for some alternative strategies, including those that invest in externally managed pooled funds for which the asset owner relies on valuations provided by the fund external managers. When using preliminary, estimated values as fair value, it is important to remember the underlying principles of the GIPS standards: fair representation and full disclosure. If using preliminary, estimated values, asset owners must disclose this fact in the relevant GIPS Asset Owner Report (Provision 24.C.32). It is recommended that the asset owner also present the percentage of assets in the total fund or composite that were valued using preliminary, estimated values as of each annual period end. Doing so provides important information that allows the oversight body to better assess the valuations and performance record presented.

Provision 24.B.10

For REAL ESTATE COMPOSITES, the ASSET OWNER SHOULD present COMPOSITE and BENCHMARK COMPONENT RETURNS for all periods presented.

Discussion

For real estate composites, it is recommended that asset owners also present composite and benchmark component returns in addition to total returns. Component returns separate the total return into a capital return and an income return. Component returns provide additional information to the oversight body regarding the sources of the total return and the nature of the investment strategy. The income return is generally viewed as more stable than the capital return. When evaluating real estate investments, it is helpful for the oversight body to know the contribution from the income and capital returns.

Given the unique nature of internal investment management costs, which typically do not flow through the portfolios and are not reflected in net investment income, the net-of-fees capital return formula assumes that these costs need to be reflected as a separate item that must be deducted in order to calculate the net-of-fees capital return. It is also assumed that all investment management costs are allocated to the capital component. Given these assumptions, internal investment management costs are not reflected in the numerator of the gross-of-fees or net-of-external-costs-only component returns. Internal investment management costs must be subtracted in the numerator of the net-of-fees total return.

The following are examples of formulas that may be used to calculate the income returns and capital returns for a real estate investment. The formulas presented use the following terms:

r_t^{GFI} = gross-of-fees income return for period t

r_t^{NECI} = net-of-external-costs-only income return for period t

r_t^{NFI} = net-of-fees income return for period t

r_t^{GFC} = gross-of-fees capital return for period t

r_t^{NECC} = net-of-external-costs-only capital return for period t

r_t^{NFC} = net-of-fees capital return for period t

r_t^{GFT} = gross-of-fees total return for period t

r_t^{NECT} = net-of-external-costs-only total return for period t

r_t^{NFT} = net-of-fees total return for period t

NII_t = net investment income (after interest expense, advisory fees, and any performance-based fees allocated to the income component for performance calculation purposes) for period t

IMC_t^C = investment management costs allocated to the capital component (for performance calculation purposes) for period t

AF_t = advisory fee (asset-based portion of investment management fee expensed, excluding any performance-based fees) for externally managed segregated accounts for period t. AF_t does not include investment management fees for externally managed pooled funds.

PF_t^C = performance-based fees allocated to the capital component (for performance calculation purposes) for externally managed segregated accounts for period t. PF_t^C does not include performance-based fees for externally managed pooled funds.

PF_t^I = performance-based fees allocated to the income component (for performance calculation purposes) for externally managed segregated accounts for period t. PF_t^I does not include performance-based fees for externally managed pooled funds.

V_t^B = the beginning value of the portfolio for period t

V_t^E = the ending value of the portfolio for period t

j = the number of external cash flows $(1, 2, 3, \ldots, J)$ in period t

|

$CF_{j,t}$ = the value of cash flow j in period t

$W_{j,t}$ = the weight of cash flow j in period t (assuming the cash flow occurred at the end of the day) as calculated according to the following formula:

$$w_{j,t} = \frac{D_t - D_{j,t}}{D_t},$$

where

$w_{j,t}$ = the weight of cash flow j in period t, assuming the cash flow occurred at the end of the day

D_t = the total number of calendar days in period t

$D_{j,t}$ = the number of calendar days from the beginning of period t to cash flow j

For directly owned real estate investments, the acquisition, disposition, and financing services performed by the asset owner or a third party on a particular transaction are considered transaction costs and must be deducted from gross-of-fees, net-of-external-costs-only, and net-of-fees returns. These items (also referred to as "brokerage expenses") are direct costs incurred upon implementation of a particular investment transaction. It is recommended that these transaction costs be reflected in the capital returns.

The term "net investment income" is intended to reflect the effect of ownership and financing structures and includes all underlying property-level activity. Investment-level returns are distinct from property-level returns. Investment-level returns reflect the effect of ownership and financing structures and include all underlying property-level activity. Property-level returns exclude all of the non-property (investment-level) balance sheet items, as well as income and expenses, and include only the income and expenses that directly relate to operation of the property. Property-level returns are not used for reporting performance in compliance with the GIPS standards, although they may be shown as supplemental information.

Income Return

The income return measures the investment income earned on all investments (including cash and cash equivalents) during the measurement period, net of all non-recoverable expenditures, interest expense on debt, and property taxes. The income return is computed as a percentage of the capital employed. Capital employed is defined as the "weighted average equity" (weighted average capital) during the measurement period. Capital employed does not include any income return or capital return earned during the measurement period. Beginning capital is adjusted by weighting the external cash flows that occurred during the period.

The numerator in the gross-of-fees income return represents the investment income for the portfolio during the period, including any income earned during the period at the investment level, and also reflects all income, fees, and expenses at the property level.

The formula for gross-of-fees income return is as follows:

$$r_t^{GFI} = \frac{NII_t + AF_t + PF_t^I}{V_t^B + \sum_{j=1}^{J}(CF_{j,t} \times W_{j,t})}.$$

The numerator in the net-of-external-costs-only income return and net-of-fees income return represents the net investment income for the portfolio during the period. This figure includes any income earned as well as expenses and fees deducted at the investment level and all income, fees, and expenses at the property level.

The formulas for net-of-external-costs-only income return and net-of-fees income return are the same and are stated as follows:

$$r_t^{NECI} \quad \text{or} \quad r_t^{NFI} = \frac{NII_t}{V_t^B + \sum_{j=1}^{J}(CF_{j,t} \times W_{j,t})}.$$

Capital Return

Capital return is the change in value of the real estate investments and cash and/or cash equivalent assets held throughout the measurement period, adjusted for all capital expenditures (subtracted) and net proceeds from sales (added). The capital return is computed as a percentage of the capital employed. Capital return is also known as "capital appreciation return" or "appreciation return."

The capital return numerator reflects the change (increase or decrease) in investment value adjusted for capital improvements, sales, refinancing, and net investment income activity. The numerator includes both realized gains/losses and the change in unrealized gains/losses from the prior period.

The net-of-fees capital return reflects the deduction of any performance-based (incentive) fees attributable to the capital component for performance calculation purposes. This figure excludes any performance-based fees attributable to the income component for performance calculation purposes. It also reflects the deduction of internal investment management costs.

The formula for gross-of-fees capital return is as follows:

$$r_t^{GFC} = \frac{V_t^E - V_t^B - \sum_{j=1}^{J}CF_{j,t} - NII_t + PF_t^C}{V_t^B + \sum_{j=1}^{J}(CF_{j,t} \times W_{j,t})}.$$

The formula for net-of-external-costs-only capital return is as follows:

$$r_t^{NECC} = \frac{V_t^E - V_t^B - \sum_{j=1}^{J}CF_{j,t} - NII_t}{V_t^B + \sum_{j=1}^{J}(CF_{j,t} \times W_{j,t})}.$$

The formula for net-of-fees capital return is as follows:

$$r_t^{NFC} = \frac{V_t^E - V_t^B - \sum_{j=1}^{J} CF_{j,t} - NII_t - IMC_t^C}{V_t^B + \sum_{j=1}^{J} (CF_{j,t} \times W_{j,t})}.$$

Total Return

The total return is the percentage change in value of real estate investments, including all capital return and income return components, expressed as a percentage of the capital employed over the measurement period. The numerator of the total return calculation measures the change (increase or decrease) in investment value from both income (loss) and realized and unrealized gains and losses. The net-of-fees total return also reflects the deduction of internal investment management costs.

The formula for gross-of-fees total return is as follows:

$$r_t^{GFT} = \frac{V_t^E - V_t^B - \sum_{j=1}^{J} CF_{j,t} + AF_t + PF_t^I + PF_t^C}{V_t^B + \sum_{j=1}^{J} (CF_{j,t} \times W_{j,t})}.$$

The formula for net-of-external-costs-only total return is as follows:

$$r_t^{NECT} = \frac{V_t^E - V_t^B - \sum_{j=1}^{J} CF_{j,t}}{V_t^B + \sum_{j=1}^{J} (CF_{j,t} \times W_{j,t})}.$$

The formula for net-of-fees total return is as follows:

$$r_t^{NFT} = \frac{V_t^E - V_t^B - \sum_{j=1}^{J} CF_{j,t} - IMC_t^C}{V_t^B + \sum_{j=1}^{J} (CF_{j,t} \times W_{j,t})}.$$

All performance results, both total returns and component returns, must be clearly identified so that the oversight body can properly interpret and compare performance. To interpret performance data, the oversight body needs to know what the performance results represent.

24.C. Disclosure—Requirements

Provision 24.C.1

Once the ASSET OWNER has met all the applicable REQUIREMENTS of the GIPS standards, the ASSET OWNER MUST disclose its compliance with the GIPS standards using one of the following compliance statements. The compliance statement MUST only be used in a GIPS ASSET OWNER REPORT.

a. For an ASSET OWNER that is verified:

"[Insert name of ASSET OWNER] claims compliance with the Global Investment Performance Standards (GIPS®) and has prepared and presented this report in compliance with the GIPS standards. [Insert name of ASSET OWNER] has been independently verified for the periods [insert dates]. The verification report(s) is/are available upon request.

"An asset owner that claims compliance with the GIPS standards must establish policies and procedures for complying with all the applicable requirements of the GIPS standards. Verification provides assurance on whether the asset owner's policies and procedures related to total fund and composite maintenance, as well as the calculation, presentation, and distribution of performance, have been designed in compliance with the GIPS standards and have been implemented on an asset owner–wide basis. Verification does not provide assurance on the accuracy of any specific performance report."

b. For TOTAL FUNDS or COMPOSITES of a verified ASSET OWNER that have also had a PERFORMANCE EXAMINATION:

"[Insert name of ASSET OWNER] claims compliance with the Global Investment Performance Standards (GIPS®) and has prepared and presented this report in compliance with the GIPS standards. [Insert name of ASSET OWNER] has been independently verified for the periods [insert dates].

"An asset owner that claims compliance with the GIPS standards must establish policies and procedures for complying with all the applicable requirements of the GIPS standards. Verification provides assurance on whether the asset owner's policies and procedures related to total fund and composite maintenance, as well as the calculation, presentation, and distribution of performance, have been designed in compliance with the GIPS standards and have been implemented on an asset owner–wide basis. The [insert name of TOTAL FUND OR COMPOSITE] has had a performance examination for the periods [insert dates]. The verification and performance examination reports are available upon request."

   |

The compliance statement for an ASSET OWNER that is verified or for TOTAL FUNDS or COMPOSITES of a verified ASSET OWNER that have also had a PERFORMANCE EXAMINATION is complete only when both paragraphs are shown together, one after the other.

c. For an ASSET OWNER that has not been verified:

"[Insert name of ASSET OWNER] claims compliance with the Global Investment Performance Standards (GIPS®) and has prepared and presented this report in compliance with the GIPS standards. [Insert name of ASSET OWNER] has not been independently verified."

The ASSET OWNER MUST NOT exclude any portion of the respective compliance statement. Any modifications to the compliance statement MUST be additive.

Discussion

An asset owner meeting all the requirements of the GIPS standards must use one of the three compliance statements in each of its GIPS Asset Owner Reports. The English version of the compliance statements is the controlling version. If an asset owner chooses to translate the compliance statement into a language for which there is no official translation of the GIPS standards, the asset owner must take care to ensure that the translation used reflects the required wording of the compliance statement used in Provision 24.C.1.a, 24.C.1.b, or 24.C.1.c.

It is acceptable to combine both paragraphs of the compliance statement for a verified asset owner (Provision 24.C.1.a) into a single paragraph. If the paragraphs are not combined, the compliance statement for a verified asset owner is complete only when both paragraphs are shown together, one after the other. An asset owner may not separate the two required paragraphs from each other.

The same is true for the compliance statement for a total fund or composite that has also had a performance examination (Provision 24.C.1.b). Both paragraphs of the compliance statement may be combined into a single paragraph. If the paragraphs are not combined, the compliance statement is complete only when both paragraphs are shown together, one after the other. An asset owner may not separate the two required paragraphs from each other.

When preparing the GIPS Asset Owner Report for a total fund or composite that has had a performance examination, the asset owner may choose to use either the verification or performance examination compliance statement. For example, an asset owner might choose to use the verification compliance statement for all GIPS Asset Owner Reports, including GIPS Asset Owner Reports for total funds and composites that have had a performance examination, if it wishes to standardize the compliance statement for all GIPS Asset Owner Reports throughout the asset owner. In this situation, the asset owner may also disclose that a specific total fund or composite has had a performance examination.

The language in each compliance statement must not exclude any portion of the respective compliance statement, with one exception. In the second paragraph of both 24.C.1.a and 24.C.1.b, there is a reference to "total fund and composite maintenance." The asset owner may delete the words "and composite" if the asset owner reports all total funds separately and has not created any total fund composites or additional composites. (An additional composite is a grouping of portfolios representing a particular strategy or asset class that the asset owner chooses to present in a GIPS Asset Owner Report.)

There may also be instances where it may be appropriate for an asset owner to modify the language slightly. For example, an asset owner may modify the language to include the name of the asset owner's verifier, if the asset owner wishes to disclose this information. An asset owner may also need to modify the language to add more details about the name of the asset owner that has been verified or the dates of the verification if the verification period was not continuous. Any modifications must be additive and must not result in a compliance statement that is false or misleading.

Provision 24.C.2

The ASSET OWNER MUST disclose the following: "GIPS® is a registered trademark of CFA Institute. CFA Institute does not endorse or promote this organization, nor does it warrant the accuracy or quality of the content contained herein."

Discussion

"GIPS®" is a registered trademark of CFA Institute, and asset owners are required to acknowledge this fact in all GIPS Asset Owner Reports. The required disclosure may appear in the body of the GIPS Asset Owner Report or in a footnote to the report. The term "this organization", which is included in the required disclosure, refers to any entity associated with the GIPS Asset Owner Report, either the asset owner or the verifier.

CFA Institute (owner of the GIPS® trademark) may take appropriate action against any asset owner that misuses the mark "GIPS®" or any compliance statement, including false claims of compliance with the GIPS standards. CFA Institute members, CFA Program charterholders, CFA candidates, CIPM Program certificants, and CIPM candidates who misuse the term "GIPS" or any compliance statement, misrepresent their performance history or the performance history of the asset owner, or falsely claim compliance with the GIPS standards are also subject to disciplinary sanctions under the CFA Institute Code of Ethics and Standards of Professional Conduct. Possible disciplinary sanctions include public censure, suspension of membership, and revocation of the CFA charter or CIPM certificate.

 |

Regulators with jurisdiction over asset owners claiming compliance with the GIPS standards may also take enforcement actions against asset owners that falsely claim compliance with the GIPS standards.

Asset owners may also use the following language to replace the first sentence in this required disclosure: "GIPS® is a registered trademark owned by CFA Institute."

See the GIPS Standards Trademark Usage Guidelines on the CFA Institute website (www.cfainstitute.org) for additional guidance on the proper use of "GIPS".

Provision 24.C.3

The ASSET OWNER MUST disclose the definition of the ASSET OWNER used to determine TOTAL ASSET OWNER ASSETS and ASSET OWNER–wide compliance.

Discussion

To claim compliance with the GIPS standards, an asset owner must comply with all applicable requirements of the GIPS standards on an asset owner–wide basis. Accordingly, the asset owner must determine exactly how it will be defined for the purpose of compliance. The GIPS standards require that an asset owner be defined as the entity that manages investments, directly and/or through the use of external managers, on behalf of participants, beneficiaries, or the organization itself. These entities include, but are not limited to, public and private pension funds, endowments, foundations, family offices, provident funds, insurers and reinsurers, sovereign wealth funds, and fiduciaries. Asset owners must have discretion over total asset owner assets, either by managing assets directly or by having the discretion to hire and fire external managers. For a public pension fund, the asset owner is generally defined by legislation. In the case of foundations, endowments, or family offices, the asset owner is the entity established by the governing body to manage the pool of assets.

In some situations, an organization may act as both an asset owner, where investment authority and ownership are vested with the organization itself, as well as a firm (asset manager) that competes for assets whose vesting lies with external clients. In such cases, the asset owner has two choices in how to define itself for the purpose of complying with the GIPS standards.

- The asset owner bifurcates its assets into two entities: one defined as an asset owner and one defined as a firm.
- The asset owner does not bifurcate its assets and instead defines itself as both an asset owner and a firm. When calculating and presenting performance to its oversight body, the asset

owner follows the GIPS Standards for Asset Owners. When calculating and presenting performance to prospective clients or prospective investors, the asset owner follows the GIPS Standards for Firms.

See Provision 21.A.24 for additional guidance on situations in which an asset owner competes for business, including those instances in which an asset owner acts as both an asset owner and a firm that competes for business.

Sample Disclosures:

Example 1:

Genius University Endowment is a university endowment fund and manages assets solely for Genius University.

Sample Disclosure for Example 1:

"For the purpose of complying with the GIPS standards, the asset owner is defined as the Genius University Endowment (GUE), established in 1972 by the Genius University Investment Committee of the Genius Corporation, and is the manager of GUE's assets."

Example 2:

Organization ABC acts as both an asset owner, managing assets for the ABC retirement system, and as an asset manager that competes for assets whose vesting lies with external clients. For the purpose of complying with the GIPS standards, Organization ABC has decided to bifurcate its assets into two entities: ABC Retirement System (ABCRS), which manages assets exclusively for the ABC Retirement System, and Firm ABC, which competes for business.

Sample Disclosure in a GIPS Asset Owner Report for Example 2:

"For the purpose of complying with the GIPS standards, ABC Retirement System (ABCRS) is defined as the division of Organization ABC that manages assets exclusively for the pension plan of Organization ABC."

Sample Disclosure in Firm ABC's GIPS Composite Report for Example 2:

"For the purpose of complying with the GIPS standards, ABC Investment Management is defined as the division of Organization ABC that is authorized by Organization ABC's governing body to compete for business."

 |

Provision 24.C.4

The ASSET OWNER MUST disclose the TOTAL FUND DESCRIPTION or COMPOSITE DESCRIPTION.

Discussion

The total fund description is defined as general information regarding the total fund's investment mandate, objective, or strategy, and it is expected to include the following:

- the total fund's asset allocation as of the most recent annual period end,
- the total fund's investment objective,
- the total fund's material risks,
- the actuarial rate of return or spending policy description,
- a description of the asset classes and/or other groupings within the total fund, such as the composition of the asset class, strategy used, types of management used (e.g., active, passive, internal, external), and relevant exposures,
- how leverage, derivatives, and short positions may be used, if they are a material part of the strategy, and
- if illiquid investments are a material part of the strategy.

The composite description is defined as general information regarding the investment mandate, objective, or strategy of the composite. The composite description may be more abbreviated than the composite definition but must include all key features of the composite and must include enough information to allow the oversight body to understand the key characteristics of the composite's investment mandate, objective, or strategy, including:

- the material risks of the composite's strategy,
- how leverage, derivatives, and short positions may be used, if they are a material part of the strategy, and
- if illiquid investments are a material part of the strategy.

The composite definition goes a step further than the composite description and includes the detailed criteria that determine the assignment of total funds or portfolios to composites, such as investment constraints or restrictions. Although the composite description is a required disclosure, the composite definition is not a required disclosure. (See Provision 23.A.4 for additional information regarding the difference between a composite definition and composite description.)

The required disclosure of the total fund description or composite description provides information about the total fund's or composite's investment strategy or asset class(es) that is intended to help the oversight body understand the total fund or composite presented in a GIPS Asset Owner Report. The disclosed strategy features will likely affect both the historical and expected risk and returns. Along with the required benchmark description (see Provision 24.C.5), the GIPS Asset Owner Report will allow the oversight body to understand both the investment strategy employed and the benchmark against which the total fund's or composite's performance is evaluated.

If leverage, derivatives, or short positions may be used, and they are a material part of the strategy, this information must be disclosed in the total fund description or composite description. Provision 24.C.14 requires that the asset owner disclose how leverage, derivatives, and short positions have been used historically, if material. Taken together, these two required disclosures provide a more complete picture about the presence, use, and extent of leverage, derivatives, and short positions. When determining what would be material, the asset owner must consider whether the disclosure of how leverage, derivatives, and/or short positions may be used and/or have been used historically is likely to affect the oversight body's view of the risk involved in the strategy. If so, it would be misleading for the asset owner to fail to disclose their use to the oversight body when describing the strategy.

Generally, all investment products or strategies have some degree of inherent risk (e.g., market risk), but it is not intended that the total fund description or composite description identifies every risk of the strategy. Instead, asset owners must identify those material risks of the strategy, if any, and must disclose those risks. For example, investment concentration, correlation (or lack thereof), liquidity, and exposure to counterparties are features that may need to be included in the total fund description or composite description. (See Provision 21.A.17 for additional guidance on the disclosure of risks in a total fund description or composite description.)

The key characteristics of some strategies may change given market events. Asset owners should periodically review total fund descriptions and composite descriptions to ensure they are current.

Sample Disclosure for a Total Fund:

"The Firefighters Total Fund includes all discretionary assets managed by Any State Retirement System for the benefit of firefighter participants. The strategy reflects the actual asset allocation approved each year by the board, based on the funded status, risk budget, and actuarial rate of return studies. Performance is measured against a blended benchmark using asset class benchmarks based on the total fund's policy weights as established at the beginning of each fiscal year. The longer-term investment objective is to earn, over moving 20-year periods, an annualized rate of return that equals or exceeds the actuarial rate of return approved by Any State Retirement System. The Total Fund's asset allocation is designed to provide high long-term return at optimal risk consistent with the board's expected long-term objectives. Investment risks are diversified across a broad range of market sectors, securities, and other investments. This strategy reduces portfolio risk to adverse developments in sectors and issuers experiencing unusual difficulties. The primary risks of the Total Fund include asset allocation risk and liquidity risk."

|

Sample Disclosure for a Composite:

"The 2018 Vintage Year Private Equity Composite includes all private equity investments with an initial capital call from limited partners in 2018. The composite focuses on investments in venture and buyout/growth funds. The risks of investing in private equity are funding risk, liquidity risk, market risk, and capital risk. Risk is diversified by investing across different types of private equity such as venture capital, leveraged buyouts, and international funds."

A Sample List of Total Fund and Composite Descriptions can be found in Appendix D of the GIPS standards.

Provision 24.C.5

The ASSET OWNER MUST disclose:

a. The BENCHMARK DESCRIPTION, which MUST include the key features of the BENCHMARK or the name of the BENCHMARK for a readily recognized index or other point of reference.

b. The PERIODICITY of the BENCHMARK if BENCHMARK returns are calculated less frequently than monthly.

Discussion

Asset owners are required to disclose a description of each benchmark included in a GIPS Asset Owner Report. The benchmark description is general information regarding the investments, structure, and characteristics of the benchmark, and it must include the key features of the benchmark. In the case of a widely recognized benchmark, such as the S&P 500® Index, the name of the benchmark will satisfy this requirement. (S&P 500® is a registered trademark of Standard & Poor's Financial Services LLC.) Each asset owner must decide for itself whether a benchmark is widely recognized. If the asset owner is not certain as to whether the benchmark is widely known, the asset owner must include the benchmark description.

If the benchmark returns are calculated less frequently than monthly, the periodicity of the benchmark must be disclosed.

Sample Disclosure for a Widely Recognized Benchmark:

"The benchmark is the S&P 500® Index."

Sample Disclosure for a Benchmark That Is Not Widely Recognized:

"The benchmark is the XYZ World Index, which is designed to measure the equity market performance of developed market countries. The benchmark is market-cap weighted and is composed of all XYZ country-specific developed market indices."

Sample Disclosure for an Index with Returns Calculated Less Frequently Than Monthly:

"The ABC Property Index (API) is a quarterly, unleveraged composite total return for private commercial real estate properties held for investment purposes only. All properties in the API have been acquired, at least in part, on behalf of tax-exempt institutional investors."

Provision 24.C.6

When presenting GROSS-OF-FEES returns, the ASSET OWNER MUST disclose if any other fees are deducted in addition to the TRANSACTION COSTS and fees and expenses for externally managed POOLED FUNDS.

Discussion

When presenting gross-of-fees returns, it is important that there are sufficient disclosures so that the oversight body can understand what the returns actually represent.

A gross-of-fees return is the return on investments reduced by transaction costs and all fees and expenses for externally managed pooled funds. If an asset owner presents a gross-of-fees return in a GIPS Asset Owner Report, the asset owner must disclose if any other fees, such as custody fees for externally managed segregated accounts, are deducted in addition to transaction costs and fees and expenses for externally managed pooled funds.

Sample Disclosure:

"Gross-of-fees returns reflect the deduction of transaction costs, fees and expenses for externally managed pooled funds, and custodian fees for externally managed segregated accounts."

Provision 24.C.7

When presenting NET-OF-EXTERNAL-COSTS-ONLY returns, the ASSET OWNER MUST disclose if any other fees are deducted in addition to the TRANSACTION COSTS, fees and expenses for externally managed POOLED FUNDS, and INVESTMENT MANAGEMENT FEES for externally managed SEGREGATED ACCOUNTS.

 |

Discussion

When presenting net-of-external-costs-only returns, it is important that there are sufficient disclosures so that the oversight body can understand what the returns actually represent.

Net-of-external-costs-only returns are required to reflect the deduction of transaction costs, all fees and expenses for externally managed pooled funds, and investment management fees for externally managed segregated accounts.[I] Investment management fees include both asset-based fees and performance-based fees or carried interest. Other expenses may also be deducted, (e.g., custody fees for segregated accounts). If other fees are deducted from the net-of-external-costs-only returns, this fact must be disclosed.

Sample Disclosure:

"Net-of-external-costs-only returns are net of transaction costs, all fees and expenses for externally managed pooled funds, and investment management fees and custodian fees for externally managed segregated accounts."

Provision 24.C.8

When presenting NET-OF-FEES returns, the ASSET OWNER MUST disclose if any other fees are deducted in addition to the TRANSACTION COSTS, fees and expenses for externally managed POOLED FUNDS, INVESTMENT MANAGEMENT FEES for externally managed SEGREGATED ACCOUNTS, and INVESTMENT MANAGEMENT COSTS.[J]

Discussion

When presenting net-of-fees returns, it is important that there be sufficient disclosures so that the oversight body can understand what the returns actually represent.

Net-of-fees returns are required to reflect the deduction of transaction costs, fees and expenses for externally managed pooled funds, investment management fees for externally managed segregated

---

[I] The definition of NET-OF-EXTERNAL-COSTS-ONLY included in the Glossary in the 2020 edition of the GIPS standards is incorrect and should state:

The GROSS-OF-FEES return reduced by ~~all costs~~ INVESTMENT MANAGEMENT FEES for externally managed SEGREGATED ACCOUNTS.

[J] The first sentence of the provision in the 2020 edition of the GIPS standards incorrectly included the word "COMPOSITE" and should state:

When presenting ~~COMPOSITE~~ NET-OF-FEES returns, the ASSET OWNER MUST disclose if any other fees are deducted in addition to the TRANSACTION COSTS, fees and expenses for externally managed POOLED FUNDS, INVESTMENT MANAGEMENT FEES for externally managed SEGREGATED ACCOUNTS, and INVESTMENT MANAGEMENT COSTS.

accounts, and investment management costs. Investment management fees include both asset-based fees and performance-based fees or carried interest. In the rare instance where other fees and expenses beyond those required to be deducted are also deducted, this information must be disclosed.

Sample Disclosure:

"Net-of-fees returns are net of transaction costs, fees and expenses for externally managed pooled funds, investment management fees for externally managed segregated accounts, investment management costs, and insurance agency costs."

Provision 24.C.9

The ASSET OWNER MUST disclose or otherwise indicate the reporting currency.

Discussion

The GIPS standards require that asset owners disclose the currency used to report the numerical information presented in a GIPS Asset Owner Report. If the asset owner presents performance in multiple currencies in the same GIPS Asset Owner Report, the asset owner must ensure it is clear which currencies are used to calculate and report performance and assets.

Labeling the columns within a GIPS Asset Owner Report with the appropriate currency symbol would satisfy this requirement, as would a written disclosure.

All required and recommended information presented in a GIPS Asset Owner Report must be presented in the same currency. (See Provision 24.A.7.)

Sample Disclosures:

"Valuations are computed and all information is reported in Canadian dollars."

"All numerical information is reported in Japanese yen."

Provision 24.C.10

The ASSET OWNER MUST disclose the TOTAL FUND INCEPTION DATE or COMPOSITE INCEPTION DATE.

Discussion

When reviewing the performance data in a GIPS Asset Owner Report, it is important that the oversight body has sufficient information regarding the length of the total fund or composite track record to put the performance presented in the GIPS Asset Owner Report in perspective. Therefore, the inception date of the total fund or composite being presented in the GIPS Asset Owner Report must be disclosed. The oversight body can then compare the periods of performance presented in the GIPS Asset Owner Report with the length of the total fund's or composite's track record, and it can request additional information for historical periods not included in the GIPS Asset Owner Report. If there has been a break in the performance record of a composite, the initial inception date before the break is the date that would be disclosed.

Sample Disclosure for a Total Fund:

"The Total Fund was established in 1989."

Sample Disclosures for Composites:

"The Domestic Equity Composite has an inception date of 1 August 1994, the date on which domestic equities were first managed as an asset class within the Total Fund."

"The Global Fixed Income Composite has an inception date of 1 November 2015. There was a break in performance from 1 March 2019 through 30 November 2019. During that period, there were no portfolios in the composite. Composite performance began again on 1 December 2019."

Provision 24.C.11

For COMPOSITES, the ASSET OWNER MUST disclose the COMPOSITE CREATION DATE.

Discussion

Asset owners must disclose the composite creation date, which is the date on which the asset owner first grouped one or more portfolios together to create the composite. The composite creation date is not necessarily the same as the composite inception date. The composite inception date is the initial date of the composite's performance record and is a required disclosure. (See Provision 24.C.10.) The composite creation date can be significantly after the composite inception date, depending on when the asset owner first grouped the individual portfolios together to create the composite. This information allows the oversight body to compare the composite creation date with the composite inception date to determine whether the asset owner grouped portfolios together into a composite retroactively or created the composite at the beginning of the composite's performance track record.

For those asset owners that created composites many years ago, it may be impossible to know the specific day a composite was created. Some asset owners disclose a composite creation date as a month, or even a year, when the composite was created in the very distant past. Newly created composites should have more-precise composite creation dates.

Sample Disclosures:

"The Real Estate Composite was created on 17 July 2019. This is the date on which portfolios were first grouped together to create the composite."

"The Core Fixed Income Composite was created in November 2009."

Provision 24.C.12

If the ASSET OWNER chooses to create additional COMPOSITES, or if the ASSET OWNER has more than one REQUIRED TOTAL FUND, the ASSET OWNER MUST disclose that the ASSET OWNER'S list of TOTAL FUND DESCRIPTIONS and COMPOSITE DESCRIPTIONS is available upon request.

Discussion

An additional composite is a grouping of portfolios representing a particular strategy or asset class that the asset owner chooses to present in a GIPS Asset Owner Report. If the asset owner chooses to create additional composites representing one or more strategies within a total fund, or if the asset owner has more than one required GIPS Asset Owner Report for its total funds, a list of total fund descriptions and composite descriptions must be maintained and made available to the oversight body upon request. (See Provisions 21.A.17 and 21.A.18 for additional guidance on the creation and distribution of the list of total fund descriptions and composite descriptions.) The asset owner must disclose, in each GIPS Asset Owner Report, that a list of total fund descriptions and composite descriptions is available upon request. When an asset owner competes for business and chooses to claim compliance with the GIPS standards while competing for business, this list must include the strategies from the part of the organization that competes for business.

If the asset owner has only one total fund or only one total fund composite and has not chosen to create any additional composites, the GIPS Asset Owner Report for the total fund or the total fund composite represents the asset owner's list of total fund descriptions and composite descriptions. This is because the description of the total fund or the total fund composite is required to be included in the relevant GIPS Asset Owner Report, and so the GIPS Asset Owner Report can be used to meet this requirement. In such cases, the asset owner is not required to disclose that this list is available upon request.

The list of total fund descriptions and composite descriptions itself does not need to be included in each GIPS Asset Owner Report but must be available upon request. The list of total fund descriptions and composite descriptions must include the total fund description or composite description for each current total fund, total fund composite, or additional composite, as well as a description for all total funds or composites that have terminated in the past five years. The total fund descriptions and composite descriptions disclosed in GIPS Asset Owner Reports must be consistent with the descriptions included in the list of total fund descriptions and composite descriptions. (Please see Provision 23.A.4 for a discussion of total fund descriptions and composite descriptions.)

A Sample List of Total Fund and Composite Descriptions can be found in Appendix D of the GIPS standards.

This requirement exists to provide the oversight body with a complete picture of the asset owner's total funds and composites.

Sample Disclosure:

"A list of total fund descriptions and composite descriptions is available upon request."

Provision 24.C.13

The ASSET OWNER MUST disclose that policies for valuing investments, calculating performance, and preparing GIPS ASSET OWNER REPORTS are available upon request.

Discussion

In each GIPS Asset Owner Report, asset owners must disclose the availability of policies for valuing investments, calculating performance, and preparing GIPS Asset Owner Reports. The policies are not required to be included in each GIPS Asset Owner Report but must be available upon request. Asset owners are not required to provide the related procedures, in addition to the policies, but may do so.

Sample Disclosure:

"Centerville Police and Fire Retirement System's policies for valuing portfolios, calculating performance, and preparing GIPS Asset Owner Reports are available upon request."

Provision 24.C.14

The ASSET OWNER MUST disclose how leverage, derivatives, and short positions have been used historically, if material.

Discussion

Asset owners must provide enough information in a GIPS Asset Owner Report to allow the oversight body to understand how leverage, derivatives, and short positions have been employed historically and may be used going forward. Although the total fund description or composite description includes disclosure of the asset owner's ability to use leverage, derivatives, and short positions (see Provision 24.C.4), this provision requires that the asset owner disclose the leverage, derivatives, and short positions that have been used historically, if material. Taken together, these two required disclosures provide a more complete picture of the presence, use, and extent of leverage, derivatives, and short positions.

For example, assume an asset owner discloses in a composite description that the strategy may employ up to 200% leverage. To satisfy the disclosure requirement in Provision 24.C.14, the asset owner might state, "Since the inception of the strategy, the leverage has averaged 110% of the composite's value; however, during 2019 the leverage averaged 160%, which greatly increased the sensitivity to market volatility and the potential for realized gains and/or losses."

No disclosure is required if leverage, derivatives, and short positions have not been used or if their use has not been material. When determining what would be material, the asset owner must consider whether the disclosure of how leverage, derivatives, and/or short positions have been used historically is likely to affect the oversight body's view of the risk involved in the strategy. If so, it would be misleading for the asset owner to fail to disclose their use to the oversight body when describing the strategy.

Provision 24.C.15

If estimated TRANSACTION COSTS are used, the ASSET OWNER MUST disclose:

a. That estimated TRANSACTION COSTS were used.
b. The estimated TRANSACTION COSTS used and how they were determined

Discussion

Gross-of-fees, net-of-external-costs-only, and net-of-fees total fund and composite returns must reflect the deduction of transaction costs, which are the costs of buying or selling investments. Asset owners may use either actual or estimated transaction costs when calculating returns. Estimated transaction costs may be used only for portfolios for which the actual transaction costs are not known. Provision 22.A.10 provides guidance on the use of estimated transaction costs.

If estimated transaction costs are used in calculating returns, there must be a disclosure that estimated transaction costs were used. An asset owner must also disclose the estimated transaction

 |

costs used and how they were determined. An asset owner might, for example, determine estimated transaction costs based on other portfolios whose transaction costs are known.

Sample Disclosure for a Total Fund:

"The transaction costs for some portfolios in the total fund are not known and must be estimated. The estimated transaction costs for these portfolios are determined based on the average transaction cost per share incurred by portfolios in the total fund that trade in similar markets and under similar conditions and whose transaction costs are known. The estimated transaction costs for those portfolios for which actual transaction costs are not known is 8 Swiss francs per trade."

Sample Disclosure for a Composite:

"Some portfolios in the composite do not pay explicit transaction costs for security purchases and sales. Estimated transaction costs for these portfolios are used, and these are determined based on the average transaction cost per share incurred by portfolios in the composite that pay explicit transaction costs. The average transaction cost was determined to be $0.031 per share. A model transaction cost per share of $0.04 is applied to each investment transaction."

Provision 24.C.16

The ASSET OWNER MUST disclose all significant events that would help the OVERSIGHT BODY interpret the GIPS ASSET OWNER REPORT. This disclosure MUST be included for a minimum of one year and for as long as it is relevant to interpreting the track record.

Discussion

The GIPS standards are based on the principles of fair representation and full disclosure. Meeting these objectives requires a good faith commitment on the part of the asset owner to adhere to the spirit of the GIPS standards. The GIPS standards cannot foresee and cover every situation that might occur. Therefore, this provision requires that asset owners disclose all significant events that would help explain the asset owner's GIPS Asset Owner Report to the oversight body. The primary goal of this requirement is to provide relevant information to the oversight body so that it can understand the potential effect of the significant event on the total fund's or composite's investment strategy and the asset owner.

Significant events are determined by the asset owner and would include, as examples, a material change in personnel responsible for investment management, significant changes to the investment management process, or the loss of historical records resulting from a catastrophic event.

The departure of someone who was the single investment decision maker for one or more strategies within the total fund would likely qualify as a significant event.

Depending on the situation, a general statement describing the significant event that has occurred may be sufficient. Other situations may require asset owners to disclose specific information pertaining to the significant event. The disclosure regarding the significant event must be included in the GIPS Asset Owner Report for a minimum of one year and for as long as it is relevant to interpreting the performance track record. As an example, if there is a legislative change that requires an asset owner to manage the assets of an additional retirement system, resulting in a large increase in total asset owner assets, the asset owner may disclose this significant event for as long as the large change in total asset owner assets is included in the GIPS Asset Owner Report. In contrast, a change in an asset owner's chief investment officer (CIO) is a change that an asset owner may believe should be disclosed for one year only.

The asset owner must consider the underlying principles of the GIPS standards, which are fair representation and full disclosure, when determining how long the disclosure will be included in the GIPS Asset Owner Report.

Sample Disclosure:

"In March 2019, the portfolio manager responsible for the internal management of all fixed-income assets of the Midway State Municipal Retirement System (MSMRS) left MSMRS. Her duties have been assumed by a member of the MSMRS investment management team. No change in the fixed-income strategy is anticipated."

Provision 24.C.17

If the ASSET OWNER is redefined, the ASSET OWNER MUST disclose the date and description of the redefinition.

Discussion

An asset owner redefinition occurs when something changes with how the asset owner is structured. For example, there may be cases where there are significant changes to an asset owner due to legislation-driven changes in the case of pension funds or changes dictated by the governing body in the case of foundations, endowments, or family offices. In some cases, as a result of a significant alteration in an asset owner's structure or organization, a change can be so great that it creates a new asset owner. Changes in investment mandate or personnel are not events that typically cause an asset owner redefinition. A simple asset owner name change is also not a sufficient reason to redefine the asset owner.

|

The GIPS standards require that changes in an asset owner's organization must not lead to alteration of historical total fund or composite performance (see Provision 21.A.22).

Sample Disclosures:

"On 1 July 2018, the Prodigy University Endowment for Theater Studies was redefined by the Prodigy University Investment Committee to include the endowments for all creative art studies at Prodigy University, including theater, dance, music, writing, and visual arts, and was renamed the Prodigy University Endowment for the Creative Arts."

"On 1 August 2019, Midway City was created through the merger of the municipalities of New Town and Old Town. On that date, the retirement systems of New Town and Old Town were merged to create the Midway City Retirement System (MCRS)."

Provision 24.C.18

If a COMPOSITE is redefined, the ASSET OWNER MUST disclose the date and description of the redefinition.

Discussion

The investment mandate, objective, or strategy of a composite of total funds or an additional composite can change over time. (An additional composite is a grouping of portfolios representing a particular strategy or asset class that the asset owner chooses to present in a GIPS Asset Owner Report.) In some cases, such a change results in the termination of one composite and the creation of a new composite. In other cases, it may be appropriate to redefine the composite. If a composite is redefined, the asset owner must disclose the date and description of the redefinition. See Provision 23.A.4 for guidance on composite definitions.

Sample Disclosure for a Total Fund Composite:

"As of 1 June 2019, the Goodtown Municipal Employees Total Fund, representing Goodtown municipal employees other than firefighters and police officers, was added to the Goodtown Municipal Retirement System (GMRS) total fund composite. Prior to 1 June 2019, the GMRS total fund composite included two total funds: the Goodtown Firefighters Total Fund and the Goodtown Police Officers Total Fund. The Goodtown Municipal Employees Total Fund had previously been presented to the oversight body separately."

Sample Disclosure for an Additional Composite:

"As of 1 July 2019, the fixed-income strategy includes the use of interest rate futures to modify duration and manage interest rate risk. Prior to this date, the fixed-income strategy did not involve the active management of interest rate risk."

Provision 24.C.19

The ASSET OWNER MUST disclose changes to the name of a TOTAL FUND or COMPOSITE. This disclosure MUST be included for a minimum of one year and for as long as it is relevant to interpreting the track record.

Discussion

When an asset owner's oversight body is evaluating total funds or composites, it is important that members of that oversight body understand exactly which total funds or composites they are assessing. If an asset owner changes the name of a total fund or composite, the change must be disclosed in the GIPS Asset Owner Report. The name change must be disclosed for a minimum of one year and potentially for more than one year if the asset owner determines the disclosure is still relevant and meaningful. The asset owner must consider the underlying principles of the GIPS standards, which are fair representation and full disclosure, when determining how long the disclosure will be included in the GIPS Asset Owner Report.

Sample Disclosure for a Total Fund:

"On 1 July 2018, the ABC Endowment for the Arts Total Fund was renamed the ABC Endowment for Science and the Arts Total Fund."

Sample Disclosure for a Composite:

"As of 1 January 2016, the XYZ Index Composite was renamed the US Equity Large Cap Composite."

Provision 24.C.20

The ASSET OWNER MUST disclose if TOTAL FUND or COMPOSITE returns are gross or net of withholding taxes, if material.

 |

Discussion

Global investing requires recognition of the tax consequences of investing in different countries. The GIPS standards do not require asset owners to reflect withholding taxes, either reclaimable or non-reclaimable taxes, in a certain manner. Asset owners may choose whether or not to reflect the effect of withholding taxes when calculating performance. The GIPS standards do recommend that performance be reported net of non-reclaimable withholding taxes on dividends, interest, and capital gains and also recommend that reclaimable foreign withholding taxes be accrued (see Provision 22.B.5). If withholding taxes are material, asset owners must disclose how withholding taxes are treated when calculating performance. An asset owner must determine the level at which withholding taxes become material, document the level in its policies and procedures, and apply it consistently.

Sample Disclosure:

"Total fund returns are net of all foreign non-reclaimable withholding taxes. Reclaimable withholding taxes are recognized if and when received."

Provision 24.C.21

The ASSET OWNER MUST disclose if BENCHMARK returns are net of withholding taxes if this information is available.

Discussion

Global investing requires recognition of the tax consequences of investing in different countries. The GIPS standards do not require asset owners to reflect withholding taxes, either reclaimable or non-reclaimable taxes, in a certain manner. Asset owners may choose whether or not to reflect the effect of withholding taxes when calculating total fund or composite performance and, similarly, whether or not to use a benchmark that reflects the effect of withholding taxes.

As Provision 24.C.20 indicates, if withholding taxes are material, asset owners must disclose how withholding taxes are treated when calculating performance. To facilitate the comparison of total fund or composite returns and benchmark returns, asset owners must also disclose if the benchmark returns are net of withholding taxes if this information is available. If the benchmark name indicates that the benchmark is net of withholding taxes, no additional disclosure is necessary.

Sample Disclosures:

"Benchmark returns are net of withholding taxes."

"The benchmark is the XYZ World Net Total Return Index."

Provision 24.C.22

If the GIPS ASSET OWNER REPORT conforms with laws and/or regulations that conflict with the REQUIREMENTS of the GIPS standards, the ASSET OWNER MUST disclose this fact and disclose the manner in which the laws and/or regulations conflict with the GIPS standards.

Discussion

Asset owners must comply with all applicable laws and regulations regarding the calculation and presentation of performance. Compliance with applicable laws and regulations, however, does not necessarily result in compliance with the GIPS standards. Asset owners must also comply with all of the applicable requirements of the GIPS standards. In the rare cases where laws and regulations conflict with the GIPS standards, asset owners are required to comply with the laws and regulations and disclose the manner in which the laws and/or regulations conflict with the GIPS standards.

This disclosure will assist the oversight body in understanding the difference between the reporting requirements of applicable laws and regulations and those of the GIPS standards.

Sample Disclosure:

"Local laws do not allow the presentation of returns of less than one year, which is in conflict with the GIPS standards. Therefore, no performance is presented for this composite for the period from 1 July 2018 (the inception date of the composite) through 31 December 2018."

Provision 24.C.23

The ASSET OWNER MUST disclose the use of EXTERNAL MANAGERS and the periods EXTERNAL MANAGERS were used.[30]

Discussion

Some asset owners use an external manager to manage part or all of a particular strategy. For example, an asset owner might manage most of its fixed-income assets internally but hire external managers to manage its equity, private equity, and real estate assets. The GIPS standards require that asset owners include the performance of assets assigned to an external manager in its total fund(s) and in any additional composite that the asset own has chosen to create, provided the asset owner

---

[30] REQUIRED for periods beginning on or after 1 January 2006.

|

has the authority to allocate the assets to an external manager. (An additional composite is a grouping of portfolios representing a particular strategy or asset class that the asset owner chooses to present in a GIPS Asset Owner Report.) In the spirit of full disclosure, an asset owner must disclose the fact that an external manager was used in the management of the total fund or composite strategy and the periods for which an external manager was used. This is required for periods beginning on or after 1 January 2006. It is not necessary to disclose the name of the external manager.

Sample Disclosures for a Total Fund:

"Since 2005, the Centerville Police and Fire Retirement System (CPFRS) has hired external managers to manage all fixed-income portfolios."

"All assets in the Everytown Municipal Retirement System (EMRS) are managed externally since inception of the total fund."

Sample Disclosures for a Composite:

"The International Equity Composite has used external managers for all periods presented."

"The Global Private Equity Composite used an external manager from its inception on 1 October 2018 through 31 May 2020. It has been internally managed since 1 June 2020."

Provision 24.C.24

The ASSET OWNER MUST disclose if the TOTAL FUND's or COMPOSITE's valuation hierarchy materially differs from the RECOMMENDED valuation hierarchy.[31] (See Provision 22.B.6 for the RECOMMENDED valuation hierarchy.)

Discussion

Asset owners must establish policies and procedures for determining portfolio valuations. For periods beginning on or after 1 January 2011, those valuations must be determined in accordance with the definition of fair value. Provision 22.B.6 includes a recommended valuation hierarchy that asset owners should incorporate into their policies and procedures for determining fair value for portfolio investments. Asset owners must establish a valuation hierarchy on a total fund–specific or composite-specific basis. It is acceptable for asset owners to apply a different valuation hierarchy to specific total funds or composites provided the valuation methodology conforms to the definition of fair value. If the valuation hierarchy materially differs from the recommended

---

[31] REQUIRED for periods beginning on or after 1 January 2011.

valuation hierarchy, the asset owner must disclose this fact. The oversight body will be informed and then may request additional information about the asset owner's valuation policies.

Sample Disclosure:

"All portfolio investments in the Private Equity Composite are valued using our proprietary valuation models to determine fair value. Our valuation procedures materially differ from the recommended valuation hierarchy in the GIPS standards."

Provision 24.C.25

If the ASSET OWNER determines no appropriate BENCHMARK for the TOTAL FUND or COMPOSITE exists, the ASSET OWNER MUST disclose why no BENCHMARK is presented.

Discussion

Benchmarks are important tools that aid in the planning, implementation, and evaluation of an investment strategy. They also help facilitate discussions with the oversight body regarding the relationship between total fund or composite risk and return. As a result, the GIPS standards require asset owners to provide benchmark total returns in all GIPS Asset Owner Reports. The benchmark must reflect the investment mandate, objective, or strategy of the total fund or composite. Although there is typically an appropriate benchmark for traditional strategies, it is more common for asset owners with alternative strategies to determine that no appropriate benchmark for the alternative strategy composite exists. If this is the case, the asset owner must disclose why no benchmark is presented.

Sample Disclosure:

"Because the composite's strategy is absolute return where investments are permitted in all asset classes, no benchmark is presented because we believe that no benchmark that reflects this strategy exists."

Provision 24.C.26

If the ASSET OWNER changes the BENCHMARK, the ASSET OWNER MUST disclose:

a. For a prospective BENCHMARK change, the date and description of the change. Changes MUST be disclosed for as long as returns for the prior BENCHMARK are included in the GIPS ASSET OWNER REPORT.

b. For a retroactive BENCHMARK change, the date and description of the change. Changes MUST be disclosed for a minimum of one year and for as long as they are relevant to interpreting the track record.

Discussion

Asset owners must disclose the date and description of any changes to the benchmark over time. A benchmark change can take two forms:

- The benchmark is changed from one benchmark to another on a prospective basis only.
- The benchmark is changed for all periods (i.e., retroactively).

In most cases, the asset owner should only change the benchmark going forward and not change it retroactively.

If the asset owner changes the benchmark prospectively and presents benchmark returns that combine two different benchmarks, the date and description of the change must be disclosed for as long as returns for the prior benchmark are included in the GIPS Asset Owner Report. For example, assume an asset owner changes the benchmark for a total fund or composite in June 2015, and the change is made prospectively. As long as benchmark returns from 2015 or prior periods are included in the GIPS Asset Owner Report, the asset owner must include this disclosure. Asset owners must also carefully identify the benchmark as a custom benchmark in the GIPS Asset Owner Report and must make clear that the benchmark returns are not those of the current benchmark for all periods. It would not be appropriate to label the benchmark returns with the name of the current benchmark. The asset owner must provide information, including labelling of the benchmark, that is sufficient to allow the oversight body to distinguish the prior benchmark returns from the current benchmark returns.

There may be times when an asset owner determines that it is appropriate to change the benchmark for a given total fund or composite retroactively. For example, because benchmarks are continually evolving, if the asset owner finds that a new benchmark is a better comparison for an investment strategy, the asset owner may consider changing the benchmark retroactively. In the case of a retroactive benchmark change, there must be a disclosure of the date and description of the benchmark change, including the fact that the benchmark was changed retroactively. Disclosures related to a retroactive change in a benchmark must be included in the respective GIPS Asset Owner Report for a minimum of one year and for as long as the disclosures are relevant to interpreting the performance track record. The asset owner must consider the underlying principles of the GIPS standards, which are fair representation and full disclosure, when determining how long this disclosure will be included in the GIPS Asset Owner Report.

When an asset owner changes a benchmark retroactively, the asset owner is encouraged to continue to also present the old benchmark.

Changes to the benchmark primarily intended to make performance look better by lowering the benchmark return violate the spirit of the GIPS standards.

Sample Disclosure for a Prospective Change:

"Benchmark results presented are a combination of two indices. ABC Index was used prior to 30 September 2015; ABC Value Index is used subsequently."

Sample Disclosure for a Retroactive Change:

"In January 2017, the benchmark was changed from ABC Index to XYZ Index for all periods."

Provision 24.C.27

If a custom BENCHMARK or combination of multiple BENCHMARKS is used, the ASSET OWNER MUST:

a. Disclose the BENCHMARK components, weights, and rebalancing process, if applicable.

b. Disclose the calculation methodology.

c. Clearly label the BENCHMARK to indicate that it is a custom BENCHMARK.

Discussion

When custom benchmarks are used, the asset owner must disclose the benchmark components, weights, and rebalancing process, if applicable, as well as the calculation methodology. For example, if the asset owner combines two indices, WW Index and XX Index, to create the WWXX benchmark for the composite, the following would be an appropriate disclosure:

"The WWXX benchmark is a combination of 50% WW Index and 50% XX Index, calculated by weighting the respective index returns on a monthly basis."

It is also required that the benchmark be clearly labeled to indicate that it is a custom benchmark. For example, the label for the benchmark returns in a GIPS Asset Owner Report would read "Custom Benchmark" or "Total Fund Benchmark." The benchmark description and required disclosures might read as follows:

"<u>Custom Benchmark</u>: The international blended benchmark is calculated monthly using 75% of the XYZ World ex-U.S. 50% Hedged Index and 25% of the XYZ Emerging Markets Index. A forward rate is used to construct the hedge. "

It is becoming more common for exchange-traded funds (ETFs) to be used as benchmarks. An ETF is a pooled fund that tracks a specific investment universe that is expressed by an index or a basket of securities and that is listed on an exchange. Unlike a market index, an ETF incurs trading costs and other charges, including taxes. Because of the incurred costs, an ETF may underperform the market index that it tracks. If an ETF is chosen as the benchmark for a composite, the asset owner should present net-of-fees composite returns. As part of the benchmark description for an ETF, the asset owner must disclose the following items:

- if ETF returns are gross or net of fees and other costs, including transaction costs;
- the ETF expense ratio, if ETF net returns are presented;
- if ETF returns are based on market prices or net asset values (NAVs);
- the timing of the market close used to determine the ETF's valuations; and
- if ETF returns are gross or net of withholding taxes, if this information is available.

If the asset owner also presents composite gross-of-fees returns, it should present ETF returns that are grossed up, but it is not required to do so.

Sample Disclosures:

"The benchmark is the Special ETF, which tracks the securities included in the Special Index. The Special ETF returns reflect the deduction of all expenses and transaction costs incurred by the Special ETF and are net of withholding taxes. As of 31 December 2019, the expense ratio was 0.14%. The Special ETF returns reflect market prices, which are determined by the midpoint between the bid and ask prices as of the closing time of the New York Stock Exchange."

Provision 24.C.28

If the TOTAL FUND BENCHMARK is a blend of asset class BENCHMARKS based on the policy weights of the respective asset classes, the ASSET OWNER MUST disclose:

a. The BENCHMARKS used by each asset class along with their weights as of the most recent annual period end.

b. General information regarding the investments, structure, and/or characteristics of the BENCHMARKS.

Discussion

A total fund is typically composed of multiple asset classes. Therefore, the total fund benchmark is often a blend of asset class benchmarks based on the policy weights of the respective asset classes. If a blended benchmark, based on the asset classes in the total fund, is presented in a GIPS Asset Owner Report, the asset owner must disclose the benchmark(s) used by each asset class, along with their policy weights as of the most recent annual period end. General information for each benchmark must also be disclosed, including its investments, structure, and/or characteristics. This information will assist the oversight body in understanding the benchmark against which the performance of the total fund is being compared.

Sample Disclosure:

"The Total Fund blended benchmark is calculated monthly using a blend of the asset class benchmarks based on the Total Fund's benchmark policy weights for the respective asset classes. Each asset class uses a total return benchmark. The benchmark policy weights listed in the following table are as of 31 December 2020. Benchmark policy weights and asset classes weights for prior periods are available upon request.

Asset Class	Benchmark	Benchmark Policy Weight 31 Dec 2020 (%)
Absolute Return	Juniper 9- to 12-Month Treasury Index	23
Domestic Equity	Desmond Total Stock Index	20
Fixed Income	Juniper 1- to 3-Year Treasury Index	9
International Equity	Smith All Country World Index ex US Index	22
Natural Resources	Jackson Associates Natural Resources Index	8
Private Equity	Jackson Associates Private Equity Index	10
Real Estate	Farley US REIT Index	4
Cash	Juniper 1- to 3-Month Treasury Index	4

"Descriptions of the blended benchmark components are as follows. The Juniper 9- to 12-Month Treasury Index includes all publicly issued US Treasury bills with a remaining maturity between 9 and 12 months. The Desmond Total Stock Index tracks the US broad equity market for companies of any market capitalization size. The Juniper 1- to 3-Year Treasury Index measures the performance of US Treasury bonds maturing in one to three years. The Smith All Country World Index ex US provides a broad measure of stock performance throughout the world, excluding US-based companies. This market-capitalization-weighted index includes companies doing business in both developed and emerging markets. The Jackson Associates Natural Resources Index represents domestic securities that are classified as energy and materials sector stocks, excluding securities associated with the chemicals industry and the steel industry. The Jackson Associates Private Equity Index is composed of the top private equity funds that meet defined criteria such as liquidity, size, exposure, and activity requirements. The Farley US REIT Index is composed of equity real estate investment trusts. The index is a free float–adjusted market capitalization weighted index. The Juniper 1- to 3-Month Treasury Index includes all publicly issued US Treasury bills with a remaining maturity between one and three months."

|

Provision 24.C.29

If a PORTFOLIO-WEIGHTED CUSTOM BENCHMARK is used, the ASSET OWNER MUST disclose:

a. That the BENCHMARK is rebalanced using the weighted average returns of the BENCHMARKS of all of the PORTFOLIOS included in the COMPOSITE.

b. The frequency of the rebalancing.

c. The components that constitute the PORTFOLIO-WEIGHTED CUSTOM BENCHMARK, including the weights that each component represents, as of the most recent annual period end.

d. That the components that constitute the PORTFOLIO-WEIGHTED CUSTOM BENCHMARK, including the weights that each component represents, are available for prior periods upon request.

Discussion

Asset owners may use a portfolio-weighted custom benchmark, which is created using the benchmarks of the individual portfolios in the composite. If such a benchmark is used, asset owners must disclose that the benchmark is calculated using the weighted average returns of the benchmarks of all of the portfolios included in the composite, along with the frequency of the rebalancing. Asset owners are not required to disclose how the underlying portfolio benchmarks and weights have changed each period.

Additionally, in the spirit of full disclosure and fair representation, asset owners must disclose the components that constitute the portfolio-weighted custom benchmark, including the weight that each component represents, as of the most recent annual period end. It is also required that asset owners disclose that information regarding the components of the portfolio-weighted custom benchmark, as well as the component weights, is available for prior periods upon request.

Sample Disclosure–Custom Benchmark:

"The Long US Government/Credit Custom Benchmark is calculated using the benchmarks of the portfolios in the composite. The benchmark is rebalanced monthly based on the beginning values of portfolios included in the composite. As of 31 December 2020, the breakdown of the benchmark is 88.2% XYZ US Long Government/Credit Index and 11.8% XYZ US Long Government/Credit A+ Index. The breakdown of the custom benchmark for different time periods is available upon request."

Sample Disclosure—Total Fund Composite Benchmark:

"The Total Fund Composite includes three total funds. Each total fund has its own policy benchmark. The Total Fund Composite benchmark is a custom benchmark that is calculated using the benchmarks of the total funds. The benchmark is calculated monthly based on the beginning values of the total funds included in the composite. As of 30 June 2020, the benchmark weights were as follows:

Benchmark	Benchmark Weights 30 June 2020 (%)
XYZ 9- to 12-Month Treasury Index	12
XYZ Total Stock Index	20
XYZ All Country World Index ex US Index	22
XYZ Aggregate Fixed Income Index	18
XYZ Private Equity Index	10
XYZ US REIT Index	14
Juniper 1- to 3-Month Treasury Index	4

"The breakdown of the custom benchmark for different time periods is available upon request."

Provision 24.C.30

For COMPOSITES with at least three annual periods of performance, the ASSET OWNER MUST disclose if the three-year annualized EX POST STANDARD DEVIATION of the COMPOSITE and/or BENCHMARK is not presented because 36 monthly returns are not available.[K]

Discussion

For periods ending on or after 1 January 2011, asset owners must present the three-year annualized ex post standard deviation of the total fund or composite and the benchmark, which must be calculated using 36 monthly returns, as of each annual period end.

The 2010 edition of the GIPS standards required that an asset owner disclose, in all cases, if the three-year annualized ex post standard deviation of the total fund or composite and/or benchmark is not presented because 36 monthly returns are not available. The 2020 edition of the GIPS standards modifies this requirement. This disclosure is required only if the three-year annualized

---

[K] The provision in the 2020 edition of the GIPS standards incorrectly included TOTAL FUNDS and should state:

For ~~TOTAL FUNDS and~~ COMPOSITES with at least three annual periods of performance, the ASSET OWNER MUST disclose if the three-year annualized EX POST STANDARD DEVIATION of the ~~TOTAL FUND or~~ COMPOSITE and/or BENCHMARK is not presented because 36 monthly returns are not available.

 |

ex post standard deviation is not presented for additional composites that have at least three annual periods of performance. This change applies to all periods presented in a GIPS Asset Owner Report.

If an additional composite has at least three annual periods of performance but 36 monthly returns are not available for the additional composite, asset owners are not required to present the three-year annualized ex post standard deviation for either the benchmark or the composite. This scenario often applies to private market investment composites because they are not required to have monthly returns. Asset owners must disclose that 36 monthly returns are not available for the composite. (If private market composites do have monthly valuations and 36 monthly returns are available, the three-year annualized ex post standard deviation must be presented.) If 36 monthly returns are not available for the additional composite but are available for the benchmark, an asset owner is not required to present the three-year annualized ex post standard deviation for the benchmark but may do so.

If 36 monthly returns are not available for the benchmark but are available for the additional composite, asset owners are required to present only the three-year annualized ex post standard deviation for the additional composite. In this instance, because 36 monthly returns are not available for the benchmark, asset owners must not present a three-year annualized ex post standard deviation for the benchmark using data points other than monthly. Asset owners must disclose that 36 monthly returns are not available for the benchmark.

Sample Disclosure If 36 Monthly Returns Are Available for the Composite but Not for the Benchmark:

"The three-year annualized ex post standard deviation of the benchmark is not presented because the benchmark returns are calculated quarterly."

Sample Disclosure If 36 Monthly Returns Are Not Available for the Composite:

"The three-year annualized ex post standard deviation of the composite and benchmark are not presented because the composite returns are calculated quarterly."

Provision 24.C.31

The ASSET OWNER MUST disclose any change to the GIPS ASSET OWNER REPORT resulting from the correction of a MATERIAL ERROR. Following the correction of the GIPS ASSET OWNER REPORT, this disclosure MUST be included for a minimum of one year and for as long as it is relevant to interpreting the track record.

Discussion

Asset owners claiming compliance with the GIPS standards are likely to face situations in which errors are discovered that must be specifically addressed. An error, which can be qualitative or quantitative, can be related to any component of a GIPS Asset Owner Report that is missing or inaccurate. Errors in GIPS Asset Owner Reports can result from, but are not limited to, incorrect, incomplete, or missing:

- total fund or composite returns or assets,
- total asset owner assets,
- benchmark returns,
- number of total funds or portfolios in a composite,
- three-year annualized ex post standard deviation, or
- disclosures.

Any material error in a GIPS Asset Owner Report must be corrected and disclosed in a revised GIPS Asset Owner Report. An asset owner must define materiality within its error correction policies and procedures.

To adhere to this requirement, an asset owner must determine the criteria it will use to determine materiality. The following is a definition of materiality that asset owners might find useful as a starting point for their determination of materiality: "An error is material if the magnitude of the omission or misstatement of performance information, in light of surrounding circumstances, makes it probable that the judgment of a reasonable person relying on the information would have been changed by the omission or misstatement." An asset owner should have a defined process for determining the objective criteria it will use in determining materiality.

Disclosure of the change in the corrected GIPS Asset Owner Report resulting from a material error must be included in the GIPS Asset Owner Report for a minimum of 12 months following the correction of the report and for as long as it is relevant to interpreting the track record. The asset owner must consider the underlying principles of the GIPS standards, which are fair representation and full disclosure, when determining how long the disclosure will be included in the GIPS Asset Owner Report that contained the material error.

The discussion for Provision 21.A.16 provides additional information on error correction, including the determination of materiality, the actions that must be taken when an error in a GIPS Asset Owner Report is discovered, and an explanation of who must receive the revised GIPS Asset Owner Report.

Sample Disclosure:

"This GIPS Asset Owner Report includes a correction of the information provided for the XYZ Index. The annual return for the XYZ Index for 2017 was originally presented as 3.4%. The correct return is 4.3%, as shown in this revised GIPS Asset Owner Report."

  |

Provision 24.C.32

The ASSET OWNER MUST disclose if preliminary, estimated values are used to determine FAIR VALUE.

Discussion

The use of preliminary, estimated values as fair value is common for some alternative strategies, including those that invest in externally managed pooled funds for which the asset owner relies on valuations provided by the fund external managers. When using preliminary, estimated values as fair value, it is important to remember the underlying principles of the GIPS standards: fair representation and full disclosure. If using preliminary, estimated values, asset owners must disclose this fact in the relevant GIPS Asset Owner Report.

Asset owners that use preliminary, estimated values to determine fair value and subsequently change valuations when final values are received must determine how the asset owner's error correction policies will be applied. (Please see Provision 21.A.16 for guidance on error correction policies.) Differences between the final and estimated values are not necessarily errors but are treated in a similar manner because the correction of previously presented information may be involved.

In addition to this required disclosure, it is recommended (see Provision 24.B.9) that asset owners present the percentage of assets in the total fund or composite that were valued using preliminary, estimated values as of each annual period end. This information will help the oversight body to interpret the performance record.

Sample Disclosure:

"Preliminary, estimated values were used in determining the fair value of the total fund's private equity assets."

Provision 24.C.33

If the ASSET OWNER changes the type of return(s) presented for the COMPOSITE (e.g., changes from MONEY-WEIGHTED RETURNS to TIME-WEIGHTED RETURNS), the ASSET OWNER MUST disclose the change and the date of the change. This disclosure MUST be included for a minimum of one year and for as long as it is relevant to interpreting the track record.

Discussion

Although an asset owner must present a time-weighted return (TWR) for all total funds and composites of total funds, it may choose to present either a TWR or a money-weighted return (MWR) for an additional composite. (An additional composite is a grouping of portfolios representing a particular strategy or asset class that the asset owner chooses to present in a GIPS Asset Owner Report.) If the asset owner changes the type of return presented for an additional composite, the asset owner must disclose, in the respective GIPS Asset Owner Report, the change in the type of return (from MWR to TWR or from TWR to MWR) and the date of the change. This disclosure must be included in the GIPS Asset Owner Report for a minimum of one year and for as long as it is relevant and helpful to the asset owner's oversight body in interpreting the composite's track record. The asset owner must consider the underlying principles of the GIPS standards, which are fair representation and full disclosure, when determining how long the disclosure will be included in the GIPS Asset Owner Report.

When an asset owner changes the type of return presented for an additional composite, for example from MWRs to TWRs, the asset owner must change the returns for all periods. As an example, suppose that an asset owner is presenting performance for the period from the inception of a composite on 1 January 2013 through 31 December 2020. It decides that it will switch to present TWRs as of 1 January 2020. The asset owner cannot present MWRs through 31 December 2019 and TWRs from 1 January 2020 through 31 December 2020. Instead, the asset owner must present TWRs from 1 January 2013 (the inception date of the composite) through 31 December 2020 in the GIPS Asset Owner Report for the period ended 31 December 2020.

Sample Disclosure:

"Beginning with the GIPS Asset Owner Report for the period ended 31 December 2020, the returns presented for the XYZ Composite were changed from money-weighted returns to time-weighted returns."

Provision 24.C.34

If the ASSET OWNER presents ADDITIONAL RISK MEASURES, the ASSET OWNER MUST:

a. Describe any ADDITIONAL RISK MEASURE.

b. Disclose the name of the risk-free rate if a risk-free rate is used in the calculation of the ADDITIONAL RISK MEASURE.

 | **169**

Discussion

Understanding and interpreting investment performance requires the consideration of both risk and return. It is therefore recommended that asset owners present additional ex post risk measures (i.e., risk measures beyond those required to be presented) for the total fund or composite and the benchmark. (See Provision 24.B.7.) It is important to keep in mind that additional risk measures should be consistent with the total fund's or composite's strategy. For example, if the strategy is to track the benchmark, then tracking error would be consistent with that objective.

The GIPS Asset Owner Report must include a description of any additional risk measure presented. If a risk-free rate is used in the calculation of an additional risk measure, the name of the risk-free rate must be disclosed. Disclosure of the name of the risk-free rate used in the calculation of an additional risk measure is required because of the importance of the selection of an appropriate risk-free rate. With a disclosure regarding the risk-free rate, the asset owner's oversight body can better understand and interpret the additional risk measure(s) presented.

Sample Disclosure:

"The Sharpe Ratio measures the performance of the total fund compared to a risk-free rate, after adjusting for risk. The risk-free rate used in the Sharpe ratio calculation is the 30-day US Treasury Bill."

Provision 24.C.35

The ASSET OWNER MUST disclose if GROSS-OF-FEES, NET-OF-EXTERNAL-COSTS-ONLY, or NET-OF-FEES returns are used to calculate presented risk measures.

Discussion

To help the oversight body interpret the risk measures presented in a GIPS Asset Owner Report, the asset owner must disclosure which returns are used in the calculation of the presented risk measures. This requirement applies to both required risk measures (e.g., the three-year annualized ex post standard deviation) and any additional risk measures. As discussed in Provision 22.B.7, it is recommended that asset owners use gross-of-fees returns when calculating risk measures.

Sample Disclosures:

"Gross-of-fees returns were used to calculate the three-year annualized ex post standard deviation of the composite."

"Gross returns were used to calculate all risk measures presented in this GIPS Asset Owner Report."

"Net-of-external-costs-only returns were used to calculate the three-year annualized ex post standard deviation of the total fund."

Provision 24.C.36

For REAL ESTATE investments that are directly owned, the ASSET OWNER MUST disclose that:[32]

a. EXTERNAL VALUATIONS are obtained and the frequency with which they are obtained; or

b. The ASSET OWNER relies on valuations from financial statement audits.

Discussion

According to Provision 22.A.33, for periods beginning on or after 1 January 2012, real estate investments that are directly owned by the asset owner must:

- have an external valuation at least once every 12 months unless the oversight body stipulates otherwise, in which case real estate investments must have an external valuation at least once every 36 months or per oversight body instructions if the oversight body requires external valuations more frequently than every 36 months; or

- be subject to an annual financial statement audit performed by an independent public accounting firm. The real estate investments must be accounted for at fair value, and the most recent audited financial statements available must contain an unmodified opinion issued by an independent public accounting firm.

Because valuation is such an important issue for real estate investments, asset owners must inform the oversight body whether they externally value real estate investments and, if so, how frequently, or instead place reliance on valuations from audited financial statements. This disclosure is required for periods ending on or after 31 December 2020.

Sample Disclosures:

"Midville Police and Fire Retirement System obtains external valuations for all real estate investments annually."

"ABC Foundation relies on valuations from audited financial statements. The audits are performed by an independent public accounting firm."

---

[32] REQUIRED for periods ending on or after 31 December 2020.

Provision 24.C.37

When the GIPS ASSET OWNER REPORT includes THEORETICAL PERFORMANCE as SUPPLEMENTAL INFORMATION, the ASSET OWNER MUST:

a. Disclose that the results are theoretical, are not based on the performance of actual assets, and if the THEORETICAL PERFORMANCE was derived from the retroactive or prospective application of a model.

b. Disclose a basic description of the methodology and assumptions used to calculate the THEORETICAL PERFORMANCE sufficient for the OVERSIGHT BODY to interpret the THEORETICAL PERFORMANCE, including if it is based on model performance, backtested performance, or hypothetical performance.

c. Disclose whether the THEORETICAL PERFORMANCE reflects the deduction of actual or estimated INVESTMENT MANAGEMENT FEES, INVESTMENT MANAGEMENT COSTS, and TRANSACTION COSTS.

d. Clearly label the THEORETICAL PERFORMANCE as SUPPLEMENTAL INFORMATION.

Discussion

To be presented as supplemental information in a GIPS Asset Owner Report, theoretical performance must relate to the respective total fund or composite. The following are examples of theoretical performance that may be included in a GIPS Asset Owner Report as supplemental information:

- Results created by applying a total fund or composite investment strategy or methodology to historical data, in order to indicate how a strategy constructed with the benefit of hindsight would have performed during a certain period in the past had the strategy been in existence during that period.

- Ex ante performance that is linked to actual total fund or composite performance, or that is calculated using actual total fund or composite performance.

- Results that include the effect of currency hedging that has been applied after the fact to the total fund or composite when the total fund or composite was not originally managed using the currency hedging strategy, and the hedging is not part of the actual total fund or composite returns.

When theoretical performance is included as supplemental information in a GIPS Asset Owner Report, an asset owner is required to include a number of disclosures to ensure that the oversight body understands the nature of the information being presented. Among the required disclosures are the source of the theoretical performance, the methodology and assumptions used to calculate the theoretical performance, and the treatment of fees and costs.

Asset owners must also clearly label the theoretical performance as supplemental information.

Sample Disclosure:

"A return history has been constructed for the period from 1 January 2015 through 31 December 2018 that reflects the application of an investment model used by XYZ Endowment Fund. The results are theoretical and are not based on the performance of actual portfolios. The return history is derived from the retroactive application of a model. Taking the constituents of the large-cap index at each month end, those securities that have an above-average dividend yield and an above-average dividend payout ratio were identified and reweighted by market capitalization. The next-month's performance was then applied to those stock weights to derive a model return for the month. These monthly model returns are then linked to provide annual returns. The theoretical performance presented does not reflect the deduction of investment management fees, transaction costs, or other fees and charges."

24.D. Disclosure—Recommendations

Provision 24.D.1

The ASSET OWNER SHOULD disclose material changes to valuation policies and/or methodologies.

Discussion

Valuation is a critical component of the performance calculation. Therefore, if a change to an asset owner's valuation policies and/or methodologies is material, asset owners should disclose the change in order to enable the oversight body to understand the potential effect of such a change.

Some examples of a material change include, but are not limited to, the following:

- new valuation principles adopted by a local accounting standards board,
- adoption of new international standards in lieu of local standards,
- change of economic criteria used to value investments, and
- change from a discounted cash flow basis to a comparables basis.

 |

Sample Disclosure for a Policy Change:

"Prior to 1 March 2016, illiquid securities were valued internally. Subsequently, illiquid securities are valued using a third-party pricing service."

Sample Disclosure for a Methodology Change:

"For periods prior to 1 August 2019, real estate investments were valued on a discounted cash flow basis. As of 1 August 2019, real estate investments are valued on a comparables basis."

Provision 24.D.2

The ASSET OWNER SHOULD disclose material changes to calculation policies and/or methodologies.

Discussion

Asset owners have discretion to determine which policies and methodologies are used for calculating performance. Although these policies and methodologies must adhere to all applicable calculation requirements, asset owners may choose from a wide variety of policies and methodologies. Asset owners may change calculation policies and/or methodologies; however, asset owners must not change a calculation policy or methodology for the sole purpose of increasing performance. If a change to calculation policies and/or methodologies is material, asset owners should disclose the change in order to enable the oversight body to understand the potential effect of such a change.

Sample Disclosure:

"Effective 1 January 2010, portfolio returns are calculated daily, using a true time-weighted return methodology. Previously, portfolio returns were calculated monthly using the Modified Dietz method."

Provision 24.D.3

The ASSET OWNER SHOULD disclose material differences between the BENCHMARK and the TOTAL FUND's or COMPOSITE's investment mandate, objective, or strategy.

Discussion

Asset owners are required to disclose the total fund or composite description (see Provision 24.C.4) and the benchmark description (see Provision 24.C.5) in a GIPS Asset Owner Report. It is recommended that asset owners also disclose any material differences between the benchmark and the total fund's or composite's investment mandate, objective, or strategy. The oversight body will be better able to evaluate the performance of the strategy relative to the benchmark presented if they understand any material differences between the total fund or composite and the benchmark.

Sample Disclosures:

"The Concentrated Equity Composite invests in only the top 20 stocks (as determined by the Kora's Foundation Investment Committee) of the stocks that are included in its benchmark, the XYZ Index."

"The Absolute Return Composite invests in stocks, both long and short, regardless of country of domicile or market capitalization. The composite benchmark is the 3 Month T-bill rate, which is the hurdle rate, and is composed of materially different investments."

"The Real Estate Composite invests primarily in directly owned properties that are diversified by property type and geographic location. Up to 10% of composite assets may be invested in opportunistic commingled funds. As of 30 June 2020, debt as a percentage of composite assets was 42%. The XYZ Property Index is an unlevered composite measure of the performance of a large pool of individual commercial real estate properties acquired in the private market for investment purposes only. Benchmark returns are calculated on an unleveraged basis."

Provision 24.D.4

The ASSET OWNER SHOULD disclose the key assumptions used to value investments.

Discussion

Asset owners are required to disclose that valuation policies are available upon request. (See Provision 24.C.13.) Because valuation is a critical component of the performance calculation, it is recommended that asset owners also disclose the key assumptions used when valuing portfolio investments. This disclosure will help the oversight body better understand how the asset owner values its different types of investments.

|

Sample Disclosure:

"Investments are valued using recent market quotations. If there is no publicly traded reference, equity investments are valued using a market multiples approach for similar investments in active markets, and fixed-income investments are valued using inputs such as interest rates, yield curve shape, volatility, prepayments, and credit spreads."

Provision 24.D.5

If the ASSET OWNER adheres to any industry valuation guidelines in addition to the GIPS valuation REQUIREMENTS, the ASSET OWNER SHOULD disclose which guidelines have been applied.

Discussion

Some market segments, such as private equity, have developed their own valuation guidelines. For these markets, it is not uncommon for the GIPS standards valuation requirements to be supplemented by other local or international standards that are more stringent in their requirements.

The disclosure of which industry's valuation guidelines have been used in addition to the GIPS standards valuation requirements will demonstrate to the oversight body that the asset owner is adhering to best practices by applying the more prescriptive standards when valuing investments.

Sample Disclosure:

"The Global Diversified Distressed Composite adheres to the XYZ Venture Capital Association's valuation guidelines as well as the GIPS valuation requirements. The XYZ valuation standards are based on fair value but provide more prescriptive advice in terms of how to value specific investments, such as secondary investments and distressed debt investments."

Provision 24.D.6

When using BENCHMARKS that have limitations, such as peer group BENCHMARKS, the ASSET OWNER SHOULD disclose these limitations.

Discussion

Asset owners must determine which benchmark(s) are most appropriate for total fund(s) or composite(s). When determining which benchmarks to present in a GIPS Asset Owner Report, asset owners should be guided by the ethical spirit of the GIPS standards.

Some benchmarks with known limitations are often used for certain types of investments. For example, peer group benchmarks, such as hedge fund peer group universe indices, are often used for hedge funds and other alternative investment strategies. Although peer group benchmarks are frequently used to evaluate hedge funds, there are some common problems with hedge fund peer group benchmarks, including the following:

- self-reporting bias (only some hedge funds choose to report performance data),
- survivorship bias (historical returns of closed hedge funds are removed from the peer group benchmark),
- inability to obtain returns for the same periods as the total fund or composite, and
- lack of investability (some hedge funds within a peer group benchmark are closed to new investors).

When using benchmarks that exhibit limitations, asset owners should describe these limitations in the relevant GIPS Asset Owner Report. This description helps the oversight body understand the nature of the benchmark and be aware of any known drawbacks in comparing the risk and return of the benchmark and the total fund or composite.

Sample Disclosure:

"The benchmark is the Hedge Fund Aggregate Multi-Style Index, which includes more than 100 hedge funds of various styles and strategies. Because this index is based on the data self-reported by the constituent funds, it may have a self-reporting bias. In addition, some funds are closed to new investors and are no longer investable. We believe that no better index exists as a comparison for this composite."

Provision 24.D.7

The ASSET OWNER SHOULD disclose information about the INVESTMENT MANAGEMENT FEES and INVESTMENT MANAGEMENT COSTS of the TOTAL FUND or COMPOSITE that were incurred during the most recent annual period.

Discussion

Investment management fees are the fees payable to external managers for externally managed assets. Investment management fees are typically asset based (percentage of assets), performance based, or a combination of the two but may take different forms as well. Investment management fees also include carried interest.

|

Investment management costs include all internal costs for both internally and externally managed assets. In addition to the costs for portfolio management, they may also involve overhead and other related costs and fees, including data valuation fees, investment research services, custody fees, pro rata share of overhead (such as building and utilities), allocation of non-investment-department expenses (such as human resources, communications, and technology), and performance measurement and compliance services.[L] Investment management fees are not included in investment management costs.

Determining investment fees and costs for an asset owner, particularly investment management costs for internally managed assets, is not a straightforward process. Given the complexity of the costs incurred by an asset owner, it is recommended that the GIPS Asset Owner Report include disclosures about the investment management fees and investment management costs of the total fund or composite that were incurred during the most recent annual period. This information will help the oversight body understand the more recent fees and costs paid for the external and internal management of the total fund or composite assets.

Sample Disclosure:

"Total investment management costs deducted from the net-of-external-costs-only return to arrive at the net return were 0.14% for the fiscal year ended 30 June 2020. These costs include the allocation of internal overhead expenses and data valuation fees."

[L] The definition of INVESTMENT MANAGEMENT COSTS included in the Glossary in the 2020 edition of the GIPS standards is incorrect and should state:

All internal costs for both internally and externally managed assets. In addition to costs for PORTFOLIO management, they may also involve overhead and other related costs and fees, including data valuation fees, investment research services, CUSTODY FEES, pro rata share of overhead (such as building and utilities), allocation of non-investment-department expenses (such as human resources, communications, and technology), and performance measurement and compliance services.

25. ADDITIONAL COMPOSITE MONEY-WEIGHTED RETURN REPORT

The following provisions apply to ASSET OWNERS that calculate and report additional COMPOSITE performance in a GIPS ASSET OWNER REPORT using MONEY-WEIGHTED RETURNS. An additional COMPOSITE is a grouping of PORTFOLIOS representing a particular strategy or asset class that the ASSET OWNER chooses to present in a GIPS ASSET OWNER REPORT.

25.A. Presentation and Reporting—Requirements

Provision 25.A.1

The ASSET OWNER MUST present in each GIPS ASSET OWNER REPORT:

a. The annualized COMPOSITE SINCE-INCEPTION MONEY-WEIGHTED RETURN through the most recent annual period end. If the ASSET OWNER has no records to support this track record, the ASSET OWNER MUST present the ANNUALIZED MONEY-WEIGHTED RETURN for the longest period for which the ASSET OWNER has such records, through the most recent annual period end.

Discussion

To claim compliance, an asset owner is required to meet all applicable requirements of the GIPS standards on an asset owner–wide basis for at least a one-year period, or since inception of the asset owner if the asset owner has been in existence for less than one year.

Although a time-weighted return (TWR) is required for a GIPS Asset Owner Report for a total fund or total fund composite, an asset owner may choose to present either a TWR or money-weighted return (MWR) in a GIPS Asset Owner Report for an additional composite. (An additional composite is a grouping of portfolios representing a particular strategy or asset class that the asset owner chooses to present in a GIPS Asset Owner Report.) If an asset owner chooses to present an MWR for an additional composite, the asset owner must present the annualized composite since-inception MWR (SI-MWR) through the most recent annual period end.

For example, assume that an asset owner presents returns on a calendar-year-end basis. If a composite has an inception date of 1 March 2015 and the most recent annual period end is

31 December 2019, the asset owner must present an annualized composite SI-MWR from 1 March 2015 through 31 December 2019. Although only the annualized composite SI-MWR through the most recent annual period end is required, it is recommended that asset owners present annualized composite SI-MWRs through each annual period end. (See Provision 25.B.1.) In this example, doing so would mean presenting SI-MWRs from 1 March 2015 through 31 December 2015, 1 March 2015 through 31 December 2016, 1 March 2015 through 31 December 2017, and 1 March 2015 through 31 December 2018, in addition to the required return from 1 March 2015 through 31 December 2019. The SI-MWR from 1 March 2015 through 31 December 2015 must not be annualized because the return is for a period of less than one year.

Many asset owners, however, have very long histories, and some of the earlier records may not be sufficient to support the entire track record of the additional composite. If the asset owner does not have the records to support the track record from the composite's inception through the most recent annual period end, the asset owner must present the annualized MWR for the longest uninterrupted period for which the asset owner has such records, through the most recent annual period end.

Asset owners must clearly label the periods for which MWRs are presented. Asset owners must select the annual period end for which MWRs will be presented on a composite-specific basis and apply it consistently. For purposes of comparability, best practice would be for an asset owner to report composite MWRs for periods ending on 31 December.

Additional composite returns may be presented either gross-of-fees, net-of-fees, or net-of-external-costs-only. Asset owners may also choose to present more than one type of return in a GIPS Asset Owner Report.

Provision 25.A.1

The ASSET OWNER MUST present in each GIPS ASSET OWNER REPORT:

b. When the COMPOSITE has a track record that is less than a full year, the non-annualized COMPOSITE SINCE-INCEPTION MONEY-WEIGHTED RETURN or the COMPOSITE non-annualized MONEY-WEIGHTED RETURN for the longest period for which the ASSET OWNER has records through the initial annual period end.

Discussion

If the additional composite has a track record of less than a full year, the asset owner must present the non-annualized composite since-inception money-weighted return (SI-MWR) or the composite non-annualized MWR for the longest period for which the asset owner has records through the initial annual period end. (An additional composite is a grouping of portfolios representing a particular strategy or asset class that the asset owner chooses to present in a GIPS Asset Owner Report.) Subsequently, the asset owner must extend the measurement period for the MWR to include the next annual period and calculate an annualized MWR through the most recent annual period end.

MWRs for periods of less than a full year must not be annualized. As an example, a composite that began on 1 December 2020 and has a one-month initial return through 31 December 2020 of 3% (which equates to an annualized return of 42.6%) would be required to present that 3% as the partial year's performance. The annualized return of 42.6% must not be presented. Some spreadsheet and software applications automatically annualize all returns, and asset owners are reminded that for periods of less than a year, the asset owner must "de-annualize" any annualized returns that are calculated.

The method chosen to de-annualize a return is at the discretion of the asset owner, but it must be a geometric calculation. In the situation just presented, the 42.6% annualized return could be de-annualized by one of the following formulas:

$$\left\{ \left[(1+0.426)^{\left(\frac{1}{12}\right)} \right] -1 \right\} \times 100 = 3\% \quad \text{or} \quad \left\{ \left[(1+0.426)^{\left(\frac{31}{365}\right)} \right] -1 \right\} \times 100 = 3\%,$$

both resulting in a non-annualized one-month return of 3%.

Provision 25.A.1

The ASSET OWNER MUST present in each GIPS ASSET OWNER REPORT:

c. When the COMPOSITE terminates, the annualized COMPOSITE SINCE-INCEPTION MONEY-WEIGHTED RETURN through the COMPOSITE TERMINATION DATE or the COMPOSITE annualized MONEY-WEIGHTED RETURN for the longest period for which the ASSET OWNER has records through the COMPOSITE TERMINATION DATE.

Discussion

When an additional composite terminates, the asset owner must present the annualized composite since-inception money-weighted return (SI-MWR) through the composite termination date. (An additional composite is a grouping of portfolios representing a particular strategy or asset class that the asset owner chooses to present in a GIPS Asset Owner Report.) For example, if a composite has an inception date of 1 July 2012 and terminates on 31 August 2019, the GIPS Asset Owner Report for this composite must include a composite SI-MWR for the period from 1 July 2012 through 31 August 2019.

|

If the asset owner does not have the records to support the track record from the composite's inception through the composite's termination date, the asset owner must present the annualized MWR for the longest period for which the asset owner has such records, through the composite termination date.

Provision 25.A.1

The ASSET OWNER MUST present in each GIPS ASSET OWNER REPORT:

d. The MONEY-WEIGHTED RETURN for the BENCHMARK for the same periods as presented for the COMPOSITE, unless the ASSET OWNER determines there is no appropriate BENCHMARK.

Discussion

Benchmarks are important tools that aid in the planning, implementation, and evaluation of a composite's investment policy. They also help facilitate discussions with the oversight body regarding the relationship between risk and return. As a result, asset owners are required to present the money-weighted return (MWR) for the benchmark for the same periods as presented for the additional composite, unless the asset owner determines there is no appropriate benchmark. (An additional composite is a grouping of portfolios representing a particular strategy or asset class that the asset owner chooses to present in a GIPS Asset Owner Report.)

The benchmark presented must be one that reflects the composite's investment mandate, objective, or strategy. An asset owner may choose to present more than one benchmark in a GIPS Asset Owner Report but must include all required information for all benchmarks presented in the GIPS Asset Owner Report.

Because the benchmark selected for a composite must be appropriate for comparison with the performance of the composite, an asset owner must not compare a time-weighted return (TWR) benchmark with a composite's MWR. Public market indices by themselves are not directly comparable to an MWR because the market indices typically use TWRs. The public market equivalent (PME) is a method in which a public market index is used to create a comparable MWR from a series of cash flows that replicate those of the composite and that can be compared with the composite's MWR. When the asset owner uses a PME, the market index used must be a total return benchmark.

See Provision 21.A.15 for a discussion of total return benchmarks. See the discussion of Provision 25.C.28 for additional information regarding a PME.

> ## Provision 25.A.1
>
> The ASSET OWNER MUST present in each GIPS ASSET OWNER REPORT:
>
> e. The number of PORTFOLIOS in the COMPOSITE as of the most recent annual period end.[33]

Discussion

For periods ending on or after 31 December 2020, each GIPS Asset Owner Report for an additional composite must present the number of portfolios included in the composite as of the most recent annual period end. (An additional composite is a grouping of portfolios representing a particular strategy or asset class that the asset owner chooses to present in a GIPS Asset Owner Report.) This requirement provides information to the oversight body on the size of the composite, measured by the number of portfolios in the composite. For example, if there were four portfolios in the composite for the full period but eight portfolios in the composite at the most recent annual period end, the asset owner would present eight, the actual number of portfolios in the composite at the most recent annual period end.

For periods ending prior to 31 December 2020, if the composite contains five or fewer portfolios as of the most recent annual period end, the number of portfolios in the composite is not required to be presented, although the asset owner may choose to present this information.

> ## Provision 25.A.1
>
> The ASSET OWNER MUST present in each GIPS ASSET OWNER REPORT:
>
> f. COMPOSITE assets as of the most recent annual period end.

Discussion

Each GIPS Asset Owner Report must include the amount of composite assets as of the most recent annual period end. This requirement provides information to the oversight body on the size of the composite, measured by the amount of assets it contains. When the composite strategy uses leverage, composite assets must be presented net of the leverage and not grossed up as if the leverage did not exist. For example, if a composite has $200 million in net assets, and $50 million of those assets have been borrowed by an external manager, the composite's

---

[33] REQUIRED for periods ending on or after 31 December 2020. For periods ending prior to 31 December 2020, if the COMPOSITE contains five or fewer PORTFOLIOS at period end, the number of PORTFOLIOS is not REQUIRED.

 |

gross assets are $250 million. When calculating composite assets, the asset owner must use $200 million. If the composite uses leverage, the asset owner should also present to the oversight body assets that are grossed up as if the leverage did not exist.

Provision 25.A.1

The ASSET OWNER MUST present in each GIPS ASSET OWNER REPORT:

g. TOTAL ASSET OWNER ASSETS as of the most recent annual period end.[34]

Discussion

For periods ending on or after 31 December 2020, the asset owner must present total asset owner assets as of the most recent annual period end. For periods ending prior to this date, the asset owner must present either total asset owner assets or composite assets as a percentage of total asset owner assets. Leverage must be deducted when calculating total asset owner assets. For example, if a composite has $200 million in net assets, and $50 million of those assets have been borrowed by an external manager, the composite's gross assets are $250 million. The asset owner must use $200 million when calculating total asset owner assets, not $250 million. The inclusion of both composite assets and total asset owner assets in a GIPS Asset Owner Report will help the oversight body understand the composite size in relation to total asset owner assets. If any total funds or composites use leverage, the asset owner should also present to the oversight body assets that are grossed up as if the leverage did not exist.

Both discretionary and non-discretionary portfolios are included in total asset owner assets. Total asset owner assets include assets assigned to an external manager provided the asset owner has discretion over the selection of the external manager. Operating cash accounts that are not available for investment should not be included in total asset owner assets.

Asset owners must be sure that assets are not double-counted, because double-counting assets would not fairly represent the asset owner's assets.

See the discussion of Provision 22.A.1 for additional guidance on the calculation of total asset owner assets and Provision 22.A.8 for additional guidance on the treatment of cash and cash equivalents.

---

[34]REQUIRED for periods ending on or after 31 December 2020. For periods ending prior to 31 December 2020, ASSET OWNERS may present either TOTAL ASSET OWNER ASSETS or COMPOSITE assets as a percentage of TOTAL ASSET OWNER ASSETS.

Provision 25.A.2

The ASSET OWNER MUST present the percentage of the total FAIR VALUE of COMPOSITE assets that were valued using subjective unobservable inputs (as described in provision 22.B.6) as of the most recent annual period end, if such investments represent a material amount of COMPOSITE assets.

Discussion

Markets are not always liquid, and investment prices are not always objective and/or observable. As the last level of the recommended valuation hierarchy indicates (see Provision 22.B.6), it may be necessary for an asset owner to use subjective unobservable inputs to value an investment for which markets are not active on the measurement date. Examples of subjective unobservable inputs include an assumed discount rate, an assumed occupancy rate for a commercial building, and the default rate used for the valuation of a security in default. Examples related to insurance-linked securities include assumptions regarding hurricane damage and mortality rates. Unobservable inputs should be used to measure fair value only when observable inputs and prices are not available or appropriate. Unobservable inputs reflect the asset owner's own assumptions about the assumptions that market participants would use in pricing the investment and should be developed based on the best information available under the circumstances.

Asset owners must present the percentage of the total fair value of composite assets that were valued using subjective unobservable inputs as of the most recent annual period end, if such investments represent a material amount of composite assets. The amount of composite assets valued using subjective unobservable inputs would be considered material if it would likely influence a reader's judgment regarding the reliability of the valuation. The asset owner must decide on the criteria it will use to determine when subjective unobservable inputs represent a material amount of composite assets, include these criteria in its policy and procedures, and apply these criteria consistently.

Sample Disclosure:

"As of 31 December 2020, 29% of composite assets were valued using subjective, unobservable inputs. These inputs are not supported by market activity and instead are based on internal proprietary pricing models."

Provision 25.A.3

For COMPOSITES where the underlying PORTFOLIOS have COMMITTED CAPITAL, the ASSET OWNER MUST present the following items as of the most recent annual period end:

a. COMPOSITE SINCE-INCEPTION PAID-IN CAPITAL.

b. COMPOSITE SINCE-INCEPTION DISTRIBUTIONS.

c. COMPOSITE cumulative COMMITTED CAPITAL.

d. TOTAL VALUE TO SINCE-INCEPTION PAID-IN CAPITAL (INVESTMENT MULTIPLE or TVPI).

e. SINCE-INCEPTION DISTRIBUTIONS to SINCE-INCEPTION PAID-IN CAPITAL (REALIZATION MULTIPLE or DPI).

f. SINCE-INCEPTION PAID-IN CAPITAL to cumulative COMMITTED CAPITAL (PIC MULTIPLE).

g. RESIDUAL VALUE to SINCE-INCEPTION PAID-IN CAPITAL (UNREALIZED MULTIPLE or RVPI).

Discussion

Although the money-weighted return (MWR) is the basic metric used to report performance for composites for which the asset owner has chosen to present MWRs, it is not the only useful metric used to gauge performance. Other measures are also useful to provide additional insight. The MWR by its nature is sensitive to early cash flow events, and the MWR calculation assumes that the residual value, or fair value, of a composite is totally liquid. In reality, however, the residual value may be illiquid. Other metrics have been developed that allow the oversight body to examine aspects of performance other than simply a rate of return.

a. COMPOSITE SINCE-INCEPTION PAID-IN CAPITAL.

The composite since-inception paid-in capital consists of all capital flows to an external manager or externally managed pooled fund. These capital flows are also referred to as contributions to external managers or pooled funds by the asset owner. Paid-in capital also includes distributions to the asset owner that are subsequently recalled by external managers or pooled funds.

b. COMPOSITE SINCE-INCEPTION DISTRIBUTIONS.

The composite since-inception distributions include all cash and stock distributed from external managers or pooled funds to the asset owner. Distributions include both recallable and non-recallable distributions.

c. COMPOSITE CUMULATIVE COMMITTED CAPITAL.

The composite cumulative committed capital represents the total pledges of capital to external managers or pooled funds by the asset owner. Committed capital can be either drawn (paid-in) or undrawn (dry powder).

d. TOTAL VALUE TO SINCE-INCEPTION PAID-IN CAPITAL (INVESTMENT MULTIPLE or TVPI).

The investment multiple, or TVPI, provides the oversight body with a multiple that indicates how many times more the investment is worth compared with the original investment without taking into account the time value of money. Also known as the Multiple of Investment Capital (MOIC), it is equal to the sum of the composite since-inception distributions and its residual value (i.e., fair value) divided by the composite since-inception paid-in capital. The investment multiple is calculated as follows:

$$TVPI = \frac{Since-Inception\ Distributions + Residual\ Value}{Since-Inception\ Paid-In\ Capital}$$

TVPI can also be calculated as DPI + RVPI, where: -

DPI = realization multiple (see Provision 25.A.3.e)

RVPI = unrealized multiple (see Provision 25.A.3.g)

e. SINCE-INCEPTION DISTRIBUTIONS to SINCE-INCEPTION PAID-IN CAPITAL (REALIZATION MULTIPLE or DPI).

The DPI, or realization multiple, measures how much invested capital has actually been returned to the asset owner. It is the amount of invested capital that has been "realized" by the asset owner and is often viewed as the amount of the TVPI that is "realized." TVPI, also known as the investment multiple, is calculated as total value divided by since-inception paid-in capital (see Provision 25.A.3.d). DPI is calculated as follows:

$$DPI = \frac{Since-Inception\ Distributions}{Since-Inception\ Paid-In\ Capital}$$

f. SINCE-INCEPTION PAID-IN CAPITAL to cumulative COMMITTED CAPITAL (PIC MULTIPLE).

The paid-in capital multiple, also known as the PIC multiple or PIC ratio, gives the oversight body information regarding how much committed capital has actually been drawn down or called. It is also known as the "dry-powder ratio" because it measures how much capital has already been invested and therefore indicates how much capital is left to invest. The PIC multiple is calculated as follows:

$$PIC = \frac{Since-Inception\ Paid-In\ Capital}{Cumulative\ Committed\ Capital}$$

 |

Distributions can be either recallable or non-recallable. If a distribution is recallable, after the external manager or pooled fund distributes proceeds to the asset owner, it can draw down the same capital again, which makes it possible for the composite to draw capital in excess of its total committed capital. A recallable distribution must be treated as an actual distribution and, if and when that distribution is recalled (drawn again), it must be treated as additional paid-in capital.

Recallable distributions affect the performance metric calculations. Asset owners may wish to consider additional disclosure when there is a material effect on the PIC or realization multiples. If a recallable distribution is re-contributed and reflected as paid-in capital a second time, the result will be that cumulative paid-in capital since inception is higher than total committed capital. It also means that the realization multiple (DPI), unrealized multiple (RVPI), and investment multiple (TVPI) will be lower. (For more information on DPI, RVPI, and TVPI, please see Provisions 25.A.3.e, 25.A.3.g, and 25.A.3.d, respectively.) All else being equal, for composites that have had recallable distributions, the denominator will be increased, and the PIC multiple will be higher.

g. RESIDUAL VALUE to SINCE-INCEPTION PAID-IN-CAPITAL (UNREALIZED MULTIPLE or RVPI).

The unrealized multiple, or RVPI, is the converse of the realization multiple. It is equal to the composite's residual value (or fair value) at the end of the period divided by since-inception paid-in capital, and is calculated as follows:

$$RVPI = \frac{Residual\ Value}{Since-Inception\ Paid-In\ Capital}$$

Provision 25.A.4

The ASSET OWNER MUST clearly label or identify:

a. The periods that are presented.

b. If returns presented are GROSS-OF-FEES, NET-OF-EXTERNAL-COSTS-ONLY, or NET-OF-FEES.

Discussion

All periods presented in a GIPS Asset Owner Report must be clearly labeled or identified.

Asset owners may present either gross-of-fees returns, net-of-external-costs-only returns, or net-of-fees returns in a GIPS Asset Owner Report for an additional composite and may also choose to present more than one type of return. (An additional composite is a grouping of portfolios representing a particular strategy or asset class that the asset owner chooses to present in a GIPS Asset

Owner Report.) For the oversight body to understand the nature of the returns being presented, all returns presented must be clearly labeled or identified as gross-of-fees, net-of-external costs-only, or net-of-fees.

Provision 25.A.5

If the ASSET OWNER presents FULL GROSS-OF-FEES RETURNS, the ASSET OWNER MUST identify them as SUPPLEMENTAL INFORMATION.

Discussion

A full gross-of-fees return is the return on investments that reflects the deduction of only transaction costs. It does not reflect the deduction of investment management fees paid for any externally managed segregated accounts or the fees and expenses for any externally managed pooled funds. Because it would not be possible to invest in these externally managed assets without paying these fees and costs, full-gross-of-fees returns must be identified as supplemental information if they are included in a GIPS Asset Owner Report.

Supplemental information is any performance-related information included as part of a GIPS Asset Owner Report that supplements or enhances the requirements and/or recommendations of the GIPS standards. Supplemental information must relate directly to the composite presented in the GIPS Asset Owner Report. See Provision 25.A.8 for additional guidance on supplemental information.

Provision 25.A.6

If the ASSET OWNER includes more than one BENCHMARK in the GIPS ASSET OWNER REPORT, the ASSET OWNER MUST present and disclose all REQUIRED information for all BENCHMARKS presented.

Discussion

It is permissible to include more than one benchmark in a GIPS Asset Owner Report. All benchmarks included in a GIPS Asset Owner Report must adhere to the requirements of the GIPS standards that are applicable to benchmarks. Asset owners may label benchmarks as primary and secondary benchmarks, but the same requirements and recommendations apply to all

 |

benchmarks included in a GIPS Asset Owner Report. For example, a GIPS Asset Owner Report must include:

- a description for all benchmarks, and
- a disclosure of changes to (or deletion of) any benchmark.

If the asset owner designates benchmarks as primary and secondary benchmarks, it must disclose when these designations change (e.g., if a primary benchmark becomes a secondary benchmark), because such a change in designation is considered a benchmark change. In all instances, if multiple benchmarks are presented in a GIPS Asset Owner Report and one or more of the benchmarks is removed from the GIPS Asset Owner Report, the asset owner must disclose this fact. (See Provision 25.C.26.)

An appropriate benchmark for a composite reflects the investment mandate, objective, or strategy of the composite. Additional benchmarks beyond appropriate benchmarks may be presented in a GIPS Asset Owner Report as supplemental information. For example, an asset owner may choose to present a time-weighted return benchmark in a GIPS Asset Owner Report along with an appropriate money-weighted return benchmark. There must be sufficient disclosure so that the oversight body understands the nature of the benchmark and why it is being presented. Disclosure, however, does not necessarily prevent information from being false or misleading. An additional benchmark must never be presented for the sole purpose of providing a favorable comparison to the performance of the composite. To do so would be misleading, regardless of the disclosures accompanying the benchmark.

Provision 25.A.7

All REQUIRED and RECOMMENDED information in the GIPS ASSET OWNER REPORT MUST be presented in the same currency.

Discussion

Asset owners must present all required and recommended information in a GIPS Asset Owner Report in the same currency (e.g., composite and benchmark returns, composite assets, and total asset owner assets). Supplemental information should also be presented in the same currency. If it is not, that fact must be disclosed. Not disclosing this fact could be misleading.

If an asset owner chooses to present a composite in a different currency, the asset owner must convert all of the required information into the new currency. It is not permissible to do so by applying the exchange rate as of the current period end to historical data.

If the asset owner chooses to present performance in multiple currencies in the same GIPS Asset Owner Report, the asset owner must convert all of the required information into each of the currencies and ensure it is clear in which currencies performance is reported. The asset owner must also convert any recommended information it chooses to present in the GIPS Asset Owner Report containing the converted information.

In cases where a composite contains portfolios with different currencies, the asset owner must convert the individual portfolio cash flows and valuations to a single currency in order to calculate a composite return. It is not permissible to do so by applying the exchange rate as of the current period end to historical data.

It is up to the asset owner to determine the composite-specific conversion method. Policies and procedures for converting returns must be established, documented, and applied consistently.

Provision 25.A.8

Any SUPPLEMENTAL INFORMATION included in the GIPS ASSET OWNER REPORT:

a. MUST relate directly to the COMPOSITE.

b. MUST NOT contradict or conflict with the REQUIRED or RECOMMENDED information in the GIPS ASSET OWNER REPORT.

c. MUST be clearly labeled as SUPPLEMENTAL INFORMATION.

Discussion

Supplemental information is any performance-related information included as part of a GIPS Asset Owner Report that supplements or enhances the requirements and/or recommendations of the GIPS standards. Performance-related information includes:

- information expressed in terms of investment return and risk, and
- other information and input data that directly relate to the calculation of investment return and risk (e.g., composite holdings), as well as information derived from investment return and risk input data (e.g., performance contribution or attribution).

Supplemental information should provide users of the GIPS Asset Owner Report with the proper context in which to understand the performance results. Common examples of supplemental information for a GIPS Asset Owner Report that presents money-weighted returns (MWRs) include the following:

- projected investment-level MWRs,
- projected multiples,
- benchmark time-weighted returns, and
- a full gross-of-fees return.

Supplemental information must relate directly to the composite and must not contradict or conflict with the required or recommended information in the GIPS Asset Owner Report. Examples of information that relates directly to the composite and would be considered supplemental information include segment returns (e.g., country or sector), performance attribution, and composite or portfolio-level holdings. An example of information that would conflict with the GIPS standards is the use of a price-only benchmark when a total return benchmark is not presented.

The following is a more complete list of the principles that apply when supplemental information is presented. Supplemental information must:

- satisfy the spirit and principles of the GIPS standards—fair representation and full disclosure,
- comply with all applicable laws and regulations regarding the calculation and presentation of performance,
- not include performance or performance-related information that is false or misleading,
- relate directly to the composite and supplement or enhance the required or recommended information included in the GIPS Asset Owner Report,
- not contradict or conflict with the required or recommended information in the GIPS Asset Owner Report,
- be clearly labeled as supplemental information, and
- not be shown with greater prominence than the required composite information.

25.B. Presentation and Reporting—Recommendations

Provision 25.B.1

The ASSET OWNER SHOULD present SINCE-INCEPTION MONEY-WEIGHTED RETURNS as of each annual period end.

Discussion

Although an asset owner is required to present only the annualized composite since-inception money-weighed return (SI-MWR) through the most recent annual period end, it is recommended that the asset owner also present SI-MWRs as of each annual period end. When the asset owner does not have records to support the track record from the composite's inception, it is required to present the MWR for the longest period for which the asset owner has such records (see Provision 25.A.1.a). In addition, it is recommended that the asset owner present the annualized composite MWR for the longest period for which the asset owner has such records as of each annual period end. Doing so will provide the oversight body with a more complete picture of the performance of the composite over time.

Provision 25.B.2

For COMPOSITES where the underlying PORTFOLIOS have COMMITTED CAPITAL, the ASSET OWNER SHOULD present the following items as of each annual period end:

a. COMPOSITE SINCE-INCEPTION PAID-IN CAPITAL.

b. COMPOSITE SINCE-INCEPTION DISTRIBUTIONS.

c. COMPOSITE cumulative COMMITTED CAPITAL.

d. TOTAL VALUE TO SINCE-INCEPTION PAID-IN CAPITAL (INVESTMENT MULTIPLE or TVPI).

e. SINCE-INCEPTION DISTRIBUTIONS TO SINCE-INCEPTION PAID-IN CAPITAL (REALIZATION MULTIPLE or DPI).

f. SINCE-INCEPTION PAID-IN CAPITAL to cumulative COMMITTED CAPITAL (PIC MULTIPLE).

g. RESIDUAL VALUE TO SINCE-INCEPTION PAID-IN CAPITAL (UNREALIZED MULTIPLE or RVPI).

Discussion

Asset owners are required to present the composite since-inception money-weighted return (SI-MWR), or the MWR for the longest period for which for which the asset owner has records to support the track record of the composite (see Provision 25.A.1.a), through the most recent annual period end, as well as the since-inception paid-in capital, since-inception distributions, cumulative committed capital, investment multiple (TVPI), realization multiple (DPI), PIC multiple, and unrealized multiple (RVPI), as of the most recent annual period end. If asset owners choose to present additional SI-MWRs through prior annual period ends, asset owners are recommended to also present the same metrics as of each additional period end for which returns are presented. See Provision 25.A.3 for further discussion of these metrics.

Provision 25.B.3

The ASSET OWNER SHOULD present GROSS-OF-FEES, NET-OF-EXTERNAL-COSTS-ONLY, and NET-OF-FEES COMPOSITE returns.

 |

Discussion

For additional composites, an asset owner may choose to present either gross-of-fees, net-of-external-costs-only, or net-of-fees composite returns in a GIPS Asset Owner Report. The asset owner may also choose to present more than one type of return. (An additional composite is a grouping of portfolios representing a particular strategy or asset class that the asset owner chooses to present in a GIPS Asset Owner Report.) Each type of return provides important information to the oversight body.

A composite gross-of-fees return is the return on investments reduced by transaction costs and all fees and expenses for externally managed pooled funds. This return gives the clearest indication of the "investment return" for the assets included in the composite.

A composite net-of-external-costs-only return is the gross-of-fees return reduced by investment management fees for externally managed segregated accounts. It, therefore, is the best indication of the returns received over time, after taking into account the effect of external management fees.

A composite net-of-fees return is the return that reflects the deduction of transaction costs, all fees and expenses for externally managed pooled funds, investment management fees for externally managed segregated accounts, and investment management costs. Net-of-fees returns therefore provide the best indication to the oversight body of the returns received over time, after taking into account the effect of all internal and external investment management fees and costs. Please see the discussion of the calculation of net-of-fees, net-of-external-costs-only, and gross-of-fees returns in Provision 22.A.24.

Because gross-of-fees, net-of-external-costs-only, and net-of-fees returns all provide important information to the oversight body, it is recommended that asset owners present all three types of returns in a GIPS Asset Owner Report for an additional composite. Presenting more than one type of return in a GIPS Asset Owner Report can provide the oversight body with insight on the relative sizes of the fees and costs associated with externally managed pooled funds and segregated accounts, as well as internally managed assets.

Provision 25.B.4

The ASSET OWNER SHOULD present an appropriate EX POST risk measure for the COMPOSITE and the BENCHMARK. The same EX POST risk measure SHOULD be presented for the COMPOSITE and the BENCHMARK.

Discussion

Evaluating past performance requires an understanding of the risks taken to achieve the results. Although asset owners are required to include a qualitative narrative of material risks as part of the composite description, asset owners should also include an ex post risk measure for the composite and benchmark. Any risk measure presented must be calculated on an ex post basis and be based on actual historical data. Some examples of ex post risk measures that may be presented include drawdown measures, interest rate risk measures (e.g., duration), credit risk measures (e.g., credit spread), and liquidity risk measures. Because no quantitative risk measure is required for composites that present money-weighted returns, all risk measures presented are considered additional risk measures.

If the asset owner chooses to present an ex post risk measure for the composite and benchmark, the same ex post risk measure should be presented for the composite and benchmark. The risk measure must be one that the asset owner determines is appropriate for the composite. When choosing an appropriate ex post risk measure to present, the asset owner should satisfy itself that there are sufficient data points for the selected risk measure to be statistically significant so as not to be misleading. Asset owners are required to describe any additional risk measure that is included in the GIPS Asset Owner Report (see Provision 25.C.33).

Provision 25.B.5

If the ASSET OWNER uses preliminary, estimated values as FAIR VALUE, the ASSET OWNER SHOULD present the percentage of assets in the COMPOSITE that were valued using preliminary, estimated values as of the most recent annual period end.

Discussion

The use of preliminary, estimated values as fair value is common for some alternative strategies, including those that invest in externally managed pooled funds for which the asset owner relies on valuations provided by the fund external managers. When using preliminary, estimated values as fair value, it is important to remember the underlying principles of the GIPS standards: fair representation and full disclosure. If using preliminary, estimated values, asset owners must disclose this fact in the relevant GIPS Asset Owner Report (see Provision 25.C.31). It is recommended that the asset owner also present the percentage of assets in the composite that were valued using preliminary, estimated values as of the most recent annual period end. Doing so provides important information that allows the oversight body to better assess the valuations and performance record presented.

 |

25.C. Disclosure—Requirements

Provision 25.C.1

Once the ASSET OWNER has met all the applicable REQUIREMENTS of the GIPS standards, the ASSET OWNER MUST disclose its compliance with the GIPS standards using one of the following compliance statements. The compliance statement for a COMPOSITE MUST only be used in a GIPS ASSET OWNER REPORT.

a. For an ASSET OWNER that is verified:

"[Insert name of ASSET OWNER] claims compliance with the Global Investment Performance Standards (GIPS®) and has prepared and presented this report in compliance with the GIPS standards. [Insert name of ASSET OWNER] has been independently verified for the periods [insert dates]. The verification report(s) is/are available upon request.

"An asset owner that claims compliance with the GIPS standards must establish policies and procedures for complying with all the applicable requirements of the GIPS standards. Verification provides assurance on whether the asset owner's policies and procedures related to total fund and composite maintenance, as well as the calculation, presentation, and distribution of performance, have been designed in compliance with the GIPS standards and have been implemented on an asset owner–wide basis. Verification does not provide assurance on the accuracy of any specific performance report."

b. For COMPOSITES of a verified ASSET OWNER that have also had a PERFORMANCE EXAMINATION:

"[Insert name of ASSET OWNER] claims compliance with the Global Investment Performance Standards (GIPS®) and has prepared and presented this report in compliance with the GIPS standards. [Insert name of ASSET OWNER] has been independently verified for the periods [insert dates].

"An asset owner that claims compliance with the GIPS standards must establish policies and procedures for complying with all the applicable requirements of the GIPS standards. Verification provides assurance on whether the asset owner's policies and procedures related to total fund and composite maintenance, as well as the calculation, presentation, and distribution of performance, have been designed in compliance with the GIPS standards and have been implemented on an asset owner–wide basis. The [insert name of COMPOSITE] has had a performance examination for the periods [insert dates]. The verification and performance examination reports are available upon request."

The compliance statement for an ASSET OWNER that is verified, or for TOTAL FUNDS or COMPOSITES of a verified ASSET OWNER that have also had a PERFORMANCE EXAMINATION, is complete only when both paragraphs are shown together, one after the other.

c.   For an ASSET OWNER that has not been verified:

"[Insert name of ASSET OWNER] claims compliance with the Global Investment Performance Standards (GIPS®) and has prepared and presented this report in compliance with the GIPS standards. [Insert name of ASSET OWNER] has not been independently verified."

The ASSET OWNER MUST NOT exclude any portion of the respective compliance statement. Any modifications to the compliance statement MUST be additive.

Discussion

An asset owner meeting all the requirements of the GIPS standards must use one of the three compliance statements in each of its GIPS Asset Owner Reports. The English version of the compliance statements is the controlling version. If an asset owner chooses to translate the compliance statement into a language for which there is no official translation of the GIPS standards, the asset owner must take care to ensure that the translation used reflects the required wording of the compliance statement used in Provision 25.C.1.a, 25.C.1.b, or 25.C.1.c.

It is acceptable to combine both paragraphs of the compliance statement for a verified asset owner (Provision 25.C.1.a) into a single paragraph. If the paragraphs are not combined, the compliance statement for a verified asset owner is complete only when both paragraphs are shown together, one after the other. An asset owner may not separate the two required paragraphs from each other.

The same is true for the compliance statement for a composite that has also had a performance examination (Provision 25.C.1.b). Both paragraphs of the compliance statement may be combined into a single paragraph. If the paragraphs are not combined, the compliance statement is complete only when both paragraphs are shown together, one after the other. An asset owner may not separate the two required paragraphs from each other.

When preparing the GIPS Asset Owner Report for a composite that has had a performance examination, the asset owner may choose to use either the verification or performance examination compliance statement. For example, an asset owner might choose to use the verification compliance statement for all GIPS Asset Owner Reports, including GIPS Asset Owner Reports for composites that have had a performance examination, if it wishes to standardize the compliance statement for all GIPS Asset Owner Reports throughout the asset owner. In this situation, the asset owner may also disclose that a specific composite has had a performance examination.

The language in each compliance statement must not exclude any portion of the respective compliance statement. There may also be instances where it may be appropriate for an asset owner to modify the language slightly. For example, an asset owner may modify the language to include the name of the asset owner's verifier, if the asset owner wishes to disclose this information. An asset owner may also need to modify the language to add more details about the name of the asset owner that has been verified or the dates of the verification if the verification period was not continuous. Any modifications must be additive and must not result in a compliance statement that is false or misleading.

Provision 25.C.2

The ASSET OWNER MUST disclose the following: "GIPS® is a registered trademark of CFA Institute. CFA Institute does not endorse or promote this organization, nor does it warrant the accuracy or quality of the content contained herein."

Discussion

"GIPS®" is a registered trademark of CFA Institute, and asset owners are required to acknowledge this fact in all GIPS Asset Owner Reports. The required disclosure may appear in the body of the GIPS Asset Owner Report or in a footnote to the report. The term "this organization," which is included in the required disclosure, refers to any entity associated with the GIPS Asset Owner Report, either the asset owner or the verifier.

CFA Institute (owner of the GIPS® trademark) may take appropriate action against any asset owner that misuses the mark "GIPS®" or any compliance statement, including false claims of compliance with the GIPS standards. CFA Institute members, CFA Program charterholders, CFA candidates, CIPM Program certificants, and CIPM candidates who misuse the term "GIPS" or any compliance statement, misrepresent their performance history or the performance history of the asset owner, or falsely claim compliance with the GIPS standards are also subject to disciplinary sanctions under the CFA Institute Code of Ethics and Standards of Professional Conduct. Possible disciplinary sanctions include public censure, suspension of membership, and revocation of the CFA charter or CIPM certificate.

Regulators with jurisdiction over asset owners claiming compliance with the GIPS standards may also take enforcement actions against asset owners that falsely claim compliance with the GIPS standards.

Asset owners may also use the following language to replace the first sentence in this required disclosure: "GIPS® is a registered trademark owned by CFA Institute."

See the GIPS Standards Trademark Usage Guidelines on the CFA Institute website (www.cfainstitute.org) for additional guidance on the proper use of "GIPS".

Provision 25.C.3

The ASSET OWNER MUST disclose the definition of the ASSET OWNER used to determine TOTAL ASSET OWNER ASSETS and ASSET OWNER–wide compliance.

Discussion

To claim compliance with the GIPS standards, an asset owner must comply with all applicable requirements of the GIPS standards on an asset owner–wide basis. Accordingly, the asset owner must determine exactly how it will be defined for the purpose of compliance. The GIPS standards require that an asset owner be defined as the entity that manages investments, directly and/or through the use of external managers, on behalf of participants, beneficiaries, or the organization itself. These entities include, but are not limited to, public and private pension funds, endowments, foundations, family offices, provident funds, insurers and reinsurers, sovereign wealth funds, and fiduciaries. Asset owners must have discretion over total asset owner assets, either by managing assets directly or by having the discretion to hire and fire external managers. For a public pension fund, the asset owner is generally defined by legislation. In the case of foundations, endowments, or family offices, the asset owner is the entity established by the governing body to manage the pool of assets.

In some situations, an organization may act as both an asset owner, where investment authority and ownership are vested with the organization itself, as well as a firm (asset manager) that competes for assets whose vesting lies with external clients. In such cases, the asset owner has two choices in how to define itself for the purpose of complying with the GIPS standards.

- The asset owner bifurcates its assets into two entities: one defined as an asset owner and one defined as a firm.
- The asset owner does not bifurcate its assets and instead defines itself as both an asset owner and a firm. When calculating and presenting performance to its oversight body, the asset owner follows the GIPS Standards for Asset Owners. When calculating and presenting performance to prospective clients or prospective investors, the asset owner follows the GIPS Standards for Firms.

See Provision 21.A.24 for additional guidance on situations in which an asset owner competes for business, including those instances in which an asset owner acts as both an asset owner and a firm that competes for business.

Sample Disclosures:

Example 1:

Genius University Endowment is a university endowment fund and manages assets solely for Genius University.

Sample Disclosure for Example 1:

"For the purpose of complying with the GIPS standards, the asset owner is defined as the Genius University Endowment (GUE), established in 1972 by the Genius University Investment Committee of the Genius Corporation, and is the manager of GUE's assets."

Example 2:

Organization ABC acts as both an asset owner, managing assets for the ABC retirement system, and as an asset manager that competes for assets whose vesting lies with external clients. For the purpose of complying with the GIPS standards, Organization ABC has decided to bifurcate its assets into two entities: ABC Retirement System (ABCRS), which manages assets exclusively for the ABC Retirement System, and Firm ABC, which competes for business.

Sample Disclosure in a GIPS Asset Owner Report for Example 2:

"For the purpose of complying with the GIPS standards, ABC Retirement System (ABCRS) is defined as the division of Organization ABC that manages assets exclusively for the pension plan of Organization ABC."

Sample Disclosure in Firm ABC's GIPS Composite Report for Example 2:

"For the purpose of complying with the GIPS standards, ABC Investment Management is defined as the division of Organization ABC that is authorized by Organization ABC's governing body to compete for business."

Provision 25.C.4

The ASSET OWNER MUST disclose the COMPOSITE DESCRIPTION.

Discussion

The composite description is defined as general information regarding the investment mandate, objective, or strategy of the composite. The composite description may be more abbreviated than the composite definition but must include all key features of the composite and must include enough information to allow the oversight body to understand the key characteristics of the composite's investment mandate, objective, or strategy, including:

- the material risks of the composite's strategy,
- how leverage, derivatives, and short positions may be used, if they are a material part of the strategy, and
- if illiquid investments are a material part of the strategy.

The composite definition goes a step further than the composite description and includes the detailed criteria that determine the assignment of portfolios to composites, such as investment constraints or restrictions. Although the composite description is a required disclosure, the composite definition is not a required disclosure. (See the discussion of Provision 23.A.4 for additional information regarding the difference between a composite definition and a composite description.)

The required disclosure of the composite description provides information about the composite's investment strategy or asset class(es) that is intended to help the oversight body understand the composite presented in a GIPS Asset Owner Report. The disclosed strategy features will likely affect both the historical and expected risk and returns. Along with the required benchmark description (see Provision 25.C.5), the GIPS Asset Owner Report will allow the oversight body to understand both the investment strategy employed and the benchmark against which the composite's performance is evaluated.

If leverage, derivatives, and short positions may be used, and they are a material part of the strategy, this information must be disclosed in the composite description. Provision 25.C.14 requires that the asset owner disclose how leverage, derivatives, and short positions have been used historically, if material. Taken together, these two required disclosures provide a more complete picture about the presence, use, and extent of leverage, derivatives, and short positions. When determining what would be material, the asset owner must consider whether the disclosure of how leverage, derivatives, and/or short positions may be used and/or have been used historically is likely to affect the oversight body's view of the risk involved in the strategy. If so, it would be misleading for the asset owner to fail to disclose their use to the oversight body when describing the strategy.

Generally, all investment products or strategies have some degree of inherent risk (e.g., market risk), but it is not intended that the composite description identifies every risk of the strategy. Instead, asset owners must identify those material risks of the strategy, if any, and must disclose those risks. For example, investment concentration, correlation (or lack thereof), liquidity, and exposure to counterparties are features that may need to be included in the composite

 |

description. (See Provision 21.A.17 for additional guidance on the disclosure of risks in a composite description.)

The key characteristics of some strategies may change given market events. Asset owners should periodically review composite descriptions to ensure they are current.

Sample Disclosures:

"The Distressed Debt Composite invests at least 85% of its assets in distressed euro-denominated bonds that have credit ratings of CCC or lower by at least one major credit rating agency. Key risks include widening corporate spreads and defaults, high levels of government debt, and elevated political tensions, which could lead to abrupt changes in monetary policy by the European Central Bank (ECB). A material amount of the composite's investments may be illiquid."

"The 2018 Vintage Year Private Equity Composite includes all private equity investments with an initial capital call from limited partners in 2018. The composite focuses on investments in venture and buyout/growth funds. The risks of investing in private equity are funding risk, liquidity risk, market risk, and capital risk. Risk is diversified by investing across different types of private equity such as venture capital, leveraged buyouts, and international funds."

A Sample List of Composite Descriptions can be found in Appendix D of the GIPS standards.

Provision 25.C.5

The ASSET OWNER MUST disclose the BENCHMARK DESCRIPTION, which MUST include the key features of the BENCHMARK or the name of the BENCHMARK for a readily recognized index or other point of reference.

Discussion

Asset owners are required to disclose a description of each benchmark included in a GIPS Asset Owner Report. The benchmark description is general information regarding the investments, structure, and characteristics of the benchmark, and it must include the key features of the benchmark. In the case of a widely recognized benchmark, the name of the benchmark will satisfy this requirement. There are few money-weighted return benchmarks that would be considered widely recognized. If the asset owner presents a public market equivalent (PME) as a benchmark, the benchmark description must include the name of the market index that is used to calculate the

PME. Given the unique nature of a PME, if the market index used to calculate the PME is not readily recognized, the asset owner must also disclose the description of this benchmark. See the discussion of Provision 25.C.28 for an explanation of a PME. Each asset owner must decide for itself whether a benchmark is widely recognized. If the asset owner is not certain as to whether the benchmark is widely known, the asset owner must include the benchmark description.

Sample Disclosure:

"The custom benchmark return is calculated by applying the investment cash flows of the Distressed Debt Composite to the XYZ Eurozone Distressed Debt Bond Index. The index reflects a portfolio of euro-denominated distressed debt bonds issued in Eurozone countries that generally have credit ratings of CCC or lower from the main rating agencies and are listed on the XYZ platforms."

Provision 25.C.6

When presenting GROSS-OF-FEES returns, the ASSET OWNER MUST disclose if any other fees are deducted in addition to TRANSACTION COSTS and fees and expenses for externally managed POOLED FUNDS.

Discussion

When presenting gross-of-fees returns, it is important that there are sufficient disclosures so that the oversight body can understand what the returns actually represent.

A gross-of-fees return is the return on investments reduced by transaction costs and all fees and expenses for externally managed pooled funds. If an asset owner presents a gross-of-fees return in a GIPS Asset Owner Report, the asset owner must disclose if any other fees, such as custody fees for externally managed segregated accounts, are deducted in addition to transaction costs and fees and expenses for externally managed pooled funds.

Sample Disclosure:

"Gross-of-fees returns reflect the deduction of transaction costs, fees and expenses for externally managed pooled funds, and custodian fees for externally managed segregated accounts."

Provision 25.C.7

When presenting NET-OF-EXTERNAL-COSTS-ONLY returns, the ASSET OWNER MUST disclose if any other fees are deducted in addition to the TRANSACTION COSTS, fees and expenses for externally managed POOLED FUNDS, and INVESTMENT MANAGEMENT FEES for externally managed SEGREGATED ACCOUNTS.

Discussion

When presenting net-of-external-costs-only returns, it is important that there are sufficient disclosures so that the oversight body can understand what the returns actually represent.

Net-of-external-costs-only returns are required to reflect the deduction of transaction costs, all fees and expenses for externally managed pooled funds, and investment management fees for externally managed segregated accounts.[M] Investment management fees include both asset-based fees and performance-based fees or carried interest. Other expenses may also be deducted (e.g., custody fees for segregated accounts). If other fees are deducted from the net-of-external-costs-only returns, this information must be disclosed.

Sample Disclosure:

"Net-of-external-costs-only returns are net of transaction costs, all fees and expenses for externally managed pooled funds, and investment management fees and custodian fees for externally managed segregated accounts."

Provision 25.C.8

When presenting NET-OF-FEES returns, the ASSET OWNER MUST disclose if any other fees are deducted in addition to the TRANSACTION COSTS, fees and expenses for externally managed POOLED FUNDS, INVESTMENT MANAGEMENT FEES for externally managed SEGREGATED ACCOUNTS, and INVESTMENT MANAGEMENT COSTS.

[M] The definition of NET-OF-EXTERNAL-COSTS-ONLY included in the Glossary in the 2020 edition of the GIPS standards is incorrect and should state:

The GROSS-OF-FEES return reduced by ~~all costs~~ INVESTMENT MANAGEMENT FEES for externally managed SEGREGATED ACCOUNTS.

Discussion

When presenting net-of-fees returns, it is important that there be sufficient disclosures so that the oversight body can understand what the returns actually represent.

Net-of-fees returns are required to reflect the deduction of transaction costs, fees and expenses for externally managed pooled funds, investment management fees for externally managed segregated accounts, and investment management costs. Investment management fees include both asset-based fees and performance-based fees or carried interest. In the rare instance where other fees and expenses beyond those required to be deducted are also deducted, this information must be disclosed.

Sample Disclosure:

"Net-of-fees returns are net of transaction costs, fees and expenses for externally managed pooled funds, investment management fees for externally managed segregated accounts, investment management costs, and insurance agency costs."

Provision 25.C.9

The ASSET OWNER MUST disclose or otherwise indicate the reporting currency.

Discussion

The GIPS standards require that asset owners disclose the currency used to report the numerical information presented in a GIPS Asset Owner Report. If the asset owner presents performance in multiple currencies in the same GIPS Asset Owner Report, the asset owner must ensure it is clear which currencies are used to calculate and report performance and assets.

Labeling the columns within a GIPS Asset Owner Report with the appropriate currency symbol would satisfy this requirement, as would a written disclosure.

All required and recommended information presented in a GIPS Asset Owner Report must be presented in the same currency. (See Provision 25.A.7.)

Sample Disclosures:

"Valuations are computed and all information is reported in Canadian dollars."

"All numerical information is reported in Japanese yen."

|

Provision 25.C.10

The ASSET OWNER MUST disclose the COMPOSITE INCEPTION DATE.

Discussion

When reviewing composite performance data in a GIPS Asset Owner Report, it is important that the oversight body has sufficient information regarding the length of the composite track record to put the performance presented in the GIPS Asset Owner Report in perspective. Therefore, the inception date of the composite being presented in the GIPS Asset Owner Report must be disclosed. The composite inception date is the initial date of the composite's track record, even if the complete track record is not presented in the GIPS Asset Owner Report. Asset owners are required to present the annualized since-inception money-weighted return (SI-MWR) through the most recent annual period end. (See Provision 25.A.1.a.) There may be instances, however, where the asset owner does not have records to support the entire track record since the composite's inception. If the asset owner is not presenting the SI-MWR and is instead presenting the MWR for the longest period for which that asset owner has records, the composite inception date does not change. For example, assume a private equity composite has an inception date of 24 June 2007, but the asset owner does not have records to support performance for periods prior to 1 January 2014. The asset owner, therefore, presents an MWR with a start date of 1 January 2014. The composite inception date is 24 June 2007, even though the asset owner is not presenting the SI-MWR with a start date of 24 June 2007.

Asset owners must clearly label or identify the periods that are presented. This requirement, together with the disclosure of the composite inception date, provides a full picture of the track record being presented.

If there has been a break in the performance record of a composite, the initial inception date before the break is the date that would be disclosed.

Sample Disclosures:

"The Global Growth Composite has an inception date of 15 September 2019, the date on which the first portfolio in the composite experienced its first capital call from external managers."

"The Global Fixed Income Composite has an inception date of 1 November 2015. There was a break in performance from 1 March 2019 through 30 November 2019. During that period, there were no portfolios in the composite. Composite performance began again on 1 December 2019."

Provision 25.C.11

The ASSET OWNER MUST disclose the COMPOSITE CREATION DATE.

Discussion

Asset owners must disclose the composite creation date, which is the date on which the asset owner first grouped one or more portfolios together to create the composite. The composite creation date is not necessarily the same as the composite inception date. The composite inception date is the initial date of the composite's performance record and is a required disclosure. (See Provision 25.C.10.) The composite creation date can be significantly after the composite inception date, depending on when the asset owner first grouped the individual portfolios together to create the composite. This information allows the oversight body to compare the composite creation date with the composite inception date to determine whether the asset owner grouped portfolios together into a composite retroactively or created the composite at the beginning of the composite's performance track record.

For those asset owners that created composites many years ago, it may be impossible to know the specific day a composite was created. Some asset owners disclose a composite creation date as a month, or even a year, when the composite was created in the very distant past. Newly created composites should have more-precise composite creation dates.

Sample Disclosures:

"The Real Estate Composite was created on 17 July 2019. This is the date on which portfolios were first grouped together to create the composite."

"The Private Equity Composite was created in September 2012."

Provision 25.C.12

If the ASSET OWNER chooses to create additional COMPOSITES, or if the ASSET OWNER has more than one REQUIRED TOTAL FUND, the ASSET OWNER MUST disclose that the ASSET OWNER's list of TOTAL FUND DESCRIPTIONS and COMPOSITE DESCRIPTIONS is available upon request.

|

Discussion

An additional composite is a grouping of portfolios representing a particular strategy or asset class that the asset owner chooses to present in a GIPS Asset Owner Report. If the asset owner chooses to create additional composites representing one or more strategies within a total fund, or if the asset owner has more than one required GIPS Asset Owner Report for its total funds, a list of total fund descriptions and composite descriptions must be maintained and made available to the oversight body upon request. (See Provisions 21.A.17 and 21.A.18 for additional guidance on the creation and distribution of the list of total fund descriptions and composite descriptions.) The asset owner must disclose, in each GIPS Asset Owner Report, that a list of total fund descriptions and composite descriptions is available upon request. When an asset owner competes for business and chooses to claim compliance with the GIPS standards while competing for business, this list must include the strategies from the part of the organization that competes for business.

If the asset owner has only one total fund or only one total fund composite and has not chosen to create any additional composites, the GIPS Asset Owner Report for the total fund or the total fund composite represents the asset owner's list of total fund descriptions and composite descriptions. This is because the description of the total fund or the total fund composite is required to be included in the relevant GIPS Asset Owner Report, and so the GIPS Asset Owner Report can be used to meet this requirement. In such cases, the asset owner is not required to disclose that this list is available upon request.

The list of total fund descriptions and composite descriptions itself does not need to be included in each GIPS Asset Owner Report but must be available upon request. The list of total fund descriptions and composite descriptions must include the total fund description or composite description for each current total fund or composite, as well as a description for all total funds or composites that have terminated in the past five years. The total fund descriptions and composite descriptions disclosed in GIPS Asset Owner Reports must be consistent with the descriptions included in the list of total fund descriptions and composite descriptions. (Please see Provision 23.A.4 for a discussion of composite descriptions.)

A Sample List of Total Fund and Composite Descriptions can be found in Appendix D of the GIPS standards.

This requirement exists to provide the oversight body with a complete picture of the asset owner's total funds and composites.

Sample Disclosure:

"A list of total fund descriptions and composite descriptions is available upon request."

Provision 25.C.13

The ASSET OWNER MUST disclose that policies for valuing investments, calculating performance, and preparing GIPS ASSET OWNER REPORTS are available upon request.

Discussion

In each GIPS Asset Owner Report, asset owners must disclose the availability of policies for valuing investments, calculating performance, and preparing GIPS Asset Owner Reports. The policies are not required to be included in each GIPS Asset Owner Report but must be available upon request. Asset owners are not required to provide the related procedures, in addition to the policies, but may do so.

Sample Disclosure:

"Centerville Police and Fire Retirement System's policies for valuing portfolios, calculating performance, and preparing GIPS Asset Owner Reports are available upon request."

Provision 25.C.14

The ASSET OWNER MUST disclose how leverage, derivatives, and short positions have been used historically, if material.

Discussion

Asset owners must provide enough information in a GIPS Asset Owner Report to allow the oversight body to understand how leverage, derivatives, and short positions have been employed historically and may be used going forward. Although the composite description includes disclosure of the asset owner's ability to use leverage, derivatives, and short positions (see Provision 25.C.4), this provision requires that the asset owner disclose the leverage, derivatives, and short positions that have been used historically, if material. Taken together, these two required disclosures provide a more complete picture of the presence, use, and extent of leverage, derivatives, and short positions.

For example, assume an asset owner discloses in a composite description that the strategy may employ up to 200% leverage. To satisfy the disclosure requirement in Provision 25.C.14, the asset

 |

owner might state, "Since the inception of the strategy, the leverage has averaged 110% of the composite's value; however, during 2019 the leverage averaged 160%, which greatly increased the sensitivity to market volatility and the potential for realized gains and/or losses."

No disclosure is required if leverage, derivatives, and short positions have not been used or if their use has not been material. When determining what would be material, the asset owner must consider whether the disclosure of how leverage, derivatives, and/or short positions have been used historically is likely to affect the oversight body's view of the risk involved in the strategy. If so, it would be misleading for the asset owner to fail to disclose their use to the oversight body when describing the strategy.

Provision 25.C.15

If estimated TRANSACTION COSTS are used, the ASSET OWNER MUST disclose:

a. That estimated TRANSACTION COSTS were used.

b. The estimated TRANSACTION COSTS used and how they were determined.

Discussion

Gross-of-fees, net-of-external-costs-only, and net-of-fees composite returns must reflect the deduction of transaction costs, which are the costs of buying or selling investments. Asset owners may use either actual or estimated transaction costs when calculating returns. Estimated transaction costs may be used only for portfolios for which the actual transaction costs are not known. Provision 22.A.10 provides guidance on the use of estimated transaction costs.

If estimated transaction costs are used in calculating returns, there must be a disclosure that estimated transaction costs were used. An asset owner must also disclose the estimated transaction costs used and how they were determined. An asset owner might, for example, determine estimated transaction costs based on other portfolios whose transaction costs are known.

Sample Disclosure for a Composite:

"Some portfolios in the composite do not pay explicit transaction costs for security purchases and sales. Estimated transaction costs for these portfolios are used, and these are determined based on the average transaction cost per share incurred by portfolios in the composite that pay explicit transaction costs. The average transaction cost was determined to be $0.031 per share. A model transaction cost per share of $0.04 is applied to each investment transaction."

Provision 25.C.16

The ASSET OWNER MUST disclose all significant events that would help the OVERSIGHT BODY interpret the GIPS ASSET OWNER REPORT. This disclosure MUST be included for a minimum of one year and for as long as it is relevant to interpreting the track record.

Discussion

The GIPS standards are based on the principles of fair representation and full disclosure. Meeting these objectives requires a good faith commitment on the part of the asset owner to adhere to the spirit of the GIPS standards. The GIPS standards cannot foresee and cover every situation that might occur. Therefore, this provision requires that asset owners disclose all significant events that would help explain the asset owner's GIPS Asset Owner Report to the oversight body. The primary goal of this requirement is to provide relevant information to the oversight body so that it can understand the potential effect of the significant event on the composite's investment strategy and the asset owner.

Significant events are determined by the asset owner and would include, as examples, a material change in personnel responsible for investment management, significant changes to the investment management process, or the loss of historical records resulting from a catastrophic event. The departure of someone who was the single investment decision maker for a strategy would also qualify as a significant event.

Depending on the situation, a general statement describing the significant event that has occurred may be sufficient. Other situations may require asset owners to disclose specific information pertaining to the significant event. The disclosure regarding the significant event must be included in the GIPS Asset Owner Report for a minimum of one year and for as long as it is relevant to interpreting the performance track record. As an example, if there is a legislative change that requires an asset owner to manage the assets of an additional retirement system, resulting in a large increase in total asset owner assets, the asset owner may disclose this significant event for as long as the large change in total asset owner assets is included in the GIPS Asset Owner Report. In contrast, a change in an asset owner's chief investment officer (CIO) is a change that an asset owner may believe should be disclosed for one year only.

The asset owner must consider the underlying principles of the GIPS standards, which are fair representation and full disclosure, when determining how long the disclosure will be included in the GIPS Asset Owner Report.

Sample Disclosure:

"In March 2019, the portfolio manager responsible for the internal management of all fixed-income assets of the Midway State Municipal Retirement System (MSMRS) left MSMRS.

Her duties have been assumed by a member of the MSMRS investment management team. No change in the fixed-income strategy is anticipated."

Provision 25.C.17

If the ASSET OWNER is redefined, the ASSET OWNER MUST disclose the date and description of the redefinition.

Discussion

An asset owner redefinition occurs when something changes with how the asset owner is structured. For example, there may be cases where there are significant changes to an asset owner due to legislation-driven changes, in the case of pension funds, or changes dictated by the governing body, in the case of foundations, endowments, or family offices. In some cases, as a result of a significant alteration in an asset owner's structure or organization, a change can be so great that it creates a new asset owner. Changes in investment style or personnel are not events that typically cause an asset owner redefinition. A simple asset owner name change is also not a sufficient reason to redefine the asset owner.

The GIPS standards require that changes in an asset owner's organization must not lead to alteration of historical total fund or composite performance (see Provision 21.A.22).

Sample Disclosures:

"On 1 July 2018, the Prodigy University Endowment for Theatre Studies was redefined by the Prodigy University Investment Committee to include the endowments for all creative art studies at Prodigy University, including theatre, dance, music, writing, and visual arts, and was renamed the Prodigy University Endowment for the Creative Arts."

"On 1 August 2019, Midway City was created through the merger of the municipalities of New Town and Old Town. On that date, the retirement systems of New Town and Old Town were merged to create the Midway City Retirement System (MCRS)."

Provision 25.C.18

If a COMPOSITE is redefined, the ASSET OWNER MUST disclose the date and description of the redefinition.

Discussion

The investment mandate, objective, or strategy of an additional composite can change over time. (An additional composite is a grouping of portfolios representing a particular strategy or asset class that the asset owner chooses to present in a GIPS Asset Owner Report.) In some cases, such a change results in the termination of one composite and the creation of a new composite. In other cases, it may be appropriate to redefine the composite. If a composite is redefined, the asset owner must disclose the date and description of the redefinition. See Provision 23.A.4 for guidance on composite definitions.

Sample Disclosure:

"As of 1 July 2017, the fixed-income strategy includes the use of interest rate futures to modify duration and manage interest rate risk. Prior to this date, the Composite's strategy did not involve the active management of interest rate risk."

Provision 25.C.19

The ASSET OWNER MUST disclose changes to the name of the COMPOSITE. This disclosure MUST be included for a minimum of one year and for as long as it is relevant to interpreting the track record.

Discussion

When an asset owner's oversight body is evaluating an additional composite, it is important that it understands exactly which composite it is assessing. (An additional composite is a grouping of portfolios representing a particular strategy or asset class that the asset owner chooses to present in a GIPS Asset Owner Report.) If an asset owner changes the name of a composite, the change must be disclosed in the GIPS Asset Owner Report. The name change must be disclosed for a minimum of one year and potentially for more than one year if the asset owner determines the disclosure is still relevant and meaningful. The asset owner must consider the underlying principles of the GIPS standards, which are fair representation and full disclosure, when determining how long the disclosure will be included in the GIPS Asset Owner Report.

Sample Disclosure:

"As of 1 January 2016, the Venture Capital Composite was renamed the Opportunity Fund Composite."

 |

Provision 25.C.20

The ASSET OWNER MUST disclose if COMPOSITE returns are gross or net of withholding taxes, if material.

Discussion

Global investing requires recognition of the tax consequences of investing in different countries. The GIPS standards do not require asset owners to reflect withholding taxes, either reclaimable or non-reclaimable taxes, in a certain manner. Asset owners may choose whether or not to reflect the effect of withholding taxes when calculating performance. The GIPS standards do recommend that performance be reported net of non-reclaimable withholding taxes on dividends, interest, and capital gains and also recommend that reclaimable foreign withholding taxes be accrued (see Provision 22.B.5). If withholding taxes are material, asset owners must disclose how withholding taxes are treated when calculating performance. An asset owner must determine the level at which withholding taxes become material, document the level in its policies and procedures, and apply it consistently.

Sample Disclosure:

"Portfolio returns are net of all foreign non-reclaimable withholding taxes. Reclaimable withholding taxes are reflected as income if and when received."

Provision 25.C.21

The ASSET OWNER MUST disclose if BENCHMARK returns are net of withholding taxes if this information is available.

Discussion

Global investing requires recognition of the tax consequences of investing in different countries. The GIPS standards do not require asset owners to reflect withholding taxes, either reclaimable or non-reclaimable taxes, in a certain manner. Asset owners may choose whether or not to reflect the effect of withholding taxes when calculating composite performance and, similarly, whether or not to use a benchmark that reflects the effect of withholding taxes.

As Provision 25.C.20 indicates, if withholding taxes are material, asset owners must disclose how withholding taxes are treated when calculating performance. To facilitate the comparison of composite returns and benchmark returns, asset owners must also disclose if the benchmark returns are net of withholding taxes if this information is available. If the benchmark name indicates that the benchmark is net of withholding taxes, no additional disclosure is necessary.

Sample Disclosure:

"Benchmark returns are net of withholding taxes."

Provision 25.C.22

If the GIPS ASSET OWNER REPORT conforms with laws and/or regulations that conflict with the REQUIREMENTS of the GIPS standards, the ASSET OWNER MUST disclose this fact and disclose the manner in which the laws and/or regulations conflict with the GIPS standards.

Discussion

Asset owners must comply with all applicable laws and regulations regarding the calculation and presentation of performance. Compliance with applicable laws and regulations, however, does not necessarily result in compliance with the GIPS standards. Asset owners must also comply with all of the applicable requirements of the GIPS standards. In the rare cases where laws and regulations conflict with the GIPS standards, asset owners are required to comply with the laws and regulations and disclose the manner in which the laws and/or regulations conflict with the GIPS standards.

This disclosure will assist the oversight body in understanding the difference between the reporting requirements of applicable laws and regulations and those of the GIPS standards.

Sample Disclosure:

"We present since-inception money-weighted returns through each annual period end. Local laws do not allow the presentation of returns of less than one year, which is in conflict with the GIPS standards. Therefore, no performance is presented for this composite for the period from 1 July 2018 (the inception date of the composite) through 31 December 2018."

> ## Provision 25.C.23
>
> The ASSET OWNER MUST disclose the use of EXTERNAL MANAGERS and the periods EXTERNAL MANAGERS were used.[35]

Discussion

Some asset owners use an external manager to manage part or all of a particular strategy. For example, an asset owner might manage most of its fixed-income assets internally but hire external managers to manage its equity, private equity, and real estate assets. The GIPS standards require that asset owners include the performance of assets assigned to an external manager in its total fund(s) and in any additional composite that an asset owner has chosen to create, provided the asset owner has the authority to allocate the assets to an external manager. (An additional composite is a grouping of portfolios representing a particular strategy or asset class that the asset owner chooses to present in a GIPS Asset Owner Report.) In the spirit of full disclosure, an asset owner must disclose the fact that an external manager was used in the management of the composite strategy and the periods for which an external manager was used. This is required for periods beginning on or after 1 January 2006. It is not necessary to disclose the name of the external manager.

Sample Disclosures:

"The Global Private Equity Composite used an external manager from its inception on 1 October 2018 through 31 May 2020. It has been internally managed since 1 June 2020."

"A sub-advisor is used to manage the international equity allocation of the Asia Real Estate Composite."

> ## Provision 25.C.24
>
> The ASSET OWNER MUST disclose if the COMPOSITE's valuation hierarchy materially differs from the RECOMMENDED valuation hierarchy.[36] (See Provision 22.B.6 for the RECOMMENDED valuation hierarchy.)

Discussion

Asset owners must establish policies and procedures for determining portfolio valuations. For periods beginning on or after 1 January 2011, those valuations must be determined in accordance

---

[35] REQUIRED for periods beginning on or after 1 January 2006.
[36] REQUIRED for periods beginning on or after 1 January 2011.

with the definition of fair value. Provision 22.B.6 includes a recommended valuation hierarchy that asset owners should incorporate into their policies and procedures for determining fair value for portfolio investments. Asset owners must establish a valuation hierarchy on a composite-specific basis. It is acceptable for asset owners to apply a different valuation hierarchy to specific composites provided the valuation methodology conforms to the definition of fair value. If the valuation hierarchy materially differs from the recommended valuation hierarchy, the asset owner must disclose this fact. The oversight body will be informed and then may request additional information about the asset owner's valuation policies.

Sample Disclosure:

"All portfolio investments in the Private Equity Composite are valued using our proprietary valuation models to determine fair value. Our valuation procedures materially differ from the recommended valuation hierarchy in the GIPS standards."

Provision 25.C.25

If the ASSET OWNER determines no appropriate BENCHMARK for the COMPOSITE exists, the ASSET OWNER MUST disclose why no BENCHMARK is presented.

Discussion

Benchmarks are important tools that aid in the planning, implementation, and evaluation of an investment strategy. They also help facilitate discussions with the oversight body regarding the relationship between composite risk and return. As a result, the GIPS standards require asset owners to provide benchmark total returns in all GIPS Asset Owner Reports. The benchmark must reflect the investment mandate, objective, or strategy of the composite. Although there is typically an appropriate benchmark for traditional strategies, it is more common for managers of alternative strategies to determine that no appropriate benchmark for the composite exists. If this is the case, the asset owner must disclose why no benchmark is presented.

Sample Disclosure:

"Because the composite's strategy is absolute return where investments are permitted in all asset classes, no benchmark is presented because we believe that no benchmark that reflects this strategy exists."

 |

Provision 25.C.26

If the ASSET OWNER changes the BENCHMARK, the ASSET OWNER MUST disclose:

a. For a prospective BENCHMARK change, the date and description of the change. Changes MUST be disclosed for as long as returns for the prior BENCHMARK are included in the GIPS ASSET OWNER REPORT.

b. For a retroactive BENCHMARK change, the date and description of the change. Changes MUST be disclosed for a minimum of one year and for as long as they are relevant to interpreting the track record.

Discussion

Asset owners must disclose the date and description of any changes to the benchmark over time. A benchmark change can take two forms:

- The benchmark is changed from one benchmark to another on a prospective basis only.
- The benchmark is changed for all periods (i.e., retroactively).

In most cases, the asset owner should only change the benchmark going forward and not change the benchmark retroactively.

If the asset owner changes the benchmark prospectively and presents benchmark returns that combine two different benchmarks, the date and description of the change must be disclosed for as long as returns for the prior benchmark are included in the GIPS Asset Owner Report. Given the nature of a money-weighted return (MWR), however, it is not expected that this situation would often apply to a GIPS Asset Owner Report that includes MWRs. If this situation does occur, this change must be disclosed.

There may be times when an asset owner determines that it is appropriate to change the benchmark for a given composite retroactively. For example, because benchmarks are continually evolving, if the asset owner finds that a new benchmark is a better comparison for an investment strategy, the asset owner may consider changing the benchmark retroactively. In the case of a retroactive benchmark change, there must be a disclosure of the date and description of the benchmark change, including the fact that the benchmark was changed retroactively. Disclosures related to a retroactive change in a benchmark must be included in the respective GIPS Asset Owner Report for a minimum of one year and for as long as the disclosures are relevant to interpreting the performance track record. The asset owner must consider the underlying principles of the GIPS standards, which are fair representation and full disclosure, when determining how long this disclosure will be included in the GIPS Asset Owner Report.

When an asset owner changes a benchmark retroactively, the asset owner is encouraged to continue to also present the old benchmark.

Changes to the benchmark primarily intended to make performance look better by lowering the benchmark return violate the spirit of the GIPS standards.

Sample Disclosure:

"In January 2017, the benchmark was changed from ABC Index to XYZ Index for all periods."

Provision 25.C.27

If a custom BENCHMARK or combination of multiple BENCHMARKS is used, the ASSET OWNER MUST:

a. Disclose the BENCHMARK components, weights, and rebalancing process, if applicable.
b. Disclose the calculation methodology.
c. Clearly label the BENCHMARK to indicate that it is a custom BENCHMARK.

Discussion

When custom benchmarks are used, the asset owner must disclose the benchmark components, weights, and rebalancing process, if applicable. Given the nature of money-weighted return (MWR) calculations, this disclosure will rarely apply to a GIPS Asset Owner Report that presents MWRs.

Instead, it is expected that an asset owner would use a public market equivalent (PME) as a custom benchmark. See the discussion of Provision 25.C.28 for an explanation of a PME. A PME must be clearly labeled as such, and the methodology used to calculate the PME must be disclosed.

An asset owner may calculate a PME that is a gross-of-fees, net-of-external-costs-only, or net-of-fees return. A PME that is a net-of-fees return is calculated using the same cash flows that are used to calculate the composite's net-of-fees return. An asset owner may use a net-of-fees PME benchmark only when composite net-of-fees returns are presented. The use of a net benchmark when composite net-of-fees returns are not presented is one instance where disclosure is not sufficient to prevent the information presented from being false and misleading. The same approach must be taken when calculating a PME that is a net-of-external-costs-only return. When an asset owner includes a net-of-external-costs-only or net-of-fees benchmark in a GIPS Asset Owner Report, the asset owner must clearly label the benchmark as a custom benchmark and disclose the calculation methodology.

Sample Disclosure for a Net-of-Fees PME Benchmark

"The benchmark is the public market equivalent (PME) of the ABC Mid-Cap Equity Index, which tracks the performance of US mid-cap companies. The PME is a method by which a public market index is used to create a since-inception money-weighted return that is comparable to a composite's since-inception money-weighted return from a series of cash flows that are the same as those of the composite and uses a theoretical investment value. The theoretical investment value is derived by buying and selling the public market index using the dates and amounts of actual composite cash flows."

Provision 25.C.28

The ASSET OWNER MUST disclose the calculation methodology used for the BENCHMARK. If the ASSET OWNER presents the PUBLIC MARKET EQUIVALENT of the COMPOSITE as a BENCHMARK, the ASSET OWNER MUST disclose the index used to calculate the PUBLIC MARKET EQUIVALENT.

Discussion

The benchmark selected for a composite must be appropriate for comparison with the performance of the composite. Unlike benchmarks for publicly traded securities, however, industry benchmarks for private market investments are not as widely available or are available only through certain commercial vendors. Asset owners may use public market indices as a benchmark for private market investments, but the public market indices by themselves are not directly comparable to a money-weighted return (MWR) because the market indices typically use a time-weighted return. The public market equivalent (PME) is a method in which a public market index is used to create a comparable MWR from a series of cash flows that replicate those of the composite and that can be compared with the MWR of the composite.

The GIPS standards require that the calculation methodology for the benchmark be disclosed. This disclosure provides transparency as to the comparability of performance between the composite and the benchmark. If a PME is used as a benchmark, the asset owner must disclose which public market index is used to create the PME.

Sample Disclosure for a Non-PME Benchmark:

"The benchmark is the since-inception money-weighted return for the ACME Advisory US Venture Capital Funds Universe—2018 Vintage Year. The vintage year is determined by the date of the first capital call for each fund in the universe."

Sample Disclosure for a PME Benchmark:

"The benchmark is the public market equivalent (PME) of the ABC Mid-Cap Equity Index, which tracks the performance of US mid-cap companies. The PME is a method by which a public market index is used to create a since-inception money-weighted return that is comparable to a composite's since-inception money-weighted return from a series of cash flows that are the same as those of the composite and uses a theoretical investment value. The theoretical investment value is derived by buying and selling the public market index using the dates and amounts of actual composite cash flows."

Provision 25.C.29

The ASSET OWNER MUST disclose the frequency of EXTERNAL CASH FLOWS used in the MONEY-WEIGHTED RETURN calculation if daily frequency was not used.

Discussion

When calculating money-weighted returns (MWRs), quarterly or more frequent cash flows must be used prior to 1 January 2020, and daily cash flows must be used as of 1 January 2020. A historical cash flow stream may, therefore, include daily, monthly, and/or quarterly cash flows. When constructing such a cash flow stream historically, and daily cash flows are not used, the asset owner must assume that all quarterly and monthly cash flows occurred on a particular date in the month or quarter regardless of the actual date of the cash flow. For example, all monthly or quarterly cash flows might be dated as if they occurred on the last day of the month, regardless of the actual date of the cash flow. See Provision 22.A.23 for an example of how quarterly and monthly cash flows can be reflected in an MWR calculation.

The MWR calculation is sensitive to the relative timing of cash flows and, especially early in the life of a composite, returns calculated using a quarterly cash flow dating convention can differ from returns calculated using a monthly or daily convention. Accordingly, asset owners are required to disclose the frequency of cash flows used in the MWR calculation if daily cash flows are not used for periods prior to 1 January 2020. It is recommended that asset owners use daily cash flows for all periods.

     |

Sample Disclosure:

"The money-weighted return calculation incorporates monthly cash flows for periods prior to 1 January 2020 and daily cash flows thereafter."

Provision 25.C.30

The ASSET OWNER MUST disclose any change to the GIPS ASSET OWNER REPORT resulting from the correction of a MATERIAL ERROR. Following the correction of the GIPS ASSET OWNER REPORT, this disclosure MUST be included for a minimum of one year and for as long as it is relevant to interpreting the track record.

Discussion

Asset owners claiming compliance with the GIPS standards are likely to be faced with situations in which errors are discovered that must be specifically addressed. An error, which can be qualitative or quantitative, can be related to any component of a GIPS Asset Owner Report that is missing or inaccurate. Errors in GIPS Asset Owner Reports can result from, but are not limited to, incorrect, incomplete, or missing:

- composite returns or assets,
- total asset owner assets,
- benchmark returns,
- number of portfolios in a composite, or
- disclosures.

Any material error in a GIPS Asset Owner Report must be corrected and disclosed in a revised GIPS Asset Owner Report. An asset owner must define materiality within its error correction policies and procedures.

To adhere to this requirement, an asset owner must determine the criteria it will use to determine materiality. The following is a definition of materiality that asset owners might find useful as a starting point for their determination of materiality: "An error is material if the magnitude of the omission or misstatement of performance information, in light of surrounding circumstances, makes it probable that the judgment of a reasonable person relying on the information would have been changed by the omission or misstatement." An asset owner should have a defined process for determining the objective criteria it will use in determining materiality.

Disclosure of the change in the corrected GIPS Asset Owner Report resulting from a material error must be included in the GIPS Asset Owner Report for a minimum of 12 months following the correction of the report and for as long as it is relevant to interpreting the track record. The asset owner must consider the underlying principles of the GIPS standards, which are fair representation and full disclosure, when determining how long the disclosure will be included in the GIPS Asset Owner Report that contained the material error.

The discussion for Provision 21.A.16 provides additional information on error correction, including the determination of materiality, the actions that must be taken when an error in a GIPS Asset Owner Report is discovered, and an explanation of who must receive the revised GIPS Asset Owner Report.

Sample Disclosure:

"This GIPS Asset Owner Report includes a correction of the information provided for the XYZ Peer Universe. The since-inception internal rate of return for the XYZ Peer Universe through 31 December 2020 was originally incorrectly presented as 3.4%. The correct return is 4.3%, as shown in this revised GIPS Asset Owner Report."

Provision 25.C.31

The ASSET OWNER MUST disclose if preliminary, estimated values are used to determine FAIR VALUE.

Discussion

The use of preliminary, estimated values as fair value is common for some alternative strategies, including those that invest in externally managed pooled funds for which the asset owner relies on valuations provided by the fund external managers. When using preliminary, estimated values as fair value, it is important to remember the underlying principles of the GIPS standards: fair representation and full disclosure. If using preliminary, estimated values, asset owners must disclose this fact in the relevant GIPS Asset Owner Report.

Asset owners that use preliminary, estimated values to determine fair value and subsequently change valuations when final values are received must determine how the asset owner's error correction policies will be applied. (Please see Provision 21.A.16 for guidance on error correction policies.) Differences between the final and estimated values are not necessarily errors but are treated in a similar manner because the correction of previously presented information may be involved.

In addition to this required disclosure, it is recommended (see Provision 25.B.5) that asset owners present the percentage of assets in the composite that were valued using preliminary, estimated values as of the most recent annual period end. This information will help the oversight body to interpret the performance record.

Sample Disclosure:

"Preliminary, estimated values were used in the determination of the fair value of the composite's assets."

Provision 25.C.32

If the ASSET OWNER changes the type of return(s) presented for the COMPOSITE (e.g., changes from TIME-WEIGHTED RETURNS to MONEY-WEIGHTED RETURNS), the ASSET OWNER MUST disclose the change and the date of the change. This disclosure MUST be included for a minimum of one year and for as long as it is relevant to interpreting the track record.

Discussion

An asset owner may present time-weighted returns (TWRs) or money-weighted returns (MWRs) in a GIPS Asset Owner Report for an additional composite. An additional composite is a grouping of portfolios representing a particular strategy or asset class that the asset owner chooses to present in a GIPS Asset Owner Report. If an asset owner changes the type of return presented for a composite, the asset owner must disclose, in the respective GIPS Asset Owner Report, the change in the type of return (e.g., from TWR to MWR) and the date of the change. This disclosure must be included in the GIPS Asset Owner Report for a minimum of one year and for as long as it is relevant and helpful to the asset owner's oversight body in interpreting the composite's track record. The asset owner must consider the underlying principles of the GIPS standards, which are fair representation and full disclosure, when determining how long the disclosure will be included in the GIPS Asset Owner Report.

As an example, suppose that an asset owner is presenting TWRs for a composite from the inception of the composite on 1 January 2013 through 31 December 2019. It decides that it will switch to present MWRs as of 1 January 2020. The asset owner cannot present TWRs through 31 December 2019 and an MWR from 1 January 2020 through 31 December 2020. The asset owner must present the since-inception MWR for the period from 1 January 2013 (the inception date of the composite) through 31 December 2020 in the GIPS Asset Owner Report for the period ended 31 December 2020.

Sample Disclosure:

"Beginning with the GIPS Asset Owner Report for the period ended 31 December 2020, the returns presented for the XYZ Composite were changed from time-weighted returns to money-weighted returns."

Provision 25.C.33

If the ASSET OWNER presents ADDITIONAL RISK MEASURES, the ASSET OWNER MUST:

a. Describe any ADDITIONAL RISK MEASURE.
b. Disclose the name of the risk-free rate if a risk-free rate is used in the calculation of the ADDITIONAL RISK MEASURE.

Discussion

There is no required risk measure for a GIPS Asset Owner Report that presents composite money-weighted returns. However, understanding and interpreting investment performance requires the consideration of both risk and return. It is, therefore, recommended that asset owners present additional risk measures for the composite and the benchmark. (Because no quantitative risk measure is required for composites that present money-weighted returns, all risk measures presented are considered additional risk measures. See Provision 25.B.4.) It is important to keep in mind that additional risk measures should be consistent with the composite's strategy. For example, if the strategy includes managing foreign currency risk, the presentation of a hedge ratio would be consistent with that objective.

The GIPS Asset Owner Report must include a description of any additional risk measure presented. If a risk-free rate is used in the calculation of an additional risk measure, the name of the risk-free rate must be disclosed. Disclosure of the name of the risk-free rate used in the calculation of an additional risk measure is required because of the importance of the selection of an appropriate risk-free rate. With a disclosure regarding the risk-free rate, the asset owner's oversight body can better understand and interpret the additional risk measure(s) presented.

Provision 25.C.34

The ASSET OWNER MUST disclose if GROSS-OF-FEES, NET-OF-EXTERNAL-COSTS-ONLY, or NET-OF-FEES returns are used to calculate presented risk measures.

Discussion

To help the oversight body interpret the risk measures presented in a GIPS Asset Owner Report, the asset owner must disclose which returns—gross-of-fees, net-of-external-costs-only, or net-of-fees returns—are used in the calculation of the presented risk measures.

 |

Sample Disclosure:

"Net-of-external-costs-only returns were used to calculate drawdown."

Provision 25.C.35

For REAL ESTATE investments that are directly owned, the ASSET OWNER MUST disclose that:[37]

a. EXTERNAL VALUATIONS are obtained and the frequency with which they are obtained; or

b. The ASSET OWNER relies on valuations from financial statement audits.

Discussion

According to Provision 22.A.33, for periods beginning on or after 1 January 2012, real estate investments that are directly owned by the asset owner must:

- have an external valuation at least once every 12 months unless the oversight body stipulates otherwise, in which case real estate investments must have an external valuation at least once every 36 months or per oversight body instructions if the oversight body requires external valuations more frequently than every 36 months; or
- be subject to an annual financial statement audit performed by an independent public accounting firm. The real estate investments must be accounted for at fair value, and the most recent audited financial statements available must contain an unmodified opinion issued by an independent public accounting firm.

Because valuation is such an important issue for real estate investments, asset owners must inform the oversight body whether they externally value real estate investments and, if so, how frequently, or instead place reliance on valuations from audited financial statements. This disclosure is required for periods ending on or after 31 December 2020.

Sample Disclosures:

"Midville Police and Fire Retirement System obtains external valuations for all real estate investments annually."

"ABC Foundation relies on valuations from audited financial statements. The audits are performed by an independent public accounting firm."

---

[37] REQUIRED for periods ending on or after 31 December 2020.

Provision 25.C.36

When the GIPS ASSET OWNER REPORT includes THEORETICAL PERFORMANCE as SUPPLEMENTAL INFORMATION, the ASSET OWNER MUST:

a. Disclose that the results are theoretical, are not based on the performance of actual assets, and if the THEORETICAL PERFORMANCE was derived from the retroactive or prospective application of a model.

b. Disclose a basic description of the methodology and assumptions used to calculate the THEORETICAL PERFORMANCE sufficient for the OVERSIGHT BODY to interpret the THEORETICAL PERFORMANCE, including if it is based on model performance, backtested performance, or hypothetical performance.

c. Disclose whether the THEORETICAL PERFORMANCE reflects the deduction of actual or estimated INVESTMENT MANAGEMENT FEES, INVESTMENT MANAGEMENT COSTS, and TRANSACTION COSTS.

d. Clearly label the THEORETICAL PERFORMANCE as SUPPLEMENTAL INFORMATION.

Discussion

To be presented as supplemental information in a GIPS Asset Owner Report, theoretical performance must relate to the respective composite. The following are examples of theoretical performance that may be included in a GIPS Asset Owner Report as supplemental information:

- Results created by applying a composite investment strategy or methodology to historical data, in order to indicate how a strategy constructed with the benefit of hindsight would have performed during a certain period in the past had the strategy been in existence during that period.

- Ex ante performance that is calculated by combining actual composite cash flows with projected future cash flows.

- Results that include the effect of currency hedging that has been applied after-the-fact to the composite when the composite was not originally managed using the currency hedging strategy, and the hedging is not part of the actual composite returns.

When theoretical performance is included as supplemental information in a GIPS Asset Owner Report, an asset owner is required to include a number of disclosures to ensure that the recipients of the report, including the oversight body, understand the nature of the information being presented. Among the required disclosures are the source of the theoretical performance, the methodology and assumptions used to calculate the theoretical performance, and the treatment of fees and costs.

 |

Asset owners must also clearly label the theoretical performance as supplemental information.

Sample Disclosure:

"A return history has been constructed for the period from 1 January 2015 through 31 December 2018 that reflects the application of an investment model used by XYZ Endowment Fund. The results are theoretical and are not based on the performance of actual portfolios. The return history is derived from the retroactive application of a model. The model assumes that an investment was made in the top 20 individual funds that have been identified as funds that meet the model's ESG screening criteria currently, and it assumes an equal amount was invested in each fund on an assumed quarterly capital call. The first capital call was assumed to occur on 31 December 2014. The since-inception internal rate of return for the model does not reflect the deduction of investment management fees, transaction costs, or other fees and charges."

25.D. Disclosure—Recommendations

Provision 25.D.1

The ASSET OWNER SHOULD disclose material changes to valuation policies and/or methodologies.

Discussion

Valuation is a critical component of the performance calculation. Therefore, if a change to an asset owner's valuation policies and/or methodologies is material, asset owners should disclose the change in order to enable the oversight body to understand the potential effect of such a change.

Some examples of a material change include, but are not limited to, the following:

- new valuation principles adopted by a local accounting standards board,
- adoption of new international standards in lieu of local standards,
- change of economic criteria used to value investments, and
- change from discounted cash flows basis to a comparables basis.

Sample Disclosure for a Policy Change:

"Prior to 1 March 2016, illiquid securities were valued internally. Subsequently, illiquid securities are valued using a third-party pricing service."

Sample Disclosure for a Methodology Change:

"For periods prior to 1 August 2019, real estate investments were valued on a discounted cash flow basis. As of 1 August 2019, real estate investments are valued on a comparables basis."

Provision 25.D.2

The ASSET OWNER SHOULD disclose material changes to calculation policies and/or methodologies.

Discussion

Asset owners have discretion to determine which policies and methodologies are used for calculating performance. Although these policies and methodologies must adhere to all applicable calculation requirements, asset owners may choose from a wide variety of policies and methodologies. Asset owners may change calculation policies and/or methodologies; however, asset owners must not change a calculation policy or methodology for the sole purpose of increasing performance. If a change to the calculation policies and/or methodologies is material, asset owners should disclose the change in order to enable the oversight body to understand the potential effect of such a change.

Sample Disclosure:

"Prior to 2019, the internal rate of return method was used to calculate since-inception money-weighted returns. Subsequently, the Modified Dietz method is used for all periods."

Provision 25.D.3

The ASSET OWNER SHOULD disclose material differences between the BENCHMARK and the COMPOSITE's investment mandate, objective, or strategy.

Discussion

Asset owners are required to disclose the composite description (see Provision 25.C.4) and the benchmark description (see Provision 25.C.5) in a GIPS Asset Owner Report. It is recommended that asset owners also disclose any material differences between the benchmark and the composite's investment mandate, objective, or strategy. The oversight body will be better able to evaluate the performance of the strategy relative to the benchmark presented if they understand any material differences between the composite and the benchmark.

 |

Sample Disclosure:

"The Small-Cap Opportunities Composite is a venture capital composite that invests in small-cap start-ups in all sectors, with a focus on the health care and financial services sectors. The benchmark for the composite is the public market equivalent (PME) of the ABC Small-Cap Index, which tracks the performance of US small-cap companies. The investment strategy of the composite differs from the small-cap investment strategies represented by the PME because the composite concentrates its investments. As of 31 December 2019, 62% of the composite was invested in the health care and financial services sectors, while 18% of the index was invested in these two sectors."

Provision 25.D.4

The ASSET OWNER SHOULD disclose the key assumptions used to value investments.

Discussion

Asset owners are required to disclose that valuation policies are available upon request. (See Provision 25.C.13.) Because valuation is a critical component of the performance calculation, it is recommended that asset owners also disclose the key assumptions used when valuing portfolio investments. This disclosure will help the oversight body better understand how the asset owner values different types of investments.

Sample Disclosures:

"Investments are valued using recent market quotations. If there is no publicly traded reference, equity investments are valued using a market multiple approach for similar investments in active markets, and fixed-income investments are valued using inputs such as interest rates, yield curve shape, volatility, prepayments, and credit spreads."

"The valuation of the Private Equity Composite is based on valuations reported by the general partners of the externally managed pooled funds."

Provision 25.D.5

If the ASSET OWNER adheres to any industry valuation guidelines in addition to the GIPS valuation REQUIREMENTS, the ASSET OWNER SHOULD disclose which guidelines have been applied.

Discussion

Some market segments, such as private equity, have developed their own valuation guidelines. For these markets, it is not uncommon for the GIPS standards valuation requirements to be supplemented by other local or international standards that are more stringent in their requirements.

The disclosure of which industry's valuation guidelines have been used in addition to the GIPS standards valuation requirements will demonstrate to the oversight body that the asset owner is adhering to best practices by applying the more stringent standards when valuing investments.

Sample Disclosure:

"The Global Diversified Distressed Composite adheres to the XYZ Venture Capital Association's valuation guidelines as well as the GIPS standards valuation requirements. The XYZ valuation standards are based on fair value but provide more prescriptive advice in terms of how to value specific investments, such as secondary investments and distressed debt investments."

Provision 25.D.6

When using BENCHMARKS that have limitations, such as peer group BENCHMARKS, the ASSET OWNER SHOULD disclose these limitations.

Discussion

Asset owners must determine which benchmark(s) are most appropriate for composite(s). When determining which benchmarks to present in a GIPS Asset Owner Report, asset owners should be guided by the ethical spirit of the GIPS standards.

Some benchmarks with known limitations are often used for certain types of investments. For example, peer group benchmarks, such as hedge fund peer group universe indices, are often used for hedge funds and other alternative investment strategies. Although peer group benchmarks are frequently used to evaluate hedge funds, there are some common problems with hedge fund peer group benchmarks, including the following:

- self-reporting bias (only some hedge funds choose to report performance data),
- survivorship bias (historical returns of closed hedge funds are removed from the peer group benchmark),
- inability to obtain returns for the same periods as the composite, and
- lack of investability (some hedge funds within a peer group benchmark are closed to new investors).

|

When using benchmarks that exhibit limitations, asset owners should describe these limitations in the relevant GIPS Asset Owner Report. This helps the oversight body understand the nature of the benchmark and be aware of any known drawbacks in comparing the risk and return of the benchmark and the composite.

Sample Disclosure:

"The benchmark is the Hedge Fund Aggregate Multi-Style Index, which includes more than 100 hedge funds of various styles and strategies. Because this index is based on the data self-reported by the constituent funds, it may have a self-reporting bias. In addition, some funds are closed to new investors and are no longer investable. We believe that no better index exists as a comparison for this composite."

Provision 25.D.7

The ASSET OWNER SHOULD disclose information about the INVESTMENT MANAGEMENT FEES and INVESTMENT MANAGEMENT COSTS of the COMPOSITE that were incurred during the most recent annual period.

Discussion

Investment management fees are the fees payable to external managers for externally managed assets. Investment management fees are typically asset based (percentage of assets), performance based, or a combination of the two but may take different forms as well. Investment management fees also include carried interest.

Investment management costs include all internal costs for both internally and externally managed assets.[N] In addition to the costs for portfolio management, they may also involve overhead and other related costs and fees, including data valuation fees, investment research services, custody fees, pro rata share of overhead (such as building and utilities), allocation of non-investment-department expenses (such as human resources, communications, and technology), and performance measurement and compliance services. Investment management fees are not included in investment management costs.

[N] The definition of INVESTMENT MANAGEMENT COSTS included in the Glossary in the 2020 edition of the GIPS standards is incorrect and should state:

All _internal_ costs for both internally and externally managed assets. In addition to costs for PORTFOLIO management, they may also involve overhead and other related costs and fees, including data valuation fees, investment research services, CUSTODY FEES, pro rata share of overhead (such as building and utilities), allocation of non-investment-department expenses (such as human resources, communications, and technology), and performance measurement and compliance services.

Determining investment fees and costs for an asset owner, particularly investment management costs for internally managed assets, is not a straightforward process. Given the complexity of the costs incurred by an asset owner, it is recommended that the GIPS Asset Owner Report include disclosures about the investment management fees and investment management costs of the composite that were incurred during the most recent annual period. This will help the oversight body understand the more recent fees and costs paid for the external and internal management of the composite assets.

Sample Disclosure:

"Total investment management costs deducted from the net-of-external-costs-only return to arrive at the net return was 0.14% for the fiscal year ended 30 June 2020. These costs include the allocation of internal overhead expenses and data valuation fees."

26. GIPS ADVERTISING GUIDELINES

Purpose of The GIPS Advertising Guidelines

The GIPS Advertising Guidelines provide asset owners with options for advertising when mentioning the asset owner's claim of compliance. The GIPS Advertising Guidelines do not replace the GIPS standards, nor do they absolve asset owners from presenting GIPS Asset Owner Reports as required by the GIPS standards. These guidelines apply only to asset owners that already satisfy all the applicable requirements of the GIPS standards on an asset owner–wide basis and prepare an advertisement that adheres to the requirements of the GIPS Advertising Guidelines (a "GIPS Advertisement"). Asset owners may also choose to include a GIPS Asset Owner Report in the advertisement.

Definitions

Advertisement

For the GIPS Advertising Guidelines for asset owners, an advertisement includes any materials that are distributed to or designed for use in newspapers, magazines, asset owner brochures, letters, media, websites, or any other written or electronic material distributed to more than one party, and there is no contact between the asset owner and the reader of the advertisement.

GIPS Advertisement

A GIPS Advertisement is an advertisement by a GIPS-compliant asset owner that adheres to the requirements of the GIPS Advertising Guidelines.

Relationship of the GIPS Advertising Guidelines to Regulatory Requirements

When preparing GIPS Advertisements, asset owners must also adhere to all applicable laws and regulations governing advertisements. Asset owners are encouraged to seek legal or regulatory counsel because additional disclosures may be required. In cases where applicable laws or regulations conflict with the requirements of the GIPS standards or the GIPS Advertising Guidelines, asset owners are required to comply with the laws or regulations.

 |

Other Information

The GIPS Advertisement may include other information beyond what is required or recommended under the GIPS Advertising Guidelines, provided the information is shown with equal or lesser prominence relative to the information required or recommended by the GIPS Advertising Guidelines and the information does not conflict with the requirements or recommendations of the GIPS standards or the GIPS Advertising Guidelines. Asset owners must adhere to the principles of fair representation and full disclosure when advertising and must not present performance or performance-related information that is false or misleading.

26.A. Fundamental Requirements of the GIPS Advertising Guidelines

Provision 26.A.1

The GIPS Advertising Guidelines apply only to ASSET OWNERS that already claim compliance with the GIPS standards.

Discussion

An asset owner that claims compliance with the GIPS standards has three options with respect to preparing an advertisement:

- Prepare the advertisement in accordance with the GIPS Advertising Guidelines.
- Include a GIPS Asset Owner Report in the advertisement.
- Do not mention the GIPS standards in the advertisement.

An asset owner that chooses to claim compliance in an advertisement must either meet the requirements of the GIPS Advertising Guidelines or include a GIPS Asset Owner Report in the advertisement. Asset owners are not required to claim compliance with the GIPS standards in advertisements.

Asset owners claiming compliance with the GIPS standards must ensure that all performance or performance-related information in advertisements is not false or misleading and adheres to the guiding principles of fair representation and full disclosure, whether or not the advertisement contains a claim of compliance with the GIPS standards.

Provision 26.A.2

An ASSET OWNER that chooses to claim compliance in a GIPS ADVERTISEMENT MUST comply with all applicable REQUIREMENTS of the GIPS Advertising Guidelines.

Discussion

If an asset owner chooses to advertise its claim of compliance with the GIPS standards by creating a GIPS Advertisement, it must comply with all applicable requirements of the GIPS Advertising Guidelines. The asset owner must also adhere to all applicable laws and regulations governing advertisements.

Provision 26.A.3

The ASSET OWNER MUST maintain all data and information necessary to support all items included in a GIPS ADVERTISEMENT.

Discussion

A fundamental principle of the GIPS standards is the need for asset owners to be able to ensure the validity of their claim of compliance. It is, therefore, important for the oversight bodies, verifiers, and regulators to have confidence that all items included in a GIPS Advertisement are supported by the appropriate records.

Asset owners must maintain records to be able to recalculate their performance history as well as substantiate all other information included in a GIPS Advertisement, for all periods shown. This requirement applies to all periods for which performance is presented in the GIPS Advertisement. There may be cases where regulators require records to be kept for longer periods than those required by the GIPS standards. Care should be taken to ensure that the asset owner follows the strictest of the recordkeeping requirements applicable to the asset owner.

It is understood that the required data may not be immediately available. For example, data may need to be retrieved from an offsite location or from a third-party service provider. However, the data and information required to be maintained by this provision must be available in a usable format within a reasonable time frame. In all instances, either paper (hard-copy) records or electronically stored records will suffice. If records are stored electronically, the records must be accessible and able to be printed or downloaded, if needed. Records stored in a system that is not operable and from which data cannot be retrieved will not satisfy the recordkeeping requirements.

 | **237**

Please refer to Provision 21.A.19 for more information about the records required to be retained to support a GIPS Advertisement.

Provision 26.A.4

Returns for periods of less than one year included in a GIPS ADVERTISEMENT MUST NOT be annualized.

Discussion

Total fund or composite performance reflects only the performance of actual assets managed by the asset owner. When returns for periods of less than one year are annualized, the partial-year return is "extended" in order to create an annual return. The extrapolation of the partial-year return produces a simulated return and does not reflect the performance of actual assets. Therefore, performance for periods of less than one year must not be annualized in a GIPS Advertisement.

Care must be taken when money-weighted returns (MWRs) are calculated and the total fund or composite has less than a year of performance. Many asset owners use Excel to calculate MWRs using the XIRR function. The XIRR function calculates an annualized internal rate of return (IRR) (an IRR is a method that can be used to calculate an MWR). When calculating an XIRR for a period of less than one year, the annualized return generated must be "de-annualized."

The non-annualized since-inception IRR (SI-IRR) can be calculated as follows:

$$R_{SI-IRR} = \left[(1 + r_{SI-IRR})^{\frac{TD}{365}} \right] - 1,$$

where

R_{SI-IRR} = non-annualized since-inception internal rate of return

r_{SI-IRR} = annualized since-inception internal rate of return

TD = total number of calendar days in the measurement period (less than one year)

For example, a portfolio is funded with $1,000,000 cash on 1 September 2020. Another $75,000 is contributed on 10 September 2020. At the end of the month, 30 September 2020, the portfolio is valued at $1,100,000. Also assume that end-of-day cash flows are used. Using Excel's XIRR formula, the annualized SI-IRR is 34.41%.

Dates	External Cash Flows & Ending Valuation	Explanation
1 Sep 20	$(1,000,000)	Contribution
10 Sep 20	$(75,000)	Contribution
30 Sep 20	$1,100,000	Portfolio value as of 30 September 2020
	34.41%	Calculated annualized return using XIRR

To calculate the non-annualized return in Excel using the non-annualized SI-IRR formula above the calculation is as follows:

$$(1+0.3441)^{(29/365)}-1 = 2.38\%$$

Provision 26.A.5

TOTAL FUND or COMPOSITE returns included in a GIPS ADVERTISEMENT MUST be derived from the returns included in or that will be included in the corresponding GIPS ASSET OWNER REPORT.

Discussion

In the spirit of fair representation and full disclosure, all total fund or composite returns included in a GIPS Advertisement must be derived from the returns that have been included in or that will be included in the corresponding GIPS Asset Owner Report. This requirement is to ensure consistency in the performance reported by an asset owner. If a GIPS Advertisement is more current than the corresponding GIPS Asset Owner Report, it is permissible to include more-recent performance in the GIPS Advertisement, as long as this performance will be included in the GIPS Asset Owner Report when it is updated or would be included in the GIPS Asset Owner Report if it were issued as of the date of the GIPS Advertisement.

Provision 26.A.6

Disclosures included in a GIPS ADVERTISEMENT for a TOTAL FUND or COMPOSITE MUST be consistent with the related disclosure included in the corresponding GIPS ASSET OWNER REPORT, unless the disclosure included in the GIPS ADVERTISEMENT is more current and has not yet been reflected in the corresponding GIPS ASSET OWNER REPORT.

 |

Discussion

In the spirit of fair representation and full disclosure, all disclosures included in a GIPS Advertisement must be consistent with the disclosures included in or that will be included in the corresponding GIPS Asset Owner Report. This requirement is to ensure consistency in information reported by an asset owner. If a GIPS Advertisement is more current than the corresponding GIPS Asset Owner Report, it is permissible to include a more current disclosure in the GIPS Advertisement, as long as the more current disclosure will be included in the GIPS Asset Owner Report if it were issued as of the date of the GIPS Advertisement.

Provision 26.A.7

BENCHMARK returns included in a GIPS ADVERTISEMENT MUST be TOTAL RETURNS.

Discussion

Because the GIPS standards require that benchmark returns presented in a GIPS Advertisement be total returns, a price-only index would not satisfy the requirements of the GIPS Advertising Guidelines. This also applies to benchmarks that are components of a blended benchmark. A price-only benchmark may be presented in a GIPS Advertisement only if it is presented in addition to a total return benchmark. It must be labeled as a price-only benchmark, and there must be sufficient disclosures so that the oversight body understands the difference between the return of a price-only benchmark and the return of a total return benchmark. Asset owners must not present only a price-only benchmark in a GIPS Advertisement even if no appropriate total return benchmark is available for a specific total fund or composite. If an asset owner determines that no appropriate benchmark for the total fund or composite exists, it must not present a benchmark.

Some benchmarks may appear to be price-only benchmarks because they do not include income, but they should be considered total return benchmarks. These include the following:

- public market equivalent (PME) benchmarks,
- commodity benchmarks, and similar benchmarks, that do not have income because of the nature of the benchmark constituents, and
- target returns, such as an 8% hurdle rate.

A PME is a method in which a public market index is used to create a comparable money-weighted return (MWR) from a series of cash flows that replicate those of the total fund or composite and that can be compared with the MWR of the total fund or composite. When the asset owner uses a PME, the market index used must be a total return benchmark.

The benchmark presented in the GIPS Advertisement must be consistent with the benchmark presented in the corresponding GIPS Asset Owner Report. If more than one benchmark is included in the corresponding GIPS Asset Owner Report, the asset owner should consider whether multiple benchmarks should be presented in the GIPS Advertisement.

Provision 26.A.8

The ASSET OWNER MUST clearly label or identify:

a. The name of the COMPOSITE or TOTAL FUND for which the GIPS ADVERTISEMENT is prepared.

b. The name of any BENCHMARK included in the GIPS ADVERTISEMENT.

c. The periods that are presented in the GIPS ADVERTISEMENT.

Discussion

The items presented in a GIPS Advertisement must be clearly labeled or identified so there is clarity regarding the information being presented. Among the items included in a GIPS Advertisement that must be clearly identified or labeled are:

- the name of the composite or total fund for which the GIPS Advertisement is prepared,
- the name of any benchmark included in the GIPS Advertisement, and
- the time periods presented.

The name of the benchmark is particularly important when a customized benchmark is used. Asset owners may need to include more than the name of a customized benchmark when more information is needed for a reader to understand the information presented. For example, if an asset owner includes a custom benchmark that has a hedge applied, simply stating that the benchmark is a custom benchmark would not allow a reader to understand the benchmark returns. It would be appropriate to disclose that the benchmark is hedged and how the hedge was applied.

Provision 26.A.9

Other information beyond what is REQUIRED or RECOMMENDED under the GIPS Advertising Guidelines (e.g., COMPOSITE or TOTAL FUND returns for additional periods) MUST be presented with equal or lesser prominence relative to the information REQUIRED or RECOMMENDED by the GIPS Advertising Guidelines. This information MUST NOT conflict with the REQUIREMENTS or RECOMMENDATIONS of the GIPS standards or the GIPS Advertising Guidelines.

 |

Discussion

A GIPS Advertisement may include information beyond what is required or recommended under the GIPS Advertising Guidelines. For example, returns for periods in addition to the required periods may be shown. However, information beyond what is required or recommended must:

- be shown with equal or lesser prominence relative to the information that is required or recommended,
- not conflict with the requirements or recommendations of the GIPS standards or the GIPS Advertising Guidelines,
- not be false or misleading, and
- adhere to the principles of fair representation and full disclosure.

As an example, assume that a GIPS Advertisement for a total fund or composite includes all information required by the GIPS Advertising Guidelines in a size 10 font. Including backtested hypothetical performance in size 18 font would not be allowed because this information would not be shown with equal or lesser prominence.

Provision 26.A.10

All REQUIRED and RECOMMENDED information in a GIPS ADVERTISEMENT MUST be presented in the same currency.

Discussion

Asset owners must present all required and recommended information in a GIPS Advertisement in the same currency (e.g., total fund or composite and benchmark returns). Any information beyond what is required or recommended by the GIPS Advertising Guidelines should also be presented in the same currency. If it is not, that fact must be disclosed. It would be misleading for the asset owner to not disclose this fact.

If an asset owner chooses to present a total fund or composite in a different currency, the asset owner must convert all of the required information into the new currency. If the asset owner chooses to present performance in multiple currencies in the same GIPS Advertisement, the asset owner must convert all of the required information into each of the currencies and ensure it is clear in which currencies performance is reported. The asset owner must also convert any recommended information it chooses to present in the GIPS Advertisement containing the converted information. See Provision 24.A.7 for guidance on converting total fund or composite time-weighted returns and Provision 25.A.7 for guidance on converting composite money-weighted returns.

26.B. GIPS Advertisements That Do Not Include Performance

Provision 26.B.1

The ASSET OWNER MUST disclose the GIPS Advertising Guidelines compliance statement:

"[Insert name of ASSET OWNER] claims compliance with the Global Investment Performance Standards (GIPS®).

Discussion

An asset owner has two ways of advertising its claim of compliance with the GIPS standards: 1) by following the GIPS Advertising Guidelines or 2) by including a GIPS Asset Owner Report in its advertisement. If an asset owner has chosen to advertise its claim of compliance by following the GIPS Advertising Guidelines, it must include the following compliance statement in the GIPS Advertisement:

"[Insert name of ASSET OWNER] claims compliance with the Global Investment Performance Standards (GIPS®)."

The compliance statement required by the GIPS Advertising Guidelines is different from the compliance statement required to be disclosed in a GIPS Asset Owner Report. The GIPS Advertising Guidelines compliance statement must appear exactly as presented in this provision and may not be reworded in any way. The English version of the compliance statement is the controlling version. If an asset owner chooses to translate the compliance statement into a language for which there is no official translation of the GIPS standards, the asset owner must take care to ensure that the translation used reflects the required wording of the compliance statement.

Provision 26.B.2

The ASSET OWNER MUST disclose the following: "GIPS® is a registered trademark of CFA Institute. CFA Institute does not endorse or promote this organization, nor does it warrant the accuracy or quality of the content contained herein."

Discussion

"GIPS®" is a registered trademark of CFA Institute, and asset owners are required to acknowledge this in all GIPS Advertisements. The required disclosure may appear in the body of the GIPS Advertisement or in a footnote to the GIPS Advertisement. The term "this organization," which is

|

included in the required disclosure, refers to any entity associated with the GIPS Advertisement, either the asset owner or the verifier.

CFA Institute (owner of the GIPS® trademark) may take appropriate action against any asset owner that misuses the mark "GIPS®" or any compliance statement, including false claims of compliance with the GIPS standards. CFA Institute members, CFA Program charterholders, CFA candidates, CIPM Program certificants, and CIPM candidates who misuse the term "GIPS" or any compliance statement, misrepresent their performance history or the performance history of the asset owner, or falsely claim compliance with the GIPS standards are also subject to disciplinary sanctions under the CFA Institute Code of Ethics and Standards of Professional Conduct. Possible disciplinary sanctions include public censure, suspension of membership, and revocation of the CFA charter or CIPM certificate.

Regulators with jurisdiction over asset owners claiming compliance with the GIPS standards may also take enforcement actions against asset owners that falsely claim compliance with the GIPS standards.

Asset owners may also use the following language to replace the first sentence in this required disclosure: "GIPS® is a registered trademark owned by CFA Institute." See the GIPS Standards Trademark Usage Guidelines on the GIPS standards website (www.gipsstandards.org) for additional guidance on the use of "GIPS".

Provision 26.B.3

The ASSET OWNER MUST disclose how a participant or beneficiary may obtain GIPS-compliant performance information for the ASSET OWNER's strategies and products.

Discussion

An advertisement is typically brief and provides limited information regarding the asset owner and its strategies and products. A participant or beneficiary may want to receive additional information in order to have a more complete understanding of an asset owner's investment performance. It is, therefore, required that asset owners disclose in a GIPS Advertisement how to obtain GIPS-compliant performance information. GIPS-compliant performance information includes GIPS Asset Owner Reports and the asset owner's required lists of total fund descriptions and composite descriptions.

Sample Disclosure:

"To receive additional information regarding Centralville Police and Fire Retirement Systems (CPFRS), including GIPS-compliant performance information, contact Susan Jenry at (779) 873-XXXX or write Centralville Police and Fire Retirement Systems, One Midtown Street, Centralville, Michigan, 48XXX or susan.jenry@CPFRS.org."

26.C. GIPS Advertisements for a Total Fund or Composite That Include Performance—Requirements

Provision 26.C.1

If TIME-WEIGHTED RETURNS are presented in the corresponding GIPS ASSET OWNER REPORT, the ASSET OWNER MUST present TOTAL FUND or COMPOSITE TOTAL RETURNS according to one of the following:

a. One-, three-, and five-year annualized TOTAL FUND or COMPOSITE returns through the most recent period. If the TOTAL FUND or COMPOSITE has been in existence for less than five years, or the ASSET OWNER presents less than five years of performance in the corresponding GIPS ASSET OWNER REPORT, the ASSET OWNER MUST also present the annualized return that includes all periods presented in the corresponding GIPS ASSET OWNER REPORT.

b. The period-to-date TOTAL FUND or COMPOSITE return in addition to one-, three-, and five-year annualized TOTAL FUND or COMPOSITE returns through the same period as presented in the corresponding GIPS ASSET OWNER REPORT. If the TOTAL FUND or COMPOSITE has been in existence for less than five years, or the ASSET OWNER presents less than five years of performance in the corresponding GIPS ASSET OWNER REPORT, the ASSET OWNER MUST also present the annualized return that includes all periods presented in the corresponding GIPS ASSET OWNER REPORT.

c. The period-to-date TOTAL FUND or COMPOSITE return in addition to five years of annual TOTAL FUND or COMPOSITE returns (or for each annual period presented in the corresponding GIPS ASSET OWNER REPORT if less than five years). The annual returns MUST be calculated through the same period as presented in the corresponding GIPS ASSET OWNER REPORT.

d. The annualized TOTAL FUND or COMPOSITE return for the total period that includes all periods presented in the corresponding GIPS ASSET OWNER REPORT, through either:

i. The most recent period end, or

ii. The most recent annual period end.

Discussion

Provision 26.C.1 does not require an asset owner presenting time-weighted returns in a GIPS Advertisement to include all four options (a through d) mentioned in the provision. Rather, an asset owner must present performance in accordance with one of the options described in the provision. A GIPS Advertisement must also adhere to all applicable laws and regulations governing advertisements.

Three of the four options in Provision 26.C.1 include the presentation of annualized total fund or composite returns, which represent the geometric average annual compound return achieved over the defined period of more than one year. Annualized performance is permitted only for periods of one year or more.

The formula for calculating annualized performance is as follows:

$$\text{Annualized Return (\%)} = [(1 + R)^{1/n}] - 1,$$

where R is the cumulative return for the period, which is calculated by geometrically linking the sub-period returns during the period, and n is the number of years in the period.

For example, assume a total fund's or composite's cumulative return for a five-year period is 150.0%. It has a five-year average annual compound return, or annualized return, of 20.11%, which is calculated as:

$$[(1+1.50)^{\frac{1}{5}}] - 1 = 0.2011 = 20.11\%.$$

If instead the 150% is earned over 12.5 years, the 12.5-year average annual compound return, or annualized return, is 7.61%, which is calculated as:

$$[(1+1.50)^{\frac{1}{12.5}}] - 1 = 0.0761 = 7.61\%.$$

If the asset owner chooses to comply with Provision 26.C.1.a, it must present the one-, three-, and five-year annualized total fund or composite returns through the most recent period end. If the total fund or composite has been in existence for less than five years, or the asset owner presents less than five years of performance in the corresponding GIPS Asset Owner Report, the asset owner must also present the annualized total fund or composite return that includes all periods presented in the corresponding GIPS Asset Owner Report.

The most recent period-end date is as of the most recent month-end or quarter-end date. For example, if preparing a GIPS Advertisement in May, the most recent quarter end would be 31 March and the most recent month end would be 30 April. The asset owner may choose whether to use month-end or quarter-end periods.

If the asset owner chooses to comply with Provision 26.C.1.b, it must present the period-to-date total fund or composite return in addition to the one-, three-, and five-year annualized total fund or composite returns through the same period as presented in the corresponding GIPS Asset Owner Report. For example, if the GIPS Asset Owner Report includes calendar-year annual returns, then the annualized returns in the GIPS Advertisement must be through the most recent 31 December. If the total fund or composite has been in existence for less than five years, or the asset owner presents less than five years of performance in the corresponding GIPS Asset Owner

Report, the asset owner must also present the annualized total fund or composite return that includes all periods presented in the corresponding GIPS Asset Owner Report through the most recent period end (either month end or quarter end).

If the asset owner chooses to comply with Provision 26.C.1.c, it must present the period-to-date total fund or composite return in addition to five years of annual total fund or composite returns (or for each annual period presented in the corresponding GIPS Asset Owner Report if less than five years). The annual returns must be calculated through the same period as presented in the corresponding GIPS Asset Owner Report.

If the asset owner chooses to comply with Provision 26.C.1.d, it must present the annualized total fund or composite return for the total period that includes all periods presented in the corresponding GIPS Asset Owner Report through either: a) the most recent period end (either month end or quarter end) or b) the most recent annual period end. If the total fund or composite has been in existence for less than one year, the return must not be annualized.

In the spirit of fair representation and full disclosure, Provision 26.A.5 requires that all total fund or composite returns included in a GIPS Advertisement must be derived from the returns that have been included in or that will be included in the corresponding GIPS Asset Owner Report. This requirement is to ensure consistency in the performance reported by an asset owner. If a GIPS Advertisement is more current than the corresponding GIPS Asset Owner Report, it is permissible to include more-recent performance in the GIPS Advertisement, as long as this performance will be included in the GIPS Asset Owner Report when it is updated or would be included in the GIPS Asset Owner Report if it were issued as of the date of the GIPS Advertisement.

Provision 26.C.2

If MONEY-WEIGHTED RETURNS are presented in the corresponding GIPS ASSET OWNER REPORT, the ASSET OWNER MUST present the annualized (for periods longer than one year) or non-annualized (for periods less than one year) TOTAL FUND or COMPOSITE MONEY-WEIGHTED RETURN that has the same start date as presented in the GIPS ASSET OWNER REPORT, through either:

a. The most recent period end, or
b. The most recent annual period end.

Discussion

If the asset owner has chosen to present a money-weighted return (MWR) for a total fund in a GIPS Asset Owner Report in addition to the required time-weighted return (TWR), the asset owner may present an MWR, a TWR, or both an MWR and a TWR in the corresponding GIPS Advertisement.

If the asset owner has chosen to present an MWR for an additional composite in a GIPS Asset Owner Report, it must present an MWR for the additional composite in the corresponding GIPS Advertisement. (An additional composite is a grouping of portfolios representing a particular strategy or asset class that the asset owner chooses to present in a GIPS Asset Owner Report.)

If the MWR is for a period of longer than one year, it must be annualized. If the MWR is for a period of less than one year, it must not be annualized. The MWR must have the same start date as the MWR that is presented in the GIPS Asset Owner Report. The MWR must be calculated through either: a) the most recent period end (i.e., through the most recent month or quarter end) or b) the most recent annual period end.

In the spirit of fair representation and full disclosure, Provision 26.A.5 requires that all total fund or composite returns included in a GIPS Advertisement must be derived from the returns that have been included in or that will be included in the corresponding GIPS Asset Owner Report. This requirement is to ensure consistency in the performance reported by an asset owner. If a GIPS Advertisement is more current than the corresponding GIPS Asset Owner Report, it is permissible to include more-recent performance in the GIPS Advertisement, as long as this performance will be included in the GIPS Asset Owner Report when it is updated or would be included in the GIPS Asset Owner Report if it were issued as of the date of the GIPS Advertisement.

Provision 26.C.3

The ASSET OWNER MUST clearly label TOTAL FUND or COMPOSITE returns as GROSS-OF-FEES, NET-OF-EXTERNAL-COSTS-ONLY, or NET-OF-FEES.

Discussion

Asset owners must present net-of-fees returns in a GIPS Asset Owner Report for a total fund or total fund composite, and may also choose to present gross-of-fees and net-of-external-costs-only returns in addition to the required net-of-fees returns.

Asset owners may present gross-of-fees returns, net-of-external-costs-only returns, or net-of-fees returns for an additional composite in a GIPS Asset Owner Report. (An additional composite is a grouping of portfolios representing a particular strategy or asset class that the asset owner chooses to present in a GIPS Asset Owner Report.)

An asset owner may present returns in a GIPS Advertisement that are different from those presented in the GIPS Asset Owner Report. For example, an asset owner may present gross-of-fees returns or net-of-external-costs-only returns in a GIPS Advertisement even if the corresponding GIPS Asset Owner Report includes only net-of-fees returns, as long as the returns presented in the GIPS Advertisement are derived from the returns that would be included in the corresponding GIPS Asset Owner Report.

For readers of the advertisement to understand the nature of the returns being presented, all returns presented must be clearly labeled as gross-of-fees, net-of-external-costs-only, or net-of-fees.

Asset owners advertising performance results must adhere to all applicable laws and regulations, including those governing advertisements. Whether or not laws or regulations specify which returns must be presented in an advertisement, asset owners must clearly indicate whether returns are presented gross-of-fees, net-of-fees, or net-of-external-costs-only so that the reader of the advertisement has a clear understanding of the returns that are presented.

Provision 26.C.4

The ASSET OWNER MUST present BENCHMARK returns for the same BENCHMARK as presented in the corresponding GIPS ASSET OWNER REPORT, if the corresponding GIPS ASSET OWNER REPORT includes BENCHMARK returns. BENCHMARK returns MUST be of the same return type (TIME-WEIGHTED RETURNS or MONEY-WEIGHTED RETURNS), in the same currency, and for the same periods for which the TOTAL FUND or COMPOSITE returns are presented.

Discussion

As described in Provisions 26.C.1 and 26.C.2, asset owners that present performance in a GIPS Advertisement for a total fund or composite have various options for the time periods used in presenting time-weighted returns (TWRs) and money-weighted returns (MWRs). Once an option is selected, the asset owner must present the total returns for the benchmark(s) for the same periods as the total fund or composite returns. The benchmark must be the same benchmark as presented in the corresponding GIPS Asset Owner Report and must also be the same return type (TWR or MWR) and in the same currency as the total fund or composite returns. If more than one benchmark is included in the GIPS Asset Owner Report, the asset owner should consider whether multiple benchmarks should be presented in the GIPS Advertisement.

This requirement is an acknowledgement that a comparison of benchmark and total fund or composite returns will help the reader of the GIPS Advertisement determine how well the total fund or composite has performed relative to the benchmark.

|

Provision 26.C.5

The ASSET OWNER MUST disclose or otherwise indicate the reporting currency.

Discussion

The GIPS standards require that asset owners disclose the currency used to report the numerical information presented in a GIPS Advertisement. If the asset owner presents performance in multiple currencies in the same GIPS Advertisement, the asset owner must ensure it is clear which currencies are used to calculate and report performance. Labeling the columns within a GIPS Advertisement with the appropriate currency symbol would satisfy this requirement, as would a written disclosure.

All required and recommended information presented in a GIPS Advertisement must be presented in the same currency. (See Provision 26.A.10.)

Sample Disclosures:

"Valuations are computed and all information is reported in Canadian dollars."

"Performance is reported in Japanese yen."

Provision 26.C.6

The ASSET OWNER MUST disclose the GIPS Advertising Guidelines compliance statement:

> "[Insert name of ASSET OWNER] claims compliance with the Global Investment Performance Standards (GIPS®)."

Discussion

An asset owner has two ways of advertising its claim of compliance with the GIPS standards: 1) by following the GIPS Advertising Guidelines or 2) by including a GIPS Asset Owner Report in its advertisement. If an asset owner chooses to advertise its claim of compliance by following the GIPS Advertising Guidelines, it must include the following compliance statement in the GIPS Advertisement:

> "[Insert name of ASSET OWNER] claims compliance with the Global Investment Performance Standards (GIPS®)."

The compliance statement required by the GIPS Advertising Guidelines is different from the compliance statement required to be disclosed in a GIPS Asset Owner Report. The GIPS Advertising Guidelines compliance statement must appear exactly as presented in this provision and may not be reworded in any way. The English version of the compliance statement is the controlling version. If an asset owner chooses to translate the compliance statement into a language for which there is no official translation of the GIPS standards, the asset owner must take care to ensure that the translation used reflects the required wording of the compliance statement.

Provision 26.C.7

The ASSET OWNER MUST disclose the following: "GIPS® is a registered trademark of CFA Institute. CFA Institute does not endorse or promote this organization, nor does it warrant the accuracy or quality of the content contained herein."

Discussion

"GIPS®" is a registered trademark of CFA Institute, and asset owners are required to acknowledge this in all GIPS Advertisements. The required disclosure may appear in the body of the GIPS Advertisement or in a footnote to the GIPS Advertisement. The term "this organization," which is included in the required disclosure, refers to any entity associated with the GIPS Advertisement, either the asset owner or the verifier.

CFA Institute (owner of the GIPS® trademark) may take appropriate action against any asset owner that misuses the mark "GIPS®" or any compliance statement, including false claims of compliance with the GIPS standards. CFA Institute members, CFA Program charterholders, CFA candidates, CIPM Program certificants, and CIPM candidates who misuse the term "GIPS" or any compliance statement, misrepresent their performance history or the performance history of the asset owner, or falsely claim compliance with the GIPS standards are also subject to disciplinary sanctions under the CFA Institute Code of Ethics and Standards of Professional Conduct. Possible disciplinary sanctions include public censure, suspension of membership, and revocation of the CFA charter or CIPM certificate.

Regulators with jurisdiction over asset owners claiming compliance with the GIPS standards may also take enforcement actions against asset owners that falsely claim compliance with the GIPS standards.

Asset owners may also use the following language to replace the first sentence in this required disclosure: "GIPS® is a registered trademark owned by CFA Institute." See the GIPS Standards Trademark Usage Guidelines on the GIPS standards website (www.gipsstandards.org) for additional guidance on the use of "GIPS®".

Provision 26.C.8

The ASSET OWNER MUST disclose how to obtain a GIPS ASSET OWNER REPORT.

Discussion

An advertisement is typically brief and provides limited information regarding the asset owner and its strategies and products. A reader of a GIPS Advertisement may want to receive additional information on the asset owner's investment performance, including a GIPS Asset Owner Report for the total fund or composite presented in the advertisement. Asset owners are, therefore, required to disclose in a GIPS Advertisement how to obtain a GIPS Asset Owner Report.

Sample Disclosure:

"To receive additional information regarding Centralville Police and Fire Retirement Systems (CPFRS), including a GIPS Asset Owner Report for the total fund presented in this advertisement, contact Susan Jenry at (779) 873-XXXX or write Centralville Police and Fire Retirement Systems, One Midtown Street, Centralville, Michigan, 48XXX or susan.jenry@CPFRS.org."

Provision 26.C.9

The ASSET OWNER MUST disclose if the GIPS ADVERTISEMENT conforms with laws or regulations that conflict with the REQUIREMENTS or RECOMMENDATIONS of the GIPS standards or the GIPS Advertising Guidelines, as well as the manner in which the laws or regulations conflict with the GIPS standards or the GIPS Advertising Guidelines.

Discussion

Asset owners must comply with all applicable laws and regulations regarding the calculation and presentation of performance, including the advertising of performance. Compliance with applicable laws and regulations, however, does not necessarily result in compliance with the GIPS Advertising Guidelines. Asset owners must also comply with all of the applicable requirements of the GIPS Advertising Guidelines when preparing an advertisement in accordance with the GIPS Advertising Guidelines. When laws and regulations conflict with the GIPS Advertising Guidelines, asset owners are required to comply with the laws and regulations and disclose the manner in which the laws or regulations conflict with the GIPS Advertising Guidelines.

This disclosure will assist the reader in understanding the difference between the reporting requirements of applicable laws and regulations and those of the GIPS standards.

Sample Disclosure:

"Local laws do not allow the presentation of returns of less than one year in an advertisement, which is in conflict with the GIPS Advertising Guidelines. Therefore, no performance is presented for this composite for the period from 1 July 2018 (the inception date of the composite) through 31 December 2018."

26.D. GIPS Advertisements for a Total Fund or Composite That Include Performance—Recommendations

Provision 26.D.1

The ASSET OWNER SHOULD disclose the TOTAL FUND DESCRIPTION or COMPOSITE DESCRIPTION.

Discussion

To help a reader of a GIPS Advertisement more fully understand the total fund or composite being presented, it is recommended that an asset owner disclose the total fund description or composite description in the GIPS Advertisement. The total fund description or composite description is general information regarding the investment mandate, objective, or strategy of the total fund or composite. The total fund description or composite description must include enough information to allow a reader of the GIPS Advertisement to understand the key characteristics of the total fund's or composite's investment mandate, objective, or strategy, including the risks of the strategy; how leverage, derivatives, and short positions may be used if they are a material part of the strategy; and whether or not illiquid assets are a material part of the strategy. In addition to these factors, the total fund description should also include:

- the total fund's asset allocation as of the most recent annual period end,
- the actuarial rate of return or spending policy description, and
- a description of the asset classes and/or other groupings within the total fund, such as the composition of the asset class, strategy used, types of management used (e.g., active, passive, internal, external), and relevant exposures.

The recommended disclosure of the total fund description or composite description provides information about the total fund's or composite's investment strategy or asset class(es) that is intended to help a reader of the GIPS Advertisement understand the total fund or composite strategy. The total fund or composite description should provide sufficient information to allow readers of the GIPS Advertisement to identify the significant features of the total fund or composite strategy. The disclosed strategy features will likely affect both the historical and expected risk and returns. Along with the recommended disclosure of the benchmark description (see Provision 26.D.3), the GIPS Advertisement will allow the reader to understand both the investment strategy employed and the benchmark against which the total fund's or composite's performance is evaluated.

If leverage, derivatives, and short positions may be used, and they are a material part of the strategy, this must be disclosed in the total fund or composite description. Provision 26.D.2 recommends that the asset owner disclose how leverage, derivatives, and short positions have been used historically, if material. Taken together, these two recommended disclosures provide a more complete picture about the presence, use, and extent of leverage, derivatives, and short positions. When determining what would be material, the asset owner must consider whether the disclosure of how leverage, derivatives, and/or short positions are used and/or have been used historically is likely to affect a reader's view of the risk involved in the strategy. If so, the asset owner must consider if it would be misleading for the asset owner to fail to disclose their use to the reader when describing the strategy.

Generally, all investment products or strategies have some degree of inherent risk (e.g., market risk), but it is not intended that the total fund or composite description identifies every risk of the strategy. Instead, asset owners must identify those material risks of the strategy, if any, and must include those risks in the description of the total fund or composite. For example, investment concentration, correlation (or lack thereof), liquidity, and exposure to counterparties are features that may need to be included in the total fund or composite description. (See Provision 21.A.17 for additional guidance on total fund descriptions and composite descriptions.)

The key characteristics of some strategies may change in response to market events. Asset owners should periodically review total fund descriptions and composite descriptions to ensure they are current.

Given the abbreviated nature of an advertisement, there may be times when asset owners may wish to use a shorter total fund description or composite description in a GIPS Advertisement rather than the description used in the corresponding GIPS Asset Owner Report. The following examples illustrate how a description can be shortened for a GIPS Advertisement while still conveying the essential features of the total fund's or composite's strategy.

Sample Disclosures:

Total Fund Description

Included in a GIPS Asset Owner Report

"The Police Officers Total Fund includes all discretionary assets managed by Any State Retirement System for the benefit of police officer participants. The strategy reflects the actual asset allocation approved each year by the board, based on the funded status, risk budget, and actuarial rate of return studies. Performance is measured against a blended benchmark using asset class benchmarks based on the total fund's policy weights as established at the beginning of each fiscal year. The longer-term investment objective is to earn, over moving 20-year periods, an annualized rate of return that equals or exceeds the actuarial rate of return approved by Any State Retirement System. The Total Fund's asset allocation is designed to provide high long-term return at optimal risk consistent with the board's expected long-term objectives. Investment risks are diversified across a broad range of market sectors, securities, and other investments. This strategy reduces portfolio risk to adverse developments in sectors and issuers experiencing unusual difficulties. The primary risks of the Total Fund include asset allocation risk and liquidity risk."

Included in a GIPS Advertisement

"The Police Officers Total Fund includes all discretionary assets managed by Any State Retirement System for the benefit of police officer participants. The strategy reflects the actual asset allocation approved each year by the board, based on the funded status, risk budget, and actuarial rate of return studies. The longer-term investment objective is to earn, over moving 20-year periods, an annualized rate of return that equals or exceeds the actuarial rate of return approved by Any State Retirement System. The Total Fund's asset allocation is designed to provide high long-term return at optimal risk consistent with the board's expected long-term objectives."

Composite Description:

Included in a GIPS Asset Owner Report

"The Leveraged Bond Composite includes all portfolios invested in a diversified range of high-yield corporate and government bonds with the aim of providing a high level of income while seeking to maximize the total return. The portfolios are invested in domestic and international fixed income securities of varying maturities. The strategy allows investment in exchange-traded and OTC derivative contracts (including, but not limited to, options, futures, swaps, and forward currency contracts) for the purposes of risk, volatility, and currency exposure management. The strategy allows leverage up to but not exceeding twice the value of a portfolio's investments through the use of repurchase financing arrangements with counterparties. Inherent in derivative instrument investments is the risk of counterparty default. Leverage may also magnify losses as well as gains to the extent that leverage is used. The benchmark is the XYZ Capital Global Aggregate Bond Index."

Included in a GIPS Advertisement

"The Leveraged Bond Composite's strategy invests in a diversified range of high-yield corporate and government bonds. The portfolios are invested in domestic and international fixed income securities of varying maturities. The strategy allows investment in exchange-traded and OTC derivatives for the purposes of risk, volatility, and currency exposure management. The strategy allows leverage up to but not exceeding twice the value of a portfolio's investments. The benchmark is the XYZ Capital Global Aggregate Bond Index."

Provision 26.D.2

The ASSET OWNER SHOULD disclose how leverage, derivatives, and short positions have been used historically, if material.

Discussion

It is recommended that asset owners provide enough information in a GIPS Advertisement to allow a reader to understand how leverage, derivatives, and short positions have been employed historically and may be used going forward. Although the recommended disclosure of the total fund or composite description (Provision 26.D.1) would include disclosure of the asset owner's ability to use leverage, derivatives, and short positions, Provision 26.D.2 recommends that the asset owner disclose how leverage, derivatives, and short positions have been used historically, if material. Taken together, these two recommended disclosures provide a more complete picture of the presence, use, and extent of leverage, derivatives, and short positions.

For example, assume an asset owner discloses in a composite description that the strategy may employ up to 200% leverage. To satisfy the disclosure recommendation in Provision 26.D.2, the asset owner might state, "Since the inception of the strategy, the leverage has averaged 110% of the composite's value; during 2019, however, the leverage averaged 160%, which greatly increased the composite's sensitivity to market volatility and the potential for realized gains and/or losses."

When determining what would be material, the asset owner must consider whether the disclosure of how leverage, derivatives, and/or short positions have been used historically is likely to affect a reader's view of the risk involved in the strategy. If so, the asset owner must consider if it would be misleading to fail to disclose their use when describing the strategy.

Provision 26.D.3

The ASSET OWNER SHOULD disclose the BENCHMARK DESCRIPTION, which MUST include the key features of the BENCHMARK or the name of the BENCHMARK for a readily recognized index or other point of reference.

Discussion

Asset owners are recommended to disclose a description of each benchmark included in a GIPS Advertisement. The benchmark description is defined as general information regarding the investments, structure, and/or characteristics of the benchmark, and it must include the key features of the benchmark. In the case of a widely recognized benchmark, such as the S&P 500® Index, the name of the benchmark will satisfy this recommendation. (S&P 500® is a registered trademark of Standard & Poor's Financial Services LLC.) Each asset owner must decide for itself whether a benchmark is widely recognized. If the asset owner is not certain as to whether the benchmark is widely known, it is recommended that the asset owner include the benchmark description.

Sample Disclosure for a Widely Recognized Benchmark:

"The benchmark is the S&P 500® Index."

Sample Disclosure for a Benchmark That Is Not Widely Recognized:

"The benchmark is the XYZ World Total Return Index, which is designed to measure the equity market performance of developed market countries. The benchmark is market-cap weighted and is composed of all XYZ country-specific developed market indices."

Provision 26.D.4

If the ASSET OWNER determines no appropriate BENCHMARK for the TOTAL FUND or COMPOSITE exists, the ASSET OWNER SHOULD disclose why no BENCHMARK is presented.

Discussion

Benchmarks are important tools that aid in the planning, implementation, and evaluation of an investment strategy. They also provide information to the reader of a GIPS Advertisement regarding the relationship between a total fund's or composite's risk and return. As a result, the GIPS standards require asset owners to provide benchmark total returns in all GIPS Advertisements, unless the asset owner determines that no appropriate benchmark for the total fund or composite exists. The benchmark must reflect the investment mandate, objective, or strategy of the total fund or composite. Although there is typically an appropriate benchmark for traditional strategies, it is more common for asset owners managing alternative strategies to determine that no appropriate benchmark for the total fund or composite exists. If this is the case, it is recommended that the asset owner disclose why no benchmark is presented.

Sample Disclosure:

"Because the composite's strategy is absolute return where investments are permitted in all asset classes, no benchmark is presented because we believe that no benchmark exists that reflects this strategy."

Provision 26.D.5

The ASSET OWNER SHOULD disclose the ASSET OWNER definition.

Discussion

To claim compliance with the GIPS standards, an asset owner must comply with all applicable requirements of the GIPS standards on an asset owner–wide basis. Accordingly, the asset owner must determine exactly how it will be defined for the purpose of compliance. An asset owner is an entity that manages investments, either directly and/or indirectly through the use of external managers, on behalf of participants, beneficiaries, or the organization itself. These entities include, but are not limited to, public and private pension funds, endowments, foundations, family offices, provident funds, insurers and reinsurers, sovereign wealth funds, and fiduciaries. For a public pension fund, the asset owner is generally defined by legislation. In the case of foundations, endowments, or family offices, the asset owner would be the entity established by the governing body to manage the pool of assets.

There are situations in which an organization may act as both an asset owner, where investment authority and ownership are vested with the organization itself, as well as a firm (asset manager) that competes for assets whose vesting lies with external clients. See Provision 21.A.24 for additional guidance on situations in which an asset owner competes for business, including those instances in which an asset owner acts as both an asset owner and a firm that competes for business.

Sample Disclosures:

Example 1:

Genius University Endowment is a university endowment fund and manages assets solely for Genius University.

Sample Disclosure for Example 1:

"For the purposes of complying with the GIPS standards, the asset owner is defined as the Genius University Endowment (GUE), established in 1972 by the Genius University Investment Committee of the Genius Corporation and is the manager of GUE's assets."

Example 2:

Organization ABC acts as both an asset owner, managing assets for the ABC retirement system, and as an asset manager that competes for assets whose vesting lies with external clients. For the purpose of complying with the GIPS standards, Organization ABC has decided to bifurcate its assets into two entities: ABC Retirement System (ABCRS), which manages assets exclusively for the ABC Retirement System, and Firm ABC, which competes for business.

Sample Disclosure for Example 2:

"For the purpose of complying with the GIPS standards, ABC Retirement System (ABCRS) is defined as the division of Organization ABC that manages assets exclusively for the pension plan of Organization ABC."

www.ingramcontent.com/pod-product-compliance
Lightning Source LLC
Chambersburg PA
CBHW051408200326
41520CB00023B/7158